D1191154

THE QUEST FOR
MORAL LAW

THE QUEST FOR
MORAL LAW

By LOUISE SAXE EBY

1944
COLUMBIA UNIVERSITY PRESS
NEW YORK

A WARTIME BOOK

This complete edition is produced
in full compliance with the government's regulations for conserving
paper and other essential materials

TO MY STUDENTS
IN PHILOSOPHY 205 AND 206,
PAST AND PRESENT,
WHO HAVE INSPIRED
THIS BOOK

ACKNOWLEDGMENTS

THE AUTHOR wishes to acknowledge gratefully the kindness of the following friends who aided in the preparation of the manuscript of this book: the Reverend A. Gladstone Finnie D.D., of Immanuel Presbyterian Church, Milwaukee, Wis., and the Reverend Russell J. Clinchy, D.D., of Center Congregational Church, Hartford, Conn., for reading and criticizing the manuscript, and Dr. A. Paul Atterberry, of Milwaukee, for checking and supplementing the medical facts in Chapter XIV. She desires to thank the following colleagues at Milwaukee-Downer College: Dean Meribeth E. Cameron, Professor Gladys L. Calbick, Assistant Professor Mary S. Benson, and Dr. Inez J. Richards for their help in reading proof, for their valuable suggestions as to style, and for correcting certain facts relating to their own fields; Miss Maude Mitchell, the college librarian, and her staff for facilitating the research necessary to write the book; and Miss Claribel Danielson for her excellent typing of the manuscript and her unfailing encouragement in coping with the difficulties of its composition.

Furthermore, the author acknowledges the kindness of the following publishers for granting permission to quote from books copyrighted by them: the Oxford University Press, London, Eng., for permission to quote from the Sacred Books of the East (Vols. X, XI, XXXIX) and from Spinoza's *Ethic* translated by W. Hale White and revised by Amelia Hutchinson Sterling; J. Murray, of London, for permission to quote from *The Science of Ethics*, by Leslie Stephen, and from *The Sayings of Confucius* (Wisdom of the East Series), translated by Lionel Giles; the International Council of Religious Education for permission to quote from the American Standard Revised Version of the Bible, which has been used for the Biblical quotations throughout; the Macmillan Company for permission to quote *The Methods of Ethics*, by Henry Sidgwick, and *The Analects of Confucius*, translated by Arthur H. Waley; the President and Fellows of Harvard College for permission to reprint quotations from Plato's *Dialogues* ("Euthyphro," "Apology," "Crito," and "Phaedo"), translated by Harold N. Fowler, and Aristotle's *Nicomachean Ethics*, translated by H. Rackham, both published in the Loeb Classical Library by the Harvard University Press; Doubleday, Doran for permission for the quotation from *Personal History*, by Vincent Sheean, copyright 1934, 1935, 1936; Harper and Brothers for permission to quote from *The Warrior, the Woman, and the Christ*, by G. A. Studdert-Kennedy; W. W. Norton Company for permission to quote from *Endocrinology*, by R. G. Hoskins; Longmans, Green & Company, for permission to quote Kant's *Theory of Ethics*, edited and translated by Thomas Kingsmill Abbott; Houghton Mifflin Company for permission to quote from *Biography and the Human Heart*, by Gamaliel Bradford; Random House for permission to quote from *The Wisdom of Confucius*, edited and translated by Lin Yutang (Modern Library Edition); the Appleton-Century Company for permission to quote from *History of European Morals*, by William E. A. Lecky, Vol. I.

LOUISE S. EBY

Milwaukee, Wis.
April 1944

CONTENTS

PART ONE

SOME CLASSIC ETHICAL SYSTEMS

CHAPTER I

THE MEANING OF MORAL LAW

THE term "moral law" has lost all precision of meaning for the mind of the twentieth century. This observation holds true both for those of our contemporaries who still believe that there is some body of rules which can be properly designated as the code of moral law and for those who deny that there is any such thing at all. Among the members of the latter group a number are likely to think the term applies largely or exclusively to sex relationships; they are convinced that the chaotic condition of sex morality in the present generation proves that there is not and cannot be anything deserving the name "moral law." Expressing a view typical of this group, even so warm a humanist as Vincent Sheean has written: "Whatever morality may be—and it seems probable that *it never was anything but a series of convenient arrangements*—its recognizable influence had vanished from the more conspicuous aspects of life in Paris and London in the 1920's." [1]

A somewhat different, but widely prevalent, view is that expressed by Aldous Huxley in "The One and the Many," one of a collection of essays written in the days when Mr. Huxley was still an agnostic,[2] that the only truths we know are psychological, therefore relative and subjective. After arguing that there is no absolute truth, not even in science and logic, he asserts that while in religion monotheism and polytheism are both true, polytheism is more true than monotheism in the diverse modern world, and concludes with this opinion about the relation of religion and morality: "The established religion decayed; but the philosophical and ethical habits persisted and persist." [3]

Mr. Huxley's modern sophism clearly implies that at the present time nothing is established in morals—all is relative and subjective, a matter of clinging to old habits inspired by an outworn

[1] Sheean, *Personal History*, p. 310. Italics mine.
[2] Huxley, "The One and the Many," in his *Do What You Will.*
[3] *Ibid.*, p. 49.

religion. This belief that morality is subjective and personal, a matter of taste or the traditional holdover from a vanished religious faith is a common philosophy among our modern intellectuals, and although they could not state it so succinctly as Mr. Huxley has done, this is also the conviction upon which a large number of less articulate people are acting nowadays. The idea that there is really no securely established moral law has come into popular thinking in two ways. Among those acquainted with the results of certain sociological and anthropological studies which show the influence of custom and social approval upon moral ideas, there are some who have concluded that since much is relative and subjective, or at best a matter of tradition in that sphere, everything must be so and nothing is fixed. Others have come to a similar position because they think that the widepread breakdown of traditional codes of morality in our era (chiefly in the sphere of sex, but to some extent in other spheres as well) proves that there is not and cannot be any moral law whatever. The truth in their position is only this: that much which former generations held as certainly established moral law has not stood the test of the "acids of modernity." However, the recognition of that undoubted fact should not blind us to the truth that genuine moral law, if there is such, stands the test of the experience of any age. It covers a wide range of human relationships and is concerned with matters far deeper than tradition, opinion, or social approval. It is distinguished from manners or accepted codes of behavior in that it pertains to fundamentals of character, and its infractions involve deep-seated and permanent injuries to the personalities concerned. Manners, on the other hand, have to do only with convenient and easy modes of social intercourse; and violations of rules of etiquette entail only temporary embarrassment and minor unpleasantnesses.

Side by side with the group in modern society who do not believe there is any such thing as moral law there exists a second group of more orthodox persons who proclaim that there is a substantial body of moral law known to themselves and to all right-thinking persons. However, a glance at what this orthodox group includes within the compass of moral law reveals that they have no clearer idea of the proper meaning and scope of the term than do those who deny its existence altogether or confuse it with sex regulations. For the orthodox adherents of moral law include within the category precepts from the most diverse sources, ranging all the way from Biblical commandments to copybook maxims, and place them all on much the same level of authoritativeness.

The religious wing of this group defines moral law as comprising the Decalogue, the Sermon on the Mount, and any or all of the commands of the Old and New Testaments, which they hold to be authoritative. In other words, for them "moral law" is synonymous with "Divine Law." Yet many church people and some traditional moralists outside the church, too, unconsciously place on much the same level as these Biblical injunctions, a motley miscellany of precepts, whose source they scarcely know, and think of them all as collectively comprising the moral law. These precepts include maxims and aphorisms from seers and sages, from moralists like Benjamin Franklin's "Poor Richard," folk proverbs and platitudes all the way down to the nursery level. Included also in the body of moral law of the moral "man in the street" are a goodly number of the most familiar quotations from great writers, such as Shakespeare. He may not even know the source from which they come, but since he has heard them from his cradle, they hold for him an authority equal to that of the Bible verses with which he is likely to confuse them. Familiar quotations, such as "Neither a borrower, nor a lender be" and "To thine own self be true, and it must follow, as the night the day, thou canst not then be false to any man" are cases in point. Of course this is not to say that the wisdom of great literary geniuses does not deserve consideration as moral law, but merely to point out the uncritical way in which these maxims are lumped together as "moral law" by unthinking persons. Indeed, included with the few principles that deserve the name "moral law" are all sorts of oddments that have no right whatsoever to the name, but are merely specious generalizations of the snap-judgment variety.

Into the popular code of moral laws go also not a few items from the *credo* of the national and racial groups to which the individuals in question belong. These are held to be self-evident and axiomatic propositions which no sane person would question, largely because they come to members of that race or nation with the very air they breathe and their value is seldom called into question by anyone within the circle. The code of the English gentleman is a case in point from the British Empire. It appears that the racial teachings of Rosenberg and Goebbels and others of Herr Hitler's circle are setting a new "moral code" based on racial superiority which is implicitly believed and warmly embraced by the youth of the Third Reich. In America we have added our own peculiar national ingredients to our moral code, from the exalted principles of the Declaration of Independence and the Bill of Rights down to what Thurman Arnold has so felicitously named the "folklore of capitalism."

The final component of the average man's code of moral law is an individual one. This is the sum of the do's and the don'ts which form that synthesis of his background and training known as his conscience. The elements of this conglomerate are the standards whose authority he recognizes out of his family background and training, parental admonitions and discipline, the conduct approved by his social group, and his conception of what respectable people should and should not do. These standards which collectively form the individual's conscience, motivated as they are by social approval and disapproval, attach to imperatives and prohibitions which frequently have but small relation to genuine moral law.

Thus it may be seen that both radical and conservative groups in modern society alike bear witness to the need for clarification of our thought about the nature of moral law. For the one thinks no such thing exists; the other emphatically asserts its existence, but has no idea of the proper limitations of the term. In fact this vagueness is but one symptom of the need for clarification and reconstruction of the whole field of ethics. What we know in ethics at the present time is so mingled and confused with opinion and tradition that it is small wonder that thoughtful people question whether we know anything at all as verified and valid moral law. That we already have a substantial body of known and assured moral law is one theme of the present volume. The first section of the book will endeavor to trace the discovery and formulation of certain moral laws and techniques by great ethical teachers of the past and to study the methods they employed in their attack on ethical problems. The second part of the volume will deal with the present situation in ethics and make some suggestions for the advance of ethics from the realm of pure value judgment to the status of a science.

The first step in bringing a new science into being is to classify the data which it treats; therefore the first attempt to reduce ethics to the status of a science is to classify the various types of moral laws which the "ethicians" [4] of the past have discovered and handed on to the present.

The term "moral law" does not occur in the works of all the ethicians studied in this book; but whether they use the term or not, it is possible to infer what most of them understood by the concept from their statement of whatever moral laws they happened to formulate. The only one who did not believe that the term "law" is appropriate in ethics is Aristotle, for he states expressly in the *Nicomachean Ethics* that ethics cannot have the exactitude and precision of science, since it belongs to a very large extent to the realm of opinion and value.[5] A careful study of the use of the term "moral law" or its near equivalents in the writings of those ethicians who employ the conception either directly or inferentially shows that moral laws are not all of the same type; in fact, three distinct types may be distinguished in their systems, although Kant is the only one to discuss the precise meaning of the term at any length in his ethical treatises.

One frequent use of the term equates moral law with a certain portion of the Divine law. The best example of that usage within the scope of the present volume is to be found in the system of

---

[4] For the sake of convenient designation of those who have devoted themselves to the study of ethics, the writer has ventured to coin the word "ethician" as an English equivalent to the German word *Ethiker*, in the hope of supplying what she feels is a lack in the philosophic vocabulary of the English language. The word "moralist" has unfortunately acquired a prudish connotation; hence "ethician," being new, shall stand for the scientific investigator in the field and obviate the difficulty of the use of "moralist."

[5] Aristotle *Nicomachean Ethics*, I. iii. 1–5.

Saint Thomas Aquinas. He thinks of the moral law as an important part of the whole body of the Divine law, in both the Old and the New Testaments; but he is always careful to recognize that it is not the whole of the Divine law, which also includes a goodly number of ceremonial and other religious provisions that are quite apart from morality. Moreover, not all moral laws belong to the body of the Divine Commandments revealed to the Jews in the Old Testament and to the Christians in the New. Some articles of the moral law belong to the *lex naturalis* and consist of precepts implanted by the Creator in the reason of every human soul. Thus in the last analysis the moral laws are all Divine commands, whether revealed directly by God to the writers of the Bible or indirectly revealed through reason, in which the Creator has implanted them; but while they are of two classes, the infraction of either class constitutes a transgression against the sovereignty of God and a direct disobedience to His Will.

In the teachings of Jesus as reported in the Synoptic Gospels the term "moral law" is not used at all. However, it is evident from many of his sayings that Jesus regarded his own teachings as commands which carried with them the authority of Divine inspiration and also that in a general way he looked upon the Decalogue and other portions of the Law and the Prophets whose content he approved as direct Divine commands, of which the moral laws formed a very important part (see Mark 10:19; Matthew 23:23; Luke 11:42). Thus for Jesus, too, moral law was an essential part of the Divine law.

The second sense in which some of the ethicians of the past have used "moral law" is entirely different—as an intrinsic principle of order, purpose, or harmony, or the law of reason within man which corresponds to the principle of order and harmony in the rest of nature. A good example of this second meaning is to be found in the sayings of Confucius. There the expressions "moral law" or "the moral law" do occur occasionally; usually they designate the principle of order within man that brings him into harmonious relation with all the rest of nature. This moral law meant to him the principle of moderation, the Golden Mean.

Sometimes Saint Thomas Aquinas, in his discussion of the moral law as part of the *lex naturalis*, the innate light of reason, verges on this second conception, though the idea springs from the Aristotelian and Stoic traditions, rather than the Christian. This line of thought follows Aristotle's idea of order as form and function, teleological adherence of a thing to that design or end for which it was made. Saint Thomas thinks that moral law set this kind of pattern, designed by the Creator, and that any departure from it represents a serious divergence from the end that man, the creature, is designed by his Creator to serve. This conception of Saint Thomas's will be discussed at length in the chapter on his system of ethics, but it is mentioned here merely as an interesting variant of the second traditional use of the expression, moral law.

There is a third sense in which moral law has been used in the past. This differs completely from the other two, for it employs moral law in the sense of a necessary operative principle analogous in its inexorable connection between cause and effect to the laws of science. The two modern ethicians, Spinoza and Kant, were the first Westerners to use it in this sense, and it is by no means accidental that both of them lived after the new science had made such strides as to impress them, along with their contemporaries, with the certainty and calculability of the laws of science. However, in India more than five centuries before the birth of Christ, Gautama the Buddha had used "the Law" (*Dharma* in Sanskrit, *Dhamma* in Pâli) in the sense of a causal principle, an inevitable sequence between cause and effect; but the relationship held only partly in moral terms. In his Four Noble Truths, his Eightfold Path, and his Ten Commandments the causal connection operates chiefly against the background of relief from suffering through the eradication of desire rather than of redemption from evil; hence the moral law as he conceives it is not an imperative which directs toward the good purely for its own sake, but only for the sake of escape from suffering into the passionless state of Nirvana. The Buddha's insistence upon the causal sequence between desire and suffering caused the intrusion into his conception of moral law of several elements that had nothing to do with morality, if the latter be conceived in terms of redemption from evil and establishment of good, which have been the prevalent ideas in other systems. Perhaps it is not too much to say that while the Buddha's Dharma resembles the laws of science in that its operation is inexorable, it is nonetheless at best a problematic law of life instead of a moral law.

With Spinoza and Kant we have moral law conceived as analogous to scientific law. Spinoza thought of moral principles as being exactly like the axioms, corollaries, and propositions of geometry, and indeed wrote his *Ethic* in the form of demonstration used in geometry, proving each ethical proposition with the same kind of deductive reasoning that the mathematician employs in proving the propositions of Euclid. Spinoza himself apparently believed that his method of handling moral laws was successful and that his demonstration of the ethical propositions was as certain, necessary, and irrefutable as the mathematical principles themselves. In the chapter on Spinoza a detailed analysis and appraisal of his method will be given, but here his attempt must be mentioned as one of the three important variations of the conception of moral law as analogous to, or even identical in its formal character with, scientific law.

While Spinoza conceived of moral law as analogous to the laws of mathematics, Kant, a century later, thought of it as more nearly resembling the laws of physics as Sir Isaac Newton had stated them —with this important difference, that Kant believed moral law to be a priori and formal instead of a posteriori and empirically verifiable as Newton had shown the laws of physics to be. However, the operative character of moral law is exactly analogous to that of physical law in the Newtonian system, for Kant believed that moral laws were completely binding and cogent principles and that in them cause and effect followed each other in inexorable sequence, just as surely as in gravitation.

Kant's discussion of the nature of moral law in his ethical writings is a pioneer attempt to state the theory of its operation with exactitude and logical consistency, and although some of the categories he used as a framework, such as his a prioris, are outmoded, his treatment of the subject is still standard in many respects. He does not use the word "operative" anywhere, but his account shows clearly that he considered that moral laws must be operative in character in order to have the status of law at all. Moral laws are universal, necessary, and their opposites unthinkable, for the moral imperatives are, according to him, apodictic and a priori, since they dictate an action as necessary in itself without regard to external effects. Kant's own phrase for the moral imperatives was "categorical" instead of "operative."

Kant is not wholly consistent as to whether there is only one moral law or more than one. Sometimes he speaks as though the general categorical imperative, the "thou shalt" of duty, were the sole moral law: at other times it seems as though he included also the two great categorical imperatives he formulated, "So act that the maxim of thy will may at all times serve as a universal law," and, second, one which he frequently insisted was identical with the first, "So act as to treat humanity whether in thine own person or in that of any other as an end withal and never as a means." There are also numerous references in his writings from which it would seem that he regarded all the commands of duty as moral laws based upon direct Divine commands.

Kant had formulated his conception of moral law against the background of eighteenth-century rationalism, when a prioris and universal ideas of pure reason seemed far more valid than they were to do in the nineteenth and twentieth centuries. The historical, anthropological, and sociological studies of the next two centuries [6] brought to light the influences of many purely empirical forces upon the development of the moral life which Kant had no more suspected than had the rest of his contemporaries, and these studies undid part of his work. They changed the complexion of ethics considerably, taking it out of the realm of a priori rationalism and showing it to be wholly empirical. In many respects this shift represented an advance, for the great weakness of Kant as an ethician was his failure to recognize that if ethics is to be a science at all, it must be an empirical one. The counter side of the nineteenth-century ap-

[6] This volume will consider only the civilized situation, since the primitive is too embryonic, too submoral to yield the data out of which the science of ethics may be evolved.

proach was that the pendulum swung too far in the opposite direction and consigned ethics entirely to the realm of value judgments, where nothing was fixed and established, and opened the way for the present widespread opinion that morality is quite relative, subjective, and purely a matter of timely expedient, group opinion, or individual preference.

Now, there is, it must be granted, a large area in ethics where such is in fact the case; but this is the very area in which no valid and approved principles have as yet been discerned. However, to suppose that all ethics is relative and that there are no absolutes whatever is as great a mistake as to suppose that it consists entirely of absolute and eternal laws, accurately formulated and known to all. The truth is that some ethical principles have already been stated and verified sufficiently so that they have reached the status of moral law; some are still in the realm of value judgment and taste; and some seem about to pass from the status of opinion to that of law, that is, they are in process of verification at the present time.

The important facts are that ethics is already partially a science and that wherever opinion and value alone still prevail that portion can pass over into science as soon as the principles governing it are observed, stated, and verified. Before this transition can come about, however, we need to evolve an ethical method comparable in the sureness of its approach to the attack of the scientific method within its field. The first step in the reduction of ethics to the status of a science is the listing and classification of the moral laws that have already been established; then these must be studied in order to ascertain the degree of authority behind them, and the process by which they were discovered and verified must be carefully investigated. This investigation should throw light on the quest of moral law and furnish clews for the creation of an ethical method and the reduction of the uncertain area to a more scientific basis.

It can be clearly seen from the foregoing discussion of the senses in which moral law has been used in the classical ethical systems that it was quite generally supposed to be operative, if it held the status of law at all, either in the complete sense that its infraction brought dire consequences which were inherent in the process, or, if moral law was identified with Divine law, in the partial sense that by disobeying it one incurred punishments as a result of the Divine wrath. Nevertheless, a careful scrutiny of those principles which have already been formulated with such exactitude that they deserve the name "moral laws" reveals that there are three distinct types of moral law: operative laws, regulative principles, and normative principles.

The operative laws are those moral laws whose action is automatic, like that of the scientific law of gravitation. You may fall, jump, or be pushed from the window of the top story of a high building, but the consequences of the operation of the law of gravitation will be the same, whatever the cause of your fall. Now it is popularly supposed that all moral laws are of this operative sort, and, indeed, the ethicians themselves have been largely responsible for this misconception, for even they have not distinguished the operative laws from the other two classes in their own formulations of moral law. But we can now confidently state that a close scrutiny of the moral laws shows that comparatively few are so absolute and automatic in their functioning. "Thou shalt not kill" is one of the few strictly operative laws known to us in the moral realm, because one exterior and objective consequence is exactly the same in all cases, whether it be the savage who kills his foe to eat him, or the supposedly civilized member of an advanced society who murders his enemy as the result of an elaborately laid plan. Something irreplaceable has gone out of the world when a life has been taken. It is the inexorable character of its consequences which makes "Thou shalt not kill" a genuine operative law. This exterior and objective consequence in this case is the important one, since it far outweighs either such subjective results as the killer's possible remorse or such social ones as the effect on the group in which the deed occurs. Comparatively few moral laws are so largely concerned with exterior and objective effects as to be genuinely operative laws. "Thou shalt not steal," for example, may entail serious and very undesirable consequences, but they are not usually irreparable, and the seriousness of the offense varies considerably according to the circumstances and the motive behind it. The law against stealing, however, is an operative law with a high statistical probability on the side of bad exterior consequences. A number of moral laws are of this sort, their consequences varying according to the circumstances, the motive, and the sensitivity of the persons involved. All such should be classified, not as absolute operative laws, but as statistical probabilities (which may be larger or smaller in the case of each individual law) toward a given set of consequences.

Quite different from the moral laws which are absolutely operative or carry statistical probability in favor of certain consequences are those of the second class: the regulative principles. These are the principles governing large classes of actions, as for example, the Golden Rule or the Golden Mean. Since they set the end and sometimes also determine the process of achievement in a variety of moral situations, the regulative principles may be roughly compared to recipes. Some of these have been formulated by ethicians of the past, like the Golden Rule, which Jesus stated, and its contrary, the Silver Rule, which Confucius had formulated some centuries earlier. These correspond somewhat to one class of imperatives named by Kant, the hypothetical imperatives which operate in certain specific situations, but govern only one class of actions instead of many classes like the categorical imperatives of Kant's classification. The normative principles, in contradistinction to the regulative principles, are the ideals governing single classes of actions, the ethical principles which arise from unusual experiences, and those which emerge from circumstances so unique, infrequent, or individual that no regulative principle covers them. Potentially included in this class also are the ideal ends which seers and sages dream in imagination by contrasting the real world in which they dwell with the inner vision they have of the world that ought to be. In this area of ethics the dictum of William James that "truth happens to an idea" holds good.

The kind of authority which the regulative and normative principles bear is qualitatively different from that of the operative laws, which either carry their own penalties with their infraction, or, if they are conceived to be Divine laws, are enforced by the Deity.

The regulative principles have the same kind of authority that a good recipe has: that is, it is the mode of producing a positive and constructive creation which is beneficial to all concerned. The moral principles of this sort concern the constructive side of the moral life; they add to man's life creative moral acts which immeasurably enrich it. The omission of such creative acts is not only a lack but also a positive detriment; and following some contrary regulative principle likewise produces harmful effects. The authority of the normative principles is of the same sort, except that it is more limited, inasmuch as it governs only one class of actions instead of a great many.

The operative, regulative, and normative principles are the three types of moral law which can be clearly indicated among those already formulated by the ethicians of the past. Perhaps other classes will be discovered with the passing of time, but of these three sorts we already know and possess a substantial body. Some of each class have been formulated by individual ethicians, some are the intuitions of great religious leaders, and a few have emerged from the group mores of various peoples in various times and places. But however they come into being, we now possess enough of these laws so that as the next step in its development ethics should now pass from philosophy into science. Ethics as a science, however, is just beginning to come into being, and in fact is still largely in the alchemy stage.

CHAPTER II

THE CHINESE MIND IN ETHICS: CONFUCIUS

THE FIRST great ethical thinker of China was Confucius, or K'ung Chunghi, who was born in the country of Lu, the modern Shantung Province, in 551 B.C., and died 479 B.C. Confucius passed most of his life as a teacher, though there were intervals during which he occupied positions of some importance in the government of the state, once rising to the office of chief minister of Lu. He wrote two books, *The Book of History*, and *Spring and Autumn*, chronicles of the history of China from the earliest times to his own day, as the name indicates, and the *Book of Songs*, a collection of folksongs and ballads which he simply recorded and edited. Neither of these two works gives us his ethical system, for which we are dependent chiefly on the *Analects*, miscellaneous collections of sayings without chronological order or much indication of context, compiled by his second- and third-generation disciples, some quotations from him in the *Liki*, the *Book of Rites*, and in the works of his grandson, Tsesze, and his chief disciple, Mencius.

We do not, therefore, know his philosophic ideas at first-hand, and as is always the difficulty in such cases, there is room for misunderstanding, misinterpretation, and idealization on the part of the disciples; much was doubtless omitted, so that we do not have the teaching in its entirety; and some of it is probably distorted or preserved in such an incomplete manner that the original context and setting cannot be readily recovered. The sayings are mostly in the form of aphorisms or of answers to questions set by the disciples, and probably this was really the original form in many cases. It is likely that Confucius himself preferred the proverb, the pithy epigram, and the terse formulation of great principles to the ordered, systematic exposition of any of these in all their manifold ramifications and interconnections. Logic does not seem to have been the outstanding characteristic of his mind, and it is unlikely that even if we possessed a knowledge of the entire teaching of the Chinese sage it would be notable for careful scrutiny of premises, systematic development of argument, and freedom from fallacies of various sorts. Rather his premises seem to have been reached intuitively, with little heed to process, and his defense of his theses is not free from fallacy or even devoid of contradiction. His approach was psychological rather than logical, and his conclusions rest upon a keen and comparatively wide observation of human nature.

Confucius created the code of ethics which has served China for seventy generations. He was able to do so because he himself was a representative Chinese whose system mirrored his countrymen so exactly that it seemed final to them. Both the greatness and the limitations of Confucius are those of his country, and he perhaps more than any other of the world's principal ethical teachers gave the stamp of his own nationality to his ethical teachings. The *summum bonum* of his system, the virtues he exalted, the vices he hated are all Chinese to the very core; the techniques for the attainment of virtue, and even the mistakes he made are all characteristic of China itself.

The *summum bonum* of Confucius is the goal to be reached by the true man, or the superior man, which the sage states thus: "Confucius remarked: To find the central clue to our moral being which unites us to the universal order, that indeed is the highest human attainment. For a long time people have seldom been capable of it." [1]

This goal extends to the mystical realm only in so far as it includes the order of nature; it has no theological implications, nor does it look to a completion outside the present world. It carries with it no expectation of aid from any god or spirit; it is simply the oneness of the inner man with the same universal order that prevails without and within. Men must find this union with the central harmony for themselves, through their own worth and by their own seeking. The characteristic conservatism of Confucius causes him to add that "for a long time the people have seldom been capable of it," but the

---

[1] "The Central Harmony," originally chap. xxi of the *Liki*, in *The Wisdom of Confucius*, ed. and tr. by Lin Yutang, p. 105.

implication is that in the Golden Age which existed in the past, many more were worthy.

Thus, in the view of the sage the capacity for finding the moral goodness and truth which lead to this union with the central harmony lies in men. Confucianism is sometimes classified as a religion, but it is strictly an ethic; for while in the course of its long history it did acquire some religious accretions and overtones, in the mind of its founder it was simply a humanistic code of ethics preoccupied with the present world of men without reference to gods or an afterlife. Confucius himself was not concerned with supernatural powers and forces; if he was not downright skeptical of their existence, at least they interested him only in the sense that he made a deferential bow to them at the sacrifices and the ceremonies. It was the rites themselves rather than the gods that interested him. A few of his sayings illustrate clearly the complete absorption of the Chinese sage with the affairs of this world and his indifference to any other:

Confucius did not talk about monsters, physical exploits, unruly conduct, and the heavenly spirits.[2]

Wangsun Chia asked, "Why do people say it is better to keep on good terms with the kitchen god than with the god of the southwestern corner of the house?" Confucius replied, "Nonsense, if you have committed sins against Heaven, you haven't got a god to pray to."

Tsekung wanted to do away with the ceremony of sacrificing a lamb in winter. Confucius said, "Ah Sze, you love the lamb, but I love the ritual."

Confucius said, "Respect the heavenly and earthly spirits and keep them at a distance."[3]

Humanism dominates the entire thinking of Confucius.

Confucius said: "Truth may not depart from human nature. If what is regarded as truth departs from human nature, it may not be regarded as truth."[4]

The humanism of Confucius, however, is highly conservative and aristocratic in character rather than melioristic and democratic. It conveys no ideal of progress; for the present is but a degeneration

[2] *Ibid.*, p. 165.   [3] *Ibid.*, pp. 167–68.   [4] *Ibid.*, p. 184.

from the Golden Age that lay in the past, a time in which Confucius expressed the wish that he might have been permitted to live. Then men were good enough to realize union with the central harmony, they were worthy, their rulers were paragons of virtue, and society was a truly moral order.[5]

In old days the common people had three faults, part of which they have now lost. In old days the impetuous were merely impatient of small restraints; now they are utterly insubordinate. In old days the proud were stiff and formal; now they are touchy and quarrelsome. In old days simpletons were at any rate straightforward; but now "simplemindedness" exists only as a device of the impostor.[6]

When the great Tao prevailed [*i.e.*, in the Golden Age], the world was a common state (not belonging to any particular ruling family), rulers were elected according to their wisdom and ability and mutual confidence and peace prevailed. Therefore people not only regarded their own parents as parents and their own children as children. The old people were able to enjoy their old age, the young men were able to employ their talent, the juniors had the elders to look up to, and the helpless widows, orphans and cripples and deformed were well taken care of. The men had their respective occupations and the women had their homes. If the people didn't want to see goods lying about on the ground, they did not have to keep them for themselves, and if people had too much energy for work, they did not have to labor for their own profit. Therefore, there was no cunning or intrigue and there were no bandits or burglars, and as a result, there was no need to shut one's outer gate (at night). This was the period of the *tat'ung*, or the Great Commonwealth.[7]

This conservative trend in the temperament of Confucius, which made him refer the Golden Age to the past, is a very fundamental expression of the nature of the great people of whom he is a typical representative. It led him to stress adherence to old custom, which he assumed must be good just because it was old, and above all things led to the selection of a typical Chinese virtue as the cardinal one

[5] *Ibid.*, p. 227.
[6] Confucius, *The Analects of Confucius*, tr. by Arthur Waley, xvii. 16.
[7] *The Wisdom of Confucius*, pp. 227–28.

of his ethical scheme: filial piety. Now it may be admitted without argument that this is a virtue too little esteemed and practiced in the Western World, nonetheless to erect it to the position of the cardinal virtue of an ethical system is an idea that would not occur to anyone but a Chinese, an emphasis traceable to the Chinese patriarchal system rather than to any intrinsic superiority of a virtue restricted to only one of life's manifold relationships over other virtues which have a much wider application.

Confucius looks upon filial piety as the root of all virtues. No one who was not a good son could lay claim to any kind of goodness—a *non sequitur* traceable to the Chinese sense of values approved by tradition rather than to any empirical observation of facts. With the veneration of parents came inevitable adherence to the past, for Confucius went so far as to say, "The dutiful son does not deviate from the ways of his father, whether dead or alive." He describes filial piety as consisting in not being perverse, in adherence to the rules of propriety in relationships with parents, in ministering to them while living, and after death burying them and presenting sacrificial gifts to them. The ideal son would so cherish his parents that they would have no trouble to bear other than their own sickness. It further included support of them based upon a reverence so great that a son would never cross his parents' will except with gentle remonstrance, and if the parents were not disposed to heed that, to yield implicit obedience without any demur, no matter what he might have to suffer from them.

Even the sovereign must be a good son, else he could not be a good ruler; for then he needed only to apply the same formula to the task of governing his people. In like manner those who were good sons would make good subjects for the ruler.[8]

A second virtue of high order in the scale of Confucian values is moderation. Confucius advocated and practiced this virtue with regard to eating, drinking, the pleasures and self-indulgences of life, all of which he apparently enjoyed, but guided by both the principle of moderation as well as a fastidious taste he enjoyed them without

[8] *Ibid.*, pp. 198–99.

going to extremes. Even virtue itself was an affair of moderation, to his temperament which was neither ascetic nor libertine. He says this:

I do not expect to find a saint today. But if I can find a gentleman, I shall be quite satisfied.[9]

Confucius remarked: "I know now why the moral law is not practiced. The wise mistake moral law for something higher than what it really is; and the foolish do not know enough what moral law really is. I know now why the moral law is not understood. The noble natures want to live too high, high above their moral ordinary self; and ignoble natures do not want to live high enough, i.e., not up to their moral ordinary true self. There is no one who does not eat and drink. But few there are who really know flavor."[10]

The primary ideal of Confucius is the superior man, the gentleman. In his portrait of the superior man is to be found the whole catalogue of the virtues he esteems, contraposed against the vices he abhors, which are all, according to him, the characteristics of the inferior man. Humility, dignity, self-respect, are all prominent virtues of the superior man. Other qualities are: integrity, regard for men before material things, incorruptibility in financial affairs, justice, breadth of mind, tolerance, patience, poise, good taste, and adaptability. This model of the superior man has served the classes of China as their ideal for many generations; it is one of the great portraits of the gentleman, perhaps the greatest that we have drawn by any single ethical teacher, and the series of contrasts which the Chinese sage drew between the superior and the inferior man is worthy of application over a much wider area than China alone. The only liability from which it suffers is that there is not always clear separation between concerns of manners and of morals.

The intellectual virtues such as wisdom, sound judgment, and sound knowledge, had their place also in the portrait of the superior man, who must be a person of scholarship and learning as well as a gentleman in society. It was no uninformed culture that Confucius advocated. No one of the great ethical teachers ever stressed the

[9] *Ibid.*, p. 179.   [10] *Ibid.*, pp. 105–6.

value of education as a means to virtue more vigorously than did
Confucius. In fact, the techniques he advocates for the acquisition of
virtue are three: self-awareness, example, and education; but of
these three, by far the most important was education. Himself a
teacher, Confucius believed as strongly as any of the modern peda-
gogues who prate of "education for character-building" that it was
the primary method for achieving virtue. He believed that ignorance
is a real barrier to goodness and that instruction and enlightenment
are its friends and aids. He evolved an original and detailed scheme
of education for virtue. This consisted of three essential studies,
which he believed would make education a moral discipline rather
than a purely intellectual one: poetry, *li*, and music. "Says Confucius: 'Wake yourself up with poetry, establish your character in
li, and complete your education with music.' " [11]

The function of poetry was to arouse the individual, to waken
in him the inner meaning of things. *Li*, a very important part of the
Confucian scheme, included ritual, ceremonies, and sacrifices, propriety and decorum, the correct usages of social intercourse, in short,
that moral order in society that corresponded to the operation of
the order of Heaven in Nature. It was the theory of the sage that *li*
instilled in a man a sense of order and of the kind of unity in diversity
which arises from doing each thing according to the process most
appropriate to itself. Music, the third essential, was to give a sense
of harmony to man's inner life, and only the kind of music which
would build up such a sense of harmony was worthy of toleration.
The ideas of the Chinese sage upon the subject of music resemble
those expressed by Plato in the *Republic*. The combination of poetry,
li, and music was designed to link the individual with the central
harmony of universe that constituted the epitome of education and
the realization of his *summum bonum* for Confucius. [12]

This union with the central harmony of the universe would
produce an inner sense of poise and unity in man's life that would
manifest itself in all his social and moral conduct, a disciplined and
ordered life that would show itself in the ordered life of the family
and the state as well. It is likely that in the last opinion Confucius

[11] *Ibid.*, p. 168.   [12] *Ibid.*, p. 200–204.

was guilty of a fallacy of composition in the notion that social harmony was a simple multiplication of individual harmony; for the aptitudes that make for fine individual living do not necessarily translate into ideal group living, as is evidenced by the rudimentary sense of social solidarity that has been such a serious handicap to the unification of China during the past three decades. Confucius himself did much to make the Chinese recognize no loyalty larger than the family group, for the family rather than the individual is the unit of society for him.

To most of the subsequent ethical teachers self-awareness was the starting point and foundation stone of the good life. To Confucius, on the contrary, it seems to have been rather the product of moral education and discipline, witness the evolution of his own progress which he traces in the following quotation:

Confucius said: "At fifteen I began to be seriously interested in study. At thirty I had formed my character. At forty I had no more perplexities. At fifty I knew the will of heaven. At sixty nothing that I heard disturbed me. At seventy, I could let my thought wander without trespassing the moral law." [13]

The third technique for the acquisition and spread of virtue, in the opinion of Confucius, was example. Apparently it was his thought that the superior or the true man should serve as such an example and pattern of virtue for all about him. The ruler, for instance, had only to set an example of good character to his people to run the state successfully and to make them good as well. It is hard to escape the feeling that in the extremes to which Confucius carried it this was really a naïve idea. Of course, in personal relations, where influence can be a direct and potent factor, it is easy to see that example might exert a strong effect, but it has to be confined to a group small enough to allow the contact to be direct. Even at that, some reservations should be made about the value of example as a technique of virtue which evidently did not occur to him. There is the difficulty that such goodness is prone to become a kind of secondhand affair, coterminous with the influence of the person chosen as model, and

[13] *Ibid.*, p. 160.

that it too readily turns into mere imitation. Indeed, the principal
fault of the example technique is that goodness is so largely a peculiar
and personal adaptation of each temperament to its environment
that the mold must be discovered by each person for his own individuality and cannot be taken over from another, whose personality may be very different.

It has been remarked several times that Confucius is a representative Chinese who influenced his own people so enduringly because
he so completely incarnated in his single person their faults and
virtues and felt life so entirely as they feel it. Both the greatness
and the limitations of the Confucian system are essentially Chinese.

Among the limitations may be mentioned Confucius's conservatism in deifying the past in his theory of the Golden Age, which is
quite unwarranted by a sound knowledge of history, but above all
in his uncritical glorification of ancestor worship with all the allegiance to tradition which it entails. Indeed, this implicit and un-
discriminating obedience to parents is a prolongation into adult life
of the state of mind of the very young child when he regards his
parents as infallible; in China this regressive idea of the parental
position served to reinforce all the conservatism of the Chinese
family system.

His failure to separate morals and manners from each other is one
of the primary limitations of Confucius as an ethical teacher. To be
sure, it is often a fine line that separates the two provinces, and it
should be added that in the west the Jewish Law also failed to make
this demarcation; but with Confucius the failure arose from a somewhat different root. His arose from the typically Chinese love of
ceremony, of natural fondness for ritual even in the smallest affairs
of daily life; whereas with the Jews it was a mixture of the survival
of primitive custom and the belief that the Divine commands extended to all areas of life. Chinese as he was, it is not strange that
Confucius never discriminated between morals and manners. He was
just too Chinese to have it dawn upon him that there was any distinction. Illustrative of his national viewpoint is Confucius's location
of the moral law in *li*.

The concept of the moral law was a very precious one to Confucius, but he had no strict concept of the moral law by and for itself as over against ritual and etiquette. "The moral law is the most characteristic attribute of man," he declares; [14] but he allocates the moral law in *li*.

"Is *li* so very important as all that?" asked Tseyu again.

"This *li*," replied Confucius, "is the principle by which the ancient kings embodied the laws of heaven and regulated the expressions of human nature. Therefore he who has attained *li* lives, and he who has lost it dies." [15]

A confusion such as the above quotation displays tends to mingle with the proper principles of the moral law all sorts of extraneous accretions: traditions, customs, codes of etiquette, outmoded rituals, sacrifices, even taboos and superstitions. It places a quite undeserved ethical sanction upon the *status quo* which interferes with the honest and searching criticism of the group mores by which most of man's ethical progress has come about.

If the limitations of Confucius are those of his country, in like manner the universal values which his system contained are those which China has to give the rest of the world. Of these, perhaps the greatest universal of his teaching was Confucius's formulation of the principles of reciprocity, or *shu*. "Tsekung asked, 'Is there one single word that can serve as a principle of conduct for life?' Confucius replied, 'Perhaps the word "reciprocity" (*shu*) will do.'" [16]

It may of course be argued that reciprocity, or mutuality, is not the only key to successful human relations, that the principle of good will is wider; yet many of life's most important relations are based upon the former: friendship, trade, social co-operation, good faith in contracts, and obligations of any sort, and it constitutes one of the major foundations of good will in life. The criticism to which Confucius is chiefly open is that he did not extend his own principle far enough. This limitation was imposed by his conservative and aristocratic outlook, for he did not at all believe that relations between superiors and inferiors in social stations should be regulated

---

[14] *Ibid.*, p. 116.   [15] *Ibid.*, p. 229.   [16] *Ibid.*, p. 186.

by reciprocity; nor were the relations of parent and child to be governed by it, for the position of the parents as elders quite precluded any mutuality in family life. Indeed a consistent extension of his own principle would have led Confucius to a democratic view of life; but, not being possessed of a particularly logical mind, apparently he never thought through his own principle in all its logical implications. His stress upon the psychological rather than the logical allowed him to pass over without noticing the contradictions between his principle of *shu* and the aristocratic set-up of the feudal states about him.

While mutuality is certainly one of the important bases of good will, Confucius apparently did not see that in those relationships where mutuality does not prevail, good will upon quite another basis must supersede it. He did not teach good will to enemies and those who wrong us.

Although Confucius discerned several important principles of the moral life, none is so profound as that of good will which his individualistic and mystical contemporary, Lao-tze (604–517? B.C.), formulated; and being the originator (so far as history knows) of that great regulative principle is enough to perpetuate the latter's memory in the history of moral law. This principle was also independently enunciated by both Jesus and Socrates in the West and by Gautama in the East. The earliest statement of it, however, is Lao-tze's.

To those who are good to me, I am good; and to those who are not good to me, I am also good; and thus all get to be good. To those who are sincere with me, I am sincere; and to those who are not sincere with me, I am also sincere; and thus all get to be sincere.[17]

Recompense injury with kindness.[18]

While Confucius is a typical and representative Chinese, Lao-tze, whose system, known as Taoism, was a mystical nihilism with some affinities to that of Tolstoi in its ascetic repudiation of civilization, is an exceptional type of psychology, diverging markedly from the humanism and this-worldly preoccupation of the average Chinese.

[17] *Tao-Teh King*, 49:2.   [18] *Ibid.*, 63:1.

The stories of clashes between Confucius and Lao-tze may be legendary, but they illustrate the mystic's departure from the usual pattern of the Chinese ways of thought. It is reported that when they met on the one occasion, Lao-tze passed the judgment that Confucius was a fussy and meddlesome busybody; [19] and in the *Analects* Confucius, perhaps in retaliation, in effect expressed the opinion that the principle of returning good for evil was unreasonable: "Some one asked: How do you regard the principle of returning good for evil?—The Master said: What, then, is to be the return for good? Rather should you return justice for injustice, and good for good." [20]

Indeed Confucius's teaching did not preclude hatred, which he felt had a legitimate place in the character of the superior man:

"Only a superior man knows how to love people, and how to hate people." [21]

Lin Yutang finds in the humanism of Confucius his greatest contribution.

The finest philosophic perception of Confucius, it seems to me, is his recognition that "the measure of man is man." If it were not so, the whole system of Confucian ethics would fall to pieces and would immediately become impracticable. The whole philosophy of ritual and music is but to "set the human heart right," and the kingdom of God is truly within the man himself. The problem for any man intending to cultivate his personal life is merely to start out on a hunt for the best in his human nature and steadfastly keep to it. That is practically the essence of Confucian ethics. [22]

The paramount place of human values is indeed one of the universals of the Confucian ethic, and its *summum bonum* of central harmony of self with the order of nature is one that man can reach through his unaided efforts. This harmony is a Chinese ideal, built upon a humanism happy with and preoccupied by the affairs of this world alone. However, there is a certain lack of dynamic in an ethic too easily realizable. To become his highest ethical self, man needs the tension and compelling power of an ethic that reaches for the

[19] *Ibid.*, 34, 35.
[20] Confucius, *The Sayings of Confucius*; tr. by Lionel Giles, p. 68.
[21] *The Wisdom of Confucius*, p. 189. [22] *Ibid.*, Introduction, pp. 17–18.

stars, that not only calls upon him to realize himself, but to transcend himself. Confucianism is good in that it recognizes man's importance and his proper level. However, it is almost too content with compromise, too moderate in its demands, too ready to accept the Golden Mean even in virtue. This readiness to compromise kept the Chinese sage from reaching the lofty heights of moral grandeur attained by Jesus, the Buddha, and other ethical teachers who were not too afraid to be absolute in their demands on human nature by holding up to it an ideal immeasurably harder to realize, but fraught with a power of exaltation that the more attainable ideal of Confucius could never convey.

CHAPTER III

THE RADICAL ETHIC OF GAUTAMA, THE BUDDHA

To THE Western mind the strangest of all the ethico-religious systems is the radical ethic of Gautama, the Buddha. In the strictest sense the teaching of Gautama is neither an ethical nor a religious system, but a moral self-discipline with a metaphysical orientation in terms of peculiarly Indian categories. The salvation it envisages is not the Western notion of redemption from sin and evil, but rather of escape from the Wheel of Life, from samsara, the continuous round of existences presupposed by the two Hindu doctrines of reincarnation and karma, which Gautama took over from the background of Hinduism. This process of freeing oneself from the endless round of existences according to the original teaching of Buddhism must be brought about entirely by the efforts of the individual himself, and in them he cannot be aided by any god or other agent, human or superhuman, outside himself. Even the Buddha merely pointed the way, which each then had to follow for himself and by himself. Thus it is really inexact to call primitive Buddhism a religion; for it is a moot question whether the Buddha believed in any gods at all; and even if he accepted their existence theoretically, they were not in any way instrumental in his scheme of salvation. Indeed, the Buddhist sources boldly assume that gods and demons must also free themselves from the Wheel of Life, and they depict both classes as coming to inquire about the way of salvation from the Buddha. It is equally inexact to call primitive Buddhism a genuine ethic, since it had but the slightest consciousness of social values and contained only that measure of altruism and good will which were necessary to attain the goal of nirvana, the *summum bonum* of the system which the founder took over from the *Upanishads*, the principal philosophic treatises of Hinduism.

Not only is the student of Buddhism faced with the amazing differences between East and West which center in its doctrine, but in addition there are very complicated and involved problems concerning the sources of the teachings of the founder. There are numerous Buddhist sacred books, but of these the earliest and most authoritative are the *Tripitakas,* or *Three Baskets,* of the Pâli Canon, which although Gautama had died about 480 B.C. were not committed to writing until 88 B. C., when a group of Ceylonese monks finally set them down. During the intervening period of almost four hundred years the sutras were circulated within the Order by monks who learned them by heart and taught them to each other. As might be expected, even the Pâli Canon contains many miraculous and mythical embellishments; but, due to the work of Western scholars in the field, it is now possible to distinguish the real facts from the legendary accretions with considerable certainty and to separate the more primitive strata, such as the contents of the earlier sutras, notably of the *Vinaya Pitaka,* which were relatively fixed by the time of King Aşoka (250 B.C.). Nevertheless, a multitude of distortions, omissions, and mistakes can creep into texts that are orally transmitted for a period of four centuries, so that it is frequently problematical how close we come to the actual teachings of Gautama at individual points.

It seems probable that the facts of Gautama's early life had a very definite bearing upon the singular philosophy which he later developed; therefore the bare outline of the facts of his life is included here. Siddhartha Gautama was born about 560 B.C. in a family of landed proprietors of the Sakya clan in Nepal, not far from Benares, where he led a luxurious and sheltered life until he was twenty-nine. Then, oppressed by the sorrow and suffering of the world, which he had discovered in spite of his own comfortable life, he deserted his wife and infant son, left home, and became an ascetic. For five years he followed the usual ascetic discipline of the Indian holy man with much rigor; but he abandoned the austerities of fasting and mortification of the flesh after trial for several years had led him to the conclusion that they were futile. His great illumination came to him under the Bo tree near Benares; thereafter he became "the Buddha," or "the Enlightened." The content of his enlightenment is said to have consisted of the twelve links in the chain of causation, the Wheel of Life, the Four Noble Truths, and the Eightfold Path. These doctrines he forthwith preached to the five recluses with whom he had formerly been associated in his pursuit of holiness, and, according to the sutra Dhammakakkappavattana-Sutta (The Foundation of the Kingdom of Righteousness), which contains the sermon, the five became his first converts. Within two months he is said to have gained sixty converts, who constituted the original members of the monastic order, the Sangha, which he established. From that time, when he was about thirty-five years old, until his death at the advanced age of eighty, Gautama spent his time wandering up and down the territories of northern India, preaching and teaching his doctrines with such success that he left behind him a large and well-established order to carry on his message.

In some ways Gautama may be looked upon as a typical Indian, yet he is not nearly so representative of India as is its modern holy man, Mohandas Gandhi. Gautama, unlike so many of the Indian religious personalities, had a strong bent for rationalism that made him despise and denounce superstition of all sorts—he was skeptical instead of mystical and puritanical rather than ascetic. While the Buddha took uncritically from Hinduism such presuppositions as reincarnation, karma, and nirvana, there are also many respects in which his teaching is a protest and a heresy from Hinduism, such as his repudiation of caste and his abhorrence of ascetic austerities, superstition, and all sorts of traffic with the supernatural. Indeed, in spite of his borrowing of some of his chief premises from Hinduism, the system of Gautama is really unique in India as well as in the rest of the world.

The very borrowings from Hinduism were for the most part interpreted originally by Gautama. The spiritual democracy of his Order is a protest against caste, which in Hinduism was closely united with reincarnation and karma. According to the theory of Hinduism belonging to the highest caste was a sign that the individual in his previous incarnations had accumulated good karma; it constituted a reward for that former virtue. Membership in a low caste, or being an outcast, on the other hand, indicated an ac-

cumulation of bad karma in consequence of evil deeds in past existences. The Buddha did not interpret karma as operating in relation
to social rank; for him it was only the force of the deed that carried
over from one existence to another, binding the individual whether
for good or for evil to the Wheel of Life. It did not operate in caste,
but merely in being incarnated into a higher or lower form of life,
in being a bodhisattva nearer or farther away from his last incarnation, according to whether he had accumulated good or evil karma.
Thus, according to Gautama karma was entirely a question of ethical
ascent or descent, not of social elevation or abasement.[1] "Not by
birth does one become an outcast, not by birth does one become a
Brâhmana; by deeds one becomes an outcast, by deeds does one become a Brâhmana." [2]

Reincarnation was also somewhat changed by the Buddha from
the classic Hindu formulation; for instead of believing that some
enduring soul passed on from incarnation to incarnation, Gautama
believed that the soul, which was only one of the Five Aggregates,
an unstable compound without unity even in any given existence,
could not be the link of continuity between existences. The real
principle of continuity was provided by karma. The famous Buddhist analogy is that of the candle and the flame. The flame of one
candle lights another, but it is the flame, not the candle, that goes
on. Karma is the flame that goes on, while the soul and the body
are both aggregates that end, like the candle.[3]

The Buddhist nirvana differs considerably from the classic Hindu
statement of the doctrine in the *Upanishads*, where it is a union of
the individual soul atman with Brahma, the Cosmic Absolute, and
is accompanied by great tranquillity and bliss, "where one knows
naught without or within." [4] For the Buddha it was no union with
any supernatural being, but simply an inner state which the indi-

---

[1] Dhammapada xxvi (Sacred Books of the East, Vol. X, Part 1).

[2] "Vasalasutta," Uragavagga 7. 21 (Sacred Books of the East, Vol. X, Part 2,
p. 23).

[3] The Questions of King Milinda ii. 2. 1 (Sacred Books of the East, Vol. XXXV,
p. 64).

[4] "Brihad Aranyaka," *The Thirteen Principal Upanishads*; tr. by Robert E.
Hume, 4: 3. 21–22.

vidual reached within himself, having affects similar to those described by the *Upanishads*. Nirvana, indeed, in his parlance simply refers to that blissful, serene state of freedom from all desires or cravings, beyond thought and sensation, where all individuality ceases to be and the arhat is beyond all distractions—where all karma is exhausted so that he has reached his last incarnation. The Buddhist sources insist repeatedly that nirvana is a state of great bliss, the highest freedom and happiness that man can know; but it is hard to see how such could be the case in a state so passive and empty.[5]

Why did the state of nirvana seem to the Buddha the highest that a man could possibly attain? The answer is to be found partly in the Indian background which Gautama did not in this respect view critically, partly in his own temperament, which viewed life in terms of endless rounds of becoming, samsara, which at all stages are full of suffering. The Four Noble Truths, which he formulated at the time of his Enlightenment, express perfectly Gautama's whole estimate of the value of life and the extreme pessimism and fear of suffering with which he viewed the world. (1) All of life is suffering. (2) Thirst (in the sense of craving or desire) is the origin of suffering. (3) The extinction of desire causes the eradication of suffering. (4) The way by which suffering is removed is the pursuit of the Noble Eightfold Path.

The Noble Eightfold Path consists of: (1) right views; (2) right aspirations; (3) right speech; (4) right conduct; (5) right livelihood; (6) right effort; (7) rightmindfulness; (8) right contemplation.[6]

The first step along the Noble Eightfold Path which leads to the destruction of all desire, to the state of nirvana, is freeing the mind from the threefold fire of lust, ill will, and ignorance; the severing of the Five Bonds that hold to samsara, the endless round of becoming. The Five Bonds are: desire, temptation, ignorance, anger,

---

[5] Dhammapada xxvi *et passim* (Sacred Books of the East, Vol. X, Part 1); Dhammakakkappavattana-Sutta 231 (Sacred Books of the East, Vol. XI, p. 153).

[6] Dhammakakkappavattana-Sutta (Sacred Books of the East, Vol. XI, pp. 137–55).

and fear.[7] The destruction of these marks the end of becoming; for the karma that has been accumulating is now exhausted, then nirvana is the end of all becoming, as of all individuality (name and form), where existence itself continues only as the wheel of the potter from sheer inertia still turns a few times after the power has been withdrawn from it. In order to reach nirvana it is necessary that the bodhisattva (one on the way to enlightenment) be free from the four great evils of the mind: sensuality, individuality, delusion, and ignorance.[8] He must overcome the five hindrances: lust, passion for a body, passion for name and form (individuality), ease in sleep or sloth, the practice of asceticism.[9] He must burst the Three Fetters: delusion of self, doubt, dependence on rites and ceremonies.[10]

In Buddhism, which is a thoroughgoing monastic scheme, there are five commandments of a moral nature which all Buddhists, laity and monks alike, are expected to keep. There are, in addition, five others which the monks are expected to observe, but are not exacted of the laity. The first five consist of prohibitions against: (1) destruction of life; (2) stealing; (3) unchastity; (4) lying; (5) the use of intoxicants.

The second five commandments are intended only for the observance of the monks. These prohibit: (1) eating at forbidden hours; (2) attendance at any public spectacle: (3) the use of garlands; (4) sleeping upon high or broad beds; (5) accepting gifts of money.[11]

The second group of five commandments seems to the outsider to have slight importance for the good life; but it must be borne in mind that all of them have to do with forbidding objects which in the eyes of the Buddha pander to the senses; hence they were important, since indulging the senses in any way would be almost as serious a hindrance to attainment of nirvana as would a breach of the moral law.

[7] Tevigga Suttanta i. 30 (Sacred Books of the East, Vol. XI, p. 182).

[8] Mahâ-Parinibbâna-Suttanta, i. 12–14 (Sacred Books of the East, Vol. XI, pp. 11–12).

[9] Ketokhila-Sutta 8 (Sacred Books of the East, Vol. XI, p. 225).

[10] Sabbâsava-Sutta 9–12 (Sacred Books of the East, Vol. XI, pp. 298 f.).

[11] Mahâvagga i. 1. 5–6 (Sacred Books of the East, Vol. XIII, p. 78).

In addition and similar to the first five commandments are the Four Deadly Sins, for which the penalty to the monks was expulsion from the Order. These are: killing, stealing, unchastity, and the pretense of supernatural powers.[12] The last sin, the pretense to the possession of supernatural powers, is a reflection of Gautama's revolt from the superstition of his Indian background, in which even today the line between the holy man and the magician is no more clearly drawn than it was in the day of the Buddha. However, Gautama was not successful in eliminating superstition among his followers, for even in the Pâli Sutras he himself is often pictured as a sorcerer of great powers.[13]

This lengthy list of prohibitions, hindrances, fetters, bonds, and obstacles to be overcome might lead to the supposition that the Buddhist ethic is almost wholly negative; but, while it is inevitable that in a system that was so essentially a denial of the positive value of life the negative element should bulk large, there is also a positive side to the self-discipline which leads to nirvana. The Eightfold Path itself is positive in all its injunctions, as are also many of Gautama's exhortations to the practice of such virtues as good will, though even here it must in fairness be admitted that since the cardinal virtues of Buddhism are those which aid most directly in the realization of its *summum bonum*, the virtues are largely passive and repressive in character rather than active and expressive. Even the more social virtues, such as good will, are not final states or ends in themselves, but simply intermediate conditions that will be superseded by the passionlessness of nirvana. It is frequently and truly said that nirvana is a selfish ideal, yet perhaps that selfishness is not so radical a criticism of nirvana as is its absolute lack of content. The late G. A. Studdert-Kennedy, an English churchman of unusual spiritual penetration, quotes this significant psychological analysis of the nirvana ideal:

The desire of life must be destroyed that the soul may find its peace. Death itself, of course, is something which, strictly speaking, can neither be desired nor conceived. Being cannot conceive not being without ceasing

---

[12] *Ibid.*, i. 1.

[13] Kullavagga vii. 3. 12 (Sacred Books of the East, Vol. XX, p. 248).

to be. The nearest the mind can get to death is absolutely passive life—Nirvana. That is what Buddhism and the great ascetic family of religions promise and point the way to. Modern psychology would, I think, see in this way what is called regressive phantasy. "Life is nothing but a struggle from the cradle to the grave. It has been said that the new-born infant's cry can, from one point of view, be regarded as the child's protest against coming into this world and leaving the perfect shelter of the mother's womb, where in a state of absolute passivity all wants were gratified without effort. If we conceive such an hypothesis we may go further and think we see in all its after life an unending struggle to reproduce if possible the equivalent of such a mental state, to cease all conflict, to find a state of Nirvana." [14]

Naturally a goal like nirvana does not stimulate the Buddhist to the abundant life or to more than a limited measure of service for the world. Life itself is not a good, it is full of suffering caused by desire; therefore the only virtues to be fostered are those which exterminate desire, which prevent the accumulation of karma and aid the individual in his final escape from suffering. Why did Gautama so wholeheartedly yearn to escape from suffering? The answer must lie hidden in the mystery of his own temperament, so that perhaps not even a Freud could untangle it from the known circumstances of his life; but there is something quite pathological about such an unwillingness to endure suffering, which causes this teaching of Gautama's to contrast so unfavorably with the Jewish-Christian idea of the moral worth of enduring certain kinds of suffering.

Since nirvana is Buddhism's ultimate goal, it is not surprising that the *Dhammapada* names passionlessness as the cardinal virtue of Buddhism.[15] Related to it are self-control, recollectedness, self-conquest, and self-restraint, which are all highly praised in the *Dhammapada* as leading along the path to nirvana by means of the destruction of desire. It is to be observed that all the virtues advocated by Gautama are without exception those that aim toward the eradica-

[14] Studdert-Kennedy, *The Warrior, the Woman, and the Christ*, pp. 157–58, with quotation from C. Stanford Read, *The Struggles of Male Adolescence*, p. 1.

[15] Dhammapada xx. 273 (Sacred Books of the East, Vol. X, Part 1, p. 67).

tion of desire, whether positive or negative, active or passive. "Cut down the whole forest [of desires], not a tree only! Danger comes out of the forest [of desires]. When you have cut down both the forest [of desires] and its undergrowth, then, Bhikshus, you will be rid of the forest and of desires." [16]

The place of good will in the Buddhist scheme of the virtues well illustrates how even that greatest of all virtues serves only an intermediate function, that of eradicating ill will in order that the devotee may reach nirvana, which is beyond either good will or ill will. The Buddhist use of the term "good will" is not to be confused with personal affection of any sort, whether love or friendship or any other deep personal tie. Even the Buddha was to be revered rather than loved, and there is a tradition that the Blessed One's chief disciple Ānanda did not enter into nirvana during the lifetime of his master, because his attachment to the latter was too strong.[17] Personal affections, attachment to family or friends, are to be shunned as great creators of karma; they bind to the world, to the Wheel of Life; they are a major cause of suffering, since wherever the heart holds fast to someone or something, it is in danger of suffering from the loss of the desired object and cannot be free and detached as the arhat must be. The characteristic attitude toward the family life is shown by the classic advice of the *Dhammapada:*

A wise man should leave the dark state (of ordinary life), and follow the bright state of a Bhikshu. After going from his home to a homeless state, he should in his retirement look for enjoyment where enjoyment seemed difficult. Leaving all pleasures behind and calling nothing his own, the wise man should purge himself from all troubles of the mind.[18]

Another sutra recommends the same monastic life and bids the eschewing of even the ties of friendship, except in the case of the very wise and the good. It recommends solitude, for at the end of every verse comes the refrain, "Wander alone like a rhinoceros."

[16] *Ibid.*, 283.
[17] Mahâ-Parinibbâna-Suttanta v. 34–35 (Sacred Books of the East, Vol. XI, p. 96).
[18] Dhammapada vi. 87–88 (Sacred Books of the East, Vol. X, Part 1, p. 25).

1. Having laid aside the rod against all beings, and not hurting any of them, let no one wish for a son, much less for a companion, let him wander alone like a rhinoceros.

2. In him who has intercourse (with others) affections arise, (and then) the pain which follows affection; considering the misery that originates in affection, let one wander alone like a rhinoceros.

3. He who has compassion on his friends and confidential (companions) loses his own advantage, having a fettered mind; seeing this danger in friendship let one wander alone like a rhinoceros.

4. Just as a large bamboo tree (with its branches) entangled (in each other, such is) the care of one with wife and children; (but) like the shoot of a bamboo, not clinging to anything, let one wander alone like a rhinoceros.

5. As a beast unbound in the forest goes feeding at pleasure, so let the wise man, considering (only his) own will, wander alone like a rhinoceros.

6. There is (a constant) calling in the midst of company, both when sitting, standing, walking, and going away; (but) let one, looking (only) for freedom from desire and for following his own will, wander alone like a rhinoceros. . . .

10. Removing the marks of a gihin (a householder) like a Kovilara tree whose leaves are fallen, let one, after cutting off heroically the ties of a gihin, wander alone like a rhinoceros.

11. If one acquires a clever companion, an associate righteous and wise, let him, overcoming all dangers, wander about with him, glad and thoughtful.

12. If one does not acquire a clever companion, an associate righteous and wise, then as a king abandoning his conquered kingdom, let him wander alone like a rhinoceros.

13. Surely we ought to praise the good luck of having companions, the best (and such as are our) equals ought to be sought for; not having acquired such friends let one, enjoying (only) allowable things, wander alone like a rhinoceros.[19]

The condition of good will, pursued largely in solitude, is thus the one most suited to the seeker after nirvana. The good will of the primitive Buddhist is, in consequence, an impersonal attitude of benevolence toward all living things, none of which are to be

[19] Khaggavisânasutta 1–6, 10–13 (Sacred Books of the East, Vol. X, Part 2).

harmed, whether men or animals. Indeed, in the way in which it extends beyond the bounds of congeniality in the human realm, embracing friend, foe, and stranger alike, it resembles the Christian *agape,* except that the latter does not shut out or preclude the possibility of personal affections as the Buddhist does. Some would see a superiority in the Buddhist extension of good will to the animal realm, but while at best there is a poetic and naïve resemblance to St. Francis of Assisi's love for his little brothers of the animal kingdom, at worst it is merely equating the arhat with the fakir and the snake charmer.[20]

At its finest, the Buddhist good will toward all living creatures appears when the true Buddhist aspirant thus meditates, putting away ill will, lust, and hatred:

And he lets his mind pervade one quarter of the world with thoughts of Love, and so the second, and so the third, and so the fourth. And thus the whole wide world, above, below, around, and everywhere, does he continue to pervade with heart of Love, far-reaching, grown great, and beyond measure.[21]

Just as good will is advocated as the remedy for ill will, malice, and hatred, so purity and chastity are the cure for lust, sensuality, and impurity. Unchastity rates as one of the deadly sins for which the monks or nuns would be expelled from the Order; but chastity is advocated as the remedy for lust, since all sex desire, which is very binding and productive of evil karma, must be eradicated. The idea of sex in primitive Buddhism is sheer monasticism. Woman was looked upon as no more than an instrument of lust, all friendship or social intercourse with women was viewed by the Buddha with the utmost suspicion; hence the famous passage from Mahâ-Parinibbâna-Suttanta (The Book of the Great Decease):

"How are we to conduct ourselves, Lord, with regard to womankind?"

"Don't see them, Ânanda."

"But if we should see them, what are we to do?"

---

[20] Kullavagga vii. 3. 12 (Sacred Books of the East, Vol. XX, p. 248).
[21] Tevigga Suttanta iii. 1, *et passim* (Sacred Books of the East, Vol. XI).

"Abstain from speech, Ânanda."

"But if they should speak to us, Lord, what are we to do?"

"Keep wide awake, Ânanda." [22]

This misogyny on the part of Gautama was so great that at first he refused to allow his aunt, Maya Pajapati, to establish an Order for nuns corresponding to that of the monks. Even the intercession of Ânanda failed to move the Buddha, until at length the disciple inquired whether or not the Blessed One was of the opinion that women could become arhats. When the latter admitted that they could, he was obliged reluctantly to consent to the founding of the Order for women, but the position of the nuns remained decidedly inferior to that of the monks and the lines along which association between the monks and the nuns was permitted were very rigidly defined.[23] Thus, even in the Order the superior position of the male was strictly upheld; and outside it, although family ties were permitted to the layman, the very status of householder was in itself a confession that the person in question had renounced all hope of attaining nirvana in his present incarnation. It therefore came about that Hinayana Buddhism, faithful to the teaching of Gautama, never could build a constructive and positive ideal of the right use of sex drives in the integration of character, but ever adhered to Gautama's rigid denial of this most enslaving of all the cravings that chain man to the Wheel of Life.

Just as all the drives that center in what the modern psychoanalysts have named the "libido" are wrong, even in their finer sublimations, because they are powerful creators of karma, so are all the drives of the ego wrong for a similar reason; for they too add to the rounds of becoming (samsara). The conviction that whatever makes for individuality is wrong, that the very principle of separateness and particularity is bad, is a singular feature of the Buddhist ethic. This interpretation is all the more peculiar since here the principle is not contrasted with any ideal of social solidarity as in Western systems or yet, as is usual in the *Upanishads*, viewed as incompletion without the fulfillment of some mystical union with

[22] Mahâ-Parinibbâna-Suttanta iii. 23 (Sacred Books of the East, Vol. XI, p. 91).

[23] Kullavagga x. 1 (Sacred Books of the East, Vol. XX, pp. 320–26).

the Divine All. Individuality is so bad merely because of its limitation and impermanence. The drives that center in the ego—ambition, acquisitiveness, self-desires and wishes of all sorts, egotism, self-esteem, conceit of every variety—are harmful and pernicious in the extreme, because they are all creators of karma—most of it bad—and major causes of suffering, impediments and hindrances to the pursuit of nirvana. No distinctions are made among the drives of the ego that might be useful assets in the ethical life of the individual and constructive, even creative, in the life of the social group. Gautama's radical view, measured solely by the standard of nirvana, allowed not at all for the Western standards of culture and progress. To him there was no value in culture, no object in progress. Individuality was not a potential center of creativity. It meant only desires, suffering in consequence of these cravings, and the accumulation of more and more karma to produce more becoming, more incarnations of these confections, the soul and the body that together with the karma they carry, constitute that fleeting and impermanent thing we name the self.

> They all, all beings that have life, shall lay
> Aside their complex form—that aggregation
> Of mental and material qualities,
> That gives them, or in heaven or on earth,
> Their fleeting individuality! [24]
>
> They're transient all, each being's parts and powers,
> Growth is their nature, and decay.
> They are produced, they are dissolved again:
> And then is best, when they have sunk to rest.[25]

The chief and most important technique which the Buddha recommended for the removal of the various hindrances to nirvana is, of course, meditation carried out along lines that were carefully indicated by him. In this sense, that the mind is the chief instrument of salvation, and in no other is it true that the Buddha is the most

[24] Mahâ-Parinibbâna-Suttanta vi. 15 (Sacred Books of the East, Vol. XI, p. 116).

[25] Ibid., vi. 16 (Sacred Books of the East, Vol. XI, p. 117).

intellectual of the ethical teachers. Mind is simply the means of penetrating such illusions as individuality and of shattering ignorance, that is, of seeing the world as the Buddha saw it when he evolved the Four Noble Truths, the means by which one becomes recollected to such a degree that he can follow the Eightfold Path *for himself.*

Therefore, O Ânanda, be ye lamps unto yourselves. Be ye a refuge to yourselves. Betake yourself to no external refuge. Hold fast to the truth as to a lamp. Hold fast as a refuge to the truth. Look not for a refuge to any one besides yourselves. And how, Ânanda, is a brother to be a lamp unto himself, a refuge to himself, betaking himself to no external refuge, holding fast to the truth as a lamp, holding fast as a refuge to the truth, looking not for refuge to any one besides himself?

Herein, O Ânanda, let a brother, as he dwells in the body, so regard the body, that he, being strenuous, thoughtful, and mindful, may whilst in the world, overcome the grief which arises from bodily craving— while subject to the sensations let him continue so to regard the sensations that he, being strenuous, thoughtful, and mindful, may whilst in the world, overcome the grief which arises from the sensations—and so also as he thinks or reasons, or feels, let him overcome the grief which arises from the craving due to ideas, or to reasoning, or to feeling.[26]

The special devices for meditation enumerated by the Buddha among his last instructions to his disciples before he passed into Parinirvana are the following:

The Fourfold Great Struggle against Sin [1. to prevent sinfulness from arising; 2. to put away sinful states which have arisen; 3. to produce goodness not previously existing; 4. to increase goodness when it does exist].

The Four Roads to Saintship [1. The will to acquire it united to earnest meditation and the necessary struggle against sin; 2. the necessary exertion united to these two; 3. necessary preparation of heart united to these; 4. investigation united to these].

The Five Moral Powers or the Five Organs of Spiritual Sense [faith, energy, thought, contemplation, wisdom].

[26] *Ibid.*, ii. 33–34 (Sacred Books of the East, Vol. XI, p. 38).

The Seven Kinds of Wisdom [energy, thought, contemplation, investigation (of scripture), joy, repose, serenity].

The Eightfold Path [already given, *vide supra* p. 33].[27]

The importance of mind in this entire process of salvation may be seen at a glance, for indeed the application of the mind to the task of subduing desire is the Buddha's most important recommendation for the implementation of the good life. The reason initiates the process by piercing through the four great evils which beset the mind itself, namely: sensuality, individuality, delusion, and ignorance. Then, once having discerned the realities of life as the Buddha had declared them to be in the Four Noble Truths, the mind next goes on to produce the kind of recollectedness that characterizes the bodhisattva in all the activities of his life. It guards the five senses, shields from the pitfalls and entanglements of desire all along the steps of the Noble Eightfold Path, until the final stage of "right contemplation" or "rapture" is reached. Here in the trancelike entrance to nirvana, the mind, like the other faculties of the personality, ceases to function.

In this final abdication of the mind we see one more instance of the intermediary character of all the ways and means of the good life, whether of the individual virtues or of the methods by which they are induced. It is just this intermediary character of Gautama's ethic that is one of the most serious criticisms of him as an ethical teacher. For him the good is not an end in itself, it is simply the means to the end of nirvana, where it is then abrogated. In his own figure, the good is the raft, which is discarded after one has crossed the stream. "And ye, Brethren," says Gautama, "learn by the parable of the raft that ye must put away good conditions, not to speak of bad." [28]

The three criticisms most frequently made of Buddhism are: that it is atheistic, or at least agnostic; that it is, in consequence, pessi-

[27] *Ibid.*, iii. 65–66 and note by T. W. Rhys Davids (Sacred Books of the East, Vol. XI, p. 65).

[28] Quoted by Ananda Coomaraswamy, *Buddha and the Gospel of Buddhism*, p. 128.

mistic; and that it is directed toward a selfish and antisocial ideal. In the judgment of the writer the most serious difficulty with the goal of nirvana is not so much in its antisocial or selfish character as in the sheer emptiness of the state it offers. It is probably no more selfish than some of the older ideas of heaven in Christianity. That the nirvana ideal should be antisocial is inevitable when that *summum bonum* is held to be the crown and consummation of life; for it must emphasize solitude over against all the human ties which tend to involve the seeker in the rounds of becoming. There is a tacit confession of the antisocial character of primitive Buddhism in the shift that the Mahayana group made when it changed the ideal from arhat to bodhisattva, where the latter refuses to enter into nirvana until all mankind has been saved.

The criticism that Buddhism derived its pessimism from its atheism or agnosticism concerns a treatise on ethics only in so far as the question of religious orientation affects the quality of an ethic for better or for worse. In the case of Gautama, it appears to the writer that the pessimism of his doctrine is not due to his agnosticism primarily, but to the low esteem in which he held the process of living for the individual man and for humanity collectively. Several of the world's important ethical systems are constructed without metaphysical or religious orientation, but are nonetheless optimistic, if, like Confucianism, they hold a positive estimate of man and his powers and of the value of life.

The correctness of Gautama's view of man rests upon the validity of the first three of his Four Noble Truths. If as the first Noble Truth asserts, all of life is suffering, then it would be logical to take the pessimistic standpoint the Buddha does in fact take. If, however, the premise that all of life is suffering be questioned, a far different estimate of the worth of living would follow. If the Buddha had arrived at the first Noble Truth by an empirical process of observation instead of by the intuitive enlightenment he received under the Bo tree, it is likely that he would have been compelled to reduce his first Noble Truth from a universal to a particular proposition, such as "Suffering is a large element in human life"—which is, after all, the only proposition anyone's observation of life warrants.

Who, after all, can observe life sufficiently to assert that it is all suffering? Any such sweeping conclusion is a leap from the particular to the universal quite impossible to substantiate with known facts.

In like manner, as a second Noble Truth, Gautama erects a particular into a universal proposition. By placing all desires of the ego and the libido on the same plane he asserts categorically that the cause of suffering is desire. A more careful observation of the operation of desire would have led Gautama to the more moderate proposition, "Desire is one of the major causes of suffering," instead of the assertion that craving is the cause of suffering.[29] Correspondingly, the third Noble Truth would have been moderated to the proposition, "The eradication of the harmful cravings or desires would remove much of life's suffering." The Buddha seems to have completely ignored in his formulation of the causality of suffering that suffering can come to man from sources outside himself as well as within himself, that is, by such catastrophes as the upheaval of natural forces (which in India the Buddha had every opportunity to notice), by disease, famine and all the other evils that are external to man. But if he had thought of these evils at all, it is likely that he would have included them in the operation of karma. Gautama, with the extremity so often characteristic of the Indian temperament, did not view the world in any cautious and scientific manner, nor did he formulate the generalizations that are his first three Noble Truths on the basis of sound inductive logic, which is, after all, a Western instrument whose use is none too congenial to the Indian's subjective outlook.

To form a fair and impartial judgment of the Buddha's contribution to general ethical development is difficult for any occidental, because his teaching is motivated by considerations that set it apart not only from the major Western systems, but also from the other oriental systems outside India. In general, however, it is fair to say that Gautama's universal contributions are the elements which remain valid and unimpaired after the three peculiarly Indian pre-

---

[29] The Four Noble Truths are from Dhammakakkappavattana-Sutta (Sacred Books of the East, Vol. XI), the most primitive formulation though they recur constantly in the Pâli sutras.

suppositions of his system, reincarnation, karma, and nirvana, are canceled out. It may seem at first sight that to take away these foundation stones upon which his whole structure rests is to destroy his ethic, root and branch. Such, however, is not the case, for only what transcends these premises in his thought can properly be called an ethic. These three presuppositions, which seem so axiomatic to the Indian that even the radical mind of the Buddha accepted them without question, are indeed very large assumptions in the eyes of the Westerner, who recognizes that they cannot be demonstrated either rationally or scientifically. Therefore, only whatever elements of Gautama's ethics can be detached from these assumptions as valid per se have a chance of universal acceptance.

One element which is valid without reference to this Indian triad of premises is the emphasis upon ahimsa, nonkilling and noninjury of any living creature, a teaching which Buddhism has in common with Hinduism and Jainism, but interprets somewhat originally. At first it may seem strange that a system which places such a low valuation upon the significance of life, and has as an ultimate goal the cessation of individuality, should lay such stress on nonkilling and prohibit so strictly injury to any living creature. This prohibition is not, however, inconsistent with the major objective of emancipation from the endless round of being. Destruction of life is forbidden by the First Commandment of Buddhism, and taking life knowingly, including inciting to suicide or even praising death, is listed as one of the mortal sins for which a monk was to be expelled from the Order.[30] The fact is that death was no solution to the problem of salvation as the Buddhist conceived it, because it only postponed for the murderer or the suicide the possibility of attaining nirvana for long cycles of reincarnation, and the murdered would lose all chance of reaching it in this present incarnation. Moreover, killing or injuring any living being would be a violation of good will toward all creatures and a cause of suffering to the victim. The perpetrator of the deed would accumulate for himself so much evil karma through his deed that it would take whole cycles of reincarnation to expiate it. Thus the summum bonum of nirvana was the

[30] Pâtimokka 3 (Sacred Books of the East, Vol. XIII, p. 4).

principal determinant of the form which this teaching of ahimsa assumed in Buddhism.

The practical effects of the Buddhist ahimsa are among its highest ethical achievements, for in the human realm Buddhism has proved a great force for peace nearly everywhere it has spread in the Far East. This is one portion of Gautama's influence that was retained throughout the drastic changes that Mahayana Buddhism wrought in other fundamentals of his teaching, so that the record of Buddhism in inspiring hatred of war and preservation of peace among its devotees has been better than that of Christianity in the West. In the animal realm the Buddhists did not carry the doctrine of ahimsa to the absurd lengths that the Jainists did in not allowing the killing of anything, even vermin or pests, or to the point of economic inexpediency to which the Hindus did in their reverence for such sacred animals as the cow and the monkey. Nonetheless it must be admitted that even the Pâli sources manifest a carryover from the magic of the Indian fakir which Gautama, who loathed superstition, never would have sanctioned in the extension of good will as a means of control over fierce animals such as tigers and enraged elephants. Excellent, on the other hand, has been its effect in prohibiting wanton destruction of animal life in the hunt and the chase.

If the greatest glory of Buddhism's accomplishments has been the strong influence for peace which it has consistently exerted, a second great contribution of its founder's is to be found in the seriousness with which he took the problems that arise from the drives of the ego. Discounting his exaggerations of the harmful character of some of these, he nevertheless rendered a great service to the future of ethics in emphasizing the need to discipline and tame these harmful drives that, in modern parlance, arise from the biological heritage. It is only to be regretted that his attachment to the goal of nirvana prevented him from going on to a more constructive solution of the ego problem.

His greatest contribution on the side of the technique of the good life is the fourth Noble Truth, the Eightfold Path, which is an ideal statement of the items of good conduct requisite for any form of the good life, not just for the attainment of nirvana. Probably the assumption that the human mind can discern correctly what the essentials of this eightfold program of righteousness would be within the complex maze of human life is too large, indeed it is inconsistent with the Buddha's own belief that the mind is one of the Five Aggregates, hence unstable and untrustworthy. However, this trust in the reason is the natural counterpart of the Buddha's extreme distrust of all desire and feeling, and it must be remembered that it is only the mind enlightened by the revelation of the Dhamma in which he trusts. Just human reason working in philosophy or any other intellectual discipline he found quite as unreliable as the senses and the other aspects of the human personality. In the last analysis the mind, too, is but the temporary and intermediate instrument which guides the bodhisattva to the final step in the Eightfold Path, right rapture, where in the trance of nirvana the mind, with all its differentiations of thought and feeling, abdicates.

After a study of Gautama's ethic one can only conclude that his system, one of the most original the world has seen and perhaps the classic statement of the case for an ethic of pessimism, misses complete universality because it does not exalt the good as an end in itself, but only as the means to the passive goal of nirvana. Only that part of the ethic is universal which can be detached from its own *summum bonum* and commends itself in its own right as enduring value in all times and places.

CHAPTER IV

SOCRATES, PIONEER OF THE WESTERN ETHICAL THINKERS

THE FIRST of the great Western ethical teachers was the Greek, Socrates, who was born about 469 B.C., in Athens, where he spent his life teaching philosophy during the brilliant age of Pericles. He marks a great change in approach to the problems of ethics from that of the two orientals Confucius and the Buddha. In the hands of Socrates ethics becomes a definite branch of philosophy; for even though he left no written works, no systematic exposition of his views, we see plainly that ethics becomes a department of knowledge, integrated and ordered by the reason, quite different from the random and miscellaneous sayings of Confucius or the proverbs and parables of the Buddha. Perhaps it is fair to say that Socrates created ethics as a branch of Greek philosophy, for while he was not the first of the Greek philosophers to occupy himself with its problems, he was the first to view it as the sole and major concern of philosophy.

Our knowledge of the teaching of Socrates is, in consequence of his never having written anything, incomplete and secondhand, and it involves some problems of literary criticism. The two major sources of our knowledge of his system are Xenophon's *Memorabilia* and the earlier *Dialogues* of Plato, particularly the four which treat of his trial and death, *Euthyphro*, the *Apology*, *Crito*, and *Phaedo*. These two portrayals of Socrates differ very markedly; but modern experts on the subject are agreed that it is the Platonic dialogues which report his ideas correctly, since Xenophon in his other works puts forward in *propria persona* the views he ascribes to Socrates in the *Memorabilia*; whereas Plato in his early works put into the mouth of Socrates ideas which he probably shared with his master at that time, but which are entirely distinct from Plato's own system as we have it in his later works.[1] There is no reasonable doubt that

---

[1] For an authoritative discussion of the merits of Plato versus Xenophon as reporters of Socrates, see Burnet, *Greek Philosophy*, pp. 125–28.

especially in the four Socratic dialogues we do have the substance of Socrates's philosophic system, retouched, but not altered in major particulars, by the hand of his greatest disciple. The following discussion will therefore be based entirely upon Plato's report of his master, chiefly as contained in the four Socratic dialogues, occasionally supplemented by other early dialogues at certain points where they are known to state accurately facts about Socrates's life and ideas.

In addition to the two major sources of information concerning Socrates, there are two minor sources that have come down to us: Aristophanes's comedy *The Clouds*, which satirizes the philosopher and his ideas, but possesses no more accuracy than a burlesque, and some brief but valuable statements as to his philosophic contributions in Aristotle's *Metaphysics*.[2]

The facts of Socrates's life are so well known that only those that bear upon the development of his ethical system need be mentioned in this sketch of his ethical teaching. The son of a sculptor and a midwife, he had originally tried to follow the profession of his father, but failing at this he turned to the teaching of philosophy. All his life, however, he was fond of applying metaphors from the occupations of both his father and his mother to his own teachings, sometimes speaking of himself as a sculptor carving out ideas, sometimes as a midwife bringing ideas to birth. His method of teaching was to engage some Athenian from almost any walk of life in a discussion by asking him a harmless and seemingly obvious question, as in *Euthyphro*, where he begs Euthyphro to tell him what holiness is. This Euthyphro readily undertakes to do, and then Socrates, by a number of apparently simple, but in reality subtle, questions leads the unwary victim on to involve himself in hopeless and absurd contradictions, whereupon he departs angry over the exposing of his ignorance by the philosopher.

Such Platonic dialogues as *Protagoras, Gorgias, Hippias,* and *Parmenides* represent Socrates as having firsthand contacts with some of his most important philosophic contemporaries, and no doubt he

---

[2] Aristotle *Metaphysics*, tr. into English by W. D. Ross, 1078b (Vol. VIII of Aristotle's collected works), Oxford, Clarendon Press, 1928.

was conversant with the teachings of his philosophic predecessors
as well. We know from his own statement in the *Phaedo* that he had
read Anaxagoras,[3] and probably knew the teaching of the other
Milesians as well, since his reaction to their ideas is apparent from
his own final position. Their investigations convinced the Athenian
philosopher that the world of nature and sense did not yield truth,
but perforce ended in confusion. He therefore turned to the world
of human conduct and ideas, where he believed truth could be obtained.[4]

Besides his conviction that the search of the Milesians for scientific truth was futile, another philosophic influence helped to turn
the attention of Socrates exclusively to the problems of ethics and
epistemology. This was his reaction from the radical ethical skepti-
cism of the Sophists, who taught that since man was the measure of
all things, all ideas, including those of ethics and morals, were entirely relative and individual; and since all ideas concerning them
were equally true or, what came to the same thing for the Sophists,
equally untrue, moral questions at best were to be decided only by
the opinion of the majority and, at worst, were incapable of any
decision. Socrates's strong urge toward positive conclusions as well
as his strong mystical bent caused him to revolt from this Sophist
conclusion that there was no right or wrong to moral questions. To
this reaction is traceable his attempt to ground ethics firmly in epistemology, and it is responsible for the peculiar version of the doctrine of the forms which Socrates puts forward in the *Phaedo* as his
answer to this problem. Some suggestions for the doctrine of the
forms came to Socrates from the teachings of a third philosophic
school, the Pythagoreans, whose belief that numbers are forms is
the model for the Socratic doctrine. In all probability they also supplied him with the idea of reincarnation which he used in the development of his conceptions of reminiscence.

The understanding of the doctrine of the forms held by Socrates
is essential to the understanding of his ethical system; for this was
at once the metaphysical and epistemological foundation on which

[3] *Phaedo*, tr. by H. N. Fowler, Loeb Classical Library, p. 335.
[4] *Ibid.*, pp. 337 f.

his whole ethical structure was erected. He believed that we do not obtain knowledge of truth, goodness, beauty, and other ideal qualities by observing particular truths that come our way, or good individuals or beautiful objects, because these particulars are necessarily imperfect and incomplete reproductions of the perfect forms. Instead, he thought that the soul of every man, before his birth, had been in contact with the pure essences of these qualities, the forms, which were self-subsistent realities in those heavenly realms where all souls had dwelt before their incarnation. Now each soul, when it is incarnated, brings along with it some memory of those ideal forms, which it never quite loses. However, its union with the body, the seat of the low principle of the flesh, lamentably dims and diminishes the reminiscence of the forms, for the flesh with its constant desire for its own gratifications distracts from that memory, and the senses deceive and impair the soul's perception of truth. Yet the reminiscence is never wholly lost by the soul. The whole process of learning, therefore, consists, according to Socrates, in wakening and revivifying it. Whenever we come in contact with a good or beautiful object, the reminiscence is refreshed and strengthened by the experience, since such objects direct the soul to the pure essences of which they partake, though they have no goodness or beauty in their own right, but merely in their participation in the ideal form. The concrete objects are only partial and imperfect copies of the heavenly originals the soul knew by direct contemplation before its birth.

Education thus meant to Socrates not at all the study and observation of particular objects and facts, but only this wakening of the reminiscence of the forms. In this endeavor the principal impediments are the senses, which deceive and mislead the soul by making it think that the concrete, particular objects are the realities instead of the forms which can be known only through the inner realm of the mind itself, never by means of the senses. The true lover of wisdom, the philosopher, must therefore turn away from the senses with their pleasures and delusions and strive as nearly as it is possible in this life to contemplate the pure forms. He must never be turned aside from his quest of the forms by becoming ensnared with the imperfect earthly objects. He must use these only as means to rise into increasing contemplation of the forms they imperfectly reflect. Since even the philosopher, handicapped as he is by the demands of the body, can never rise to the heights of perfect knowledge of the forms during this life, he welcomes death as a liberation from the hindrances of the body and the restoration of the soul to the kind of pure contemplation of the essences which it enjoyed before its incarnation. As Socrates repeatedly remarks in the *Phaedo*, the philosopher welcomes death, which is the separation of the soul from the body, because with him life itself is the effort to separate the soul from the body; that is, as nearly as possible to transcend the body by reaching the forms.

The state of communion with the forms was what Socrates meant by wisdom, the object of the philosopher, its lover. Thus philosophy became a definitely religious quest to him; it was nothing less than a scheme of salvation whereby the soul achieved the highest destiny of which it was capable in this life; and in the life after death, to which the philosopher went as an initiate possessed of unusual purity and a high degree of knowledge of the eternal verities, his soul, immortal like the essences, entered into unbroken and complete communion with them. Impure souls who followed the senses and the lusts of the flesh would be punished—the very bad everlastingly in Tartarus, the mediocre purged in Acheron. Of the souls of the philosophers Socrates believed thus:

But those who are found to have excelled in holy living are freed from these regions within the earth and are released as from prisons; they mount upward into their pure abode and dwell upon the earth. And of these, all who have duly purified themselves by philosophy live henceforth altogether without bodies, and pass to still more beautiful abodes which it is not easy to describe . . .[5]

This complete communion with the pure forms is the goal, the *summum bonum* of the Socratic ethical system. It is definitely a metaphysical system developed in some degree against the picture of the afterworld painted by the popular mythology of Greece, which Socrates seems never wholly to have discarded. It is to be

[5] *Ibid.*, p. 391.

observed, however, that the idea of the forms and the salvation
achieved by the philosopher through single-hearted pursuit of them
is a variant originated by Socrates himself, upon the popular Greek
idea of the afterlife. His strong ethical interest made a place in
this background of tradition for the realities in which he so firmly
believed. Where he transcended the popular religion of his time,
it was his strong ethical interest which caused him to do so, as in
the present instance. The same strong ethical motive made him discard the popular stories of the immortal deeds of the gods. The ethical motivation in Socrates really ordered and arranged the religious
one, for in the *Euthyphro* he makes the point that holiness cannot
be defined as that which is dear to the gods, since it is not holy because they love it; rather they love it because it is the holy, one component of the great quality of righteousness.[6] The metaphysic underlying the Socratic ethics and epistemology is open to all sorts
of objections from the modern standpoint, but the purity and
strength of the ethical passion which dictated them cannot be questioned in any age.

The method by which Socrates hoped to attain his *summum
bonum* of communion with the ideal forms is one of the important
connections of his ethics with his epistemology, for it was the highly
intellectual one of the inductive method in dialectics. In the *Apology*
Socrates defends his use of the dialectic method in his discussions
with Athenians of all sorts—politicians, poets, and partisans—as a
part of that call to the pursuit of wisdom. This he believed had come
to him directly from the god Apollo, whose oracle at Delphi had
declared through the Pythia in answer to the question of one Chaero-
phon, an Athenian admirer of the philosopher, that no one was wiser
than Socrates. Socrates seems to have taken this oracle very seriously.
On hearing of Apollo's reply, he soberly set out to find some man
wiser than himself; but after his debates and discussions with all
sorts of Athenians, he was unable to discover a single man; hence
although he had at first thought the god must be propounding a
riddle, he at length concluded that the oracle could mean only one
thing: "This one of you, O human beings, is wisest, who, like Socra-

---

[6] *Euthyphro*, Loeb Classical Library, pp. 31–45.

tes, recognizes that he is in truth of no account in respect to wisdom."

Thus it was, according to Socrates's own declaration, that he embarked upon the quest of wisdom under the aegis of the god of wisdom himself, and he always treated this as a sacred trust to which he had to be faithful at all costs. Why did he choose as the means for realizing his goal the method of dissecting the answers given to his apparently harmless questions by his fellow citizens? This, too, was an integral part of the quest of wisdom according to Socrates's own explanation; for it was necessary to expose the folly and superficiality of those who made a pretense to wisdom, but did not possess it. Socrates himself knew that holding up his victims to ridicule in this manner made him enemies among Athenians of all classes, some of whom were very powerful. His philosophic purpose was that through such analysis of questions, by clear definition of terms and the logical scrutiny of the answer he received, certain universals should emerge as a result of his inductive comparison and a nearer approach to truth be made by revivifying the reminiscence of the forms in the subject. Socrates conceived of himself in these discussions as a midwife bringing to birth ideas of the good in the minds of those whom he subjected to this uncomfortable process, and he believed that, while his victims might not enjoy the stings of the "gadfly of Athens," he was giving his fellow citizens an opportunity to learn much about the nature of truth and goodness. His method fitted exactly with his belief that virtue and knowledge are identical.

The beginning of wisdom to Socrates was to be found in self-knowledge. He is said to have adopted as his own motto the words from Apollo's temple at Delphi, "Γνῶθι σεαυτόν (Know thyself)." He had started from this point in his own pursuit of wisdom, and he strove to recommend it to others as the first step along the way. That his fellow Athenians were slow to follow his lead was no fault of his, nor did that fact shake his faith in self-knowledge as the sure entrance to the path of wisdom. Thus the starting point advocated by the Western Socrates is the same as that commended by the orientals Confucius and Gautama, each from his own individual standpoint. Self-knowledge is one of the few agreements to be found among nearly all the great ethical teachers as the fundamental technique for entrance upon the good life, and it is a method that has been proved by the experience of many generations as a technique capable of universal application.

Somewhat more debatable was Socrates's second assumption concerning the means of realizing the good life, his theory that knowledge of the good is all that is necessary to bring about right conduct. He defends this faith consistently in the four Socratic dialogues and is elsewhere pictured as holding it whenever the question arises in the other early dialogues of Plato; hence it seems certain that it was a very firm faith with Socrates. In the *Euthyphro* he asserts that if Euthyphro will but tell him clearly what piety is, he will not any longer be open to the attacks of his accusers on the ground of impiety.[7] At his trial he gives out that one of the chief efforts of his defense is to get his accusers to state just how he has been corrupting the youth and in what his impiety has consisted; for if he but knows wherein he is doing wrong, he will cease to do it, since no one can do wrong voluntarily. When his accusers fail to substantiate their charges with statements of just what wrongs he has been guilty of committing, he feels that he has established that he is doing right in both regards and that their charges fall to the ground.[8] He triumphantly maintains that if he had been corrupting the youth of Athens, he had not done so voluntarily; and if he had done so involuntarily, he would have needed instruction, not punishment.

The same principle is assumed throughout the dialogue *Crito*, though it operates in a more positive way. Here Socrates takes the stand that he knows that the right course is for him to accept the death sentence which the state has passed upon him instead of trying to avoid it by accepting Crito's proffered aid to go into exile. Once having discerned that such is the right course, Socrates is not to be deterred from it by all of Crito's well-intended arguments. For himself at least, Socrates's proposition that a man does not knowingly do wrong held good. He was truly guided by the principle set forth by his better self in these words: "Care neither for your children nor for life nor for anything else more than for the right, that when

[7] *Ibid.*, p. 47.　　　　　　[8] *Apology*, Loeb Classical Library, p. 47.

you come to the home of the dead you may have all these things to say in your own defense." [9]

While it may be granted without hesitation that for Socrates himself the principle held good that a man could not wittingly do wrong, it is quite a different question to be as convinced as the philosopher seems to have been that it held equally for all men. This would involve two assumptions that are by no means so certain of affirmative answer as he seems to have believed: first, that knowledge of the right course is the only condition essential to good action; and second, that the intellect is always capable of discerning what the right course is. The first assumption is one of several in his system wherein Socrates is guilty of rationalistic oversimplification of the problem of moral action. It seems clear from the Socratic dialogues that Socrates did believe that no person would voluntarily do wrong, yet this fails to take into account a plain fact of history, that men may will to pursue the very course of action which their intellect discerns to be wrong and even disastrous. It demands a philosopher to follow the dictum of Socrates. Those to whom intellectual considerations are less vivid are prone to follow the course their emotions prefer, instead of the one their intellect discerns to be right, or they may confess with the Apostle Paul, "For the good that I would, I do not; but the evil which I would not, that I do" (Rom. 7:20). The confession of Paul is truer to the moral life of the majority of mankind, no doubt, than that of the Greek philosopher. Even Socrates himself, when he mentions defending himself in the realm of the dead, seems to have introduced an incentive contrary to his own thesis in the quotation just cited from *Crito*.

The second assumption would seem to be necessary to the theory of Socrates—that the intellect is always able to discern the right course. This probably was a natural one, which Socrates, convinced as he was of his doctrine of the soul's prenatal knowledge of the forms, never thought of questioning. We do, it is true, find him stating to Euthyphro in the course of their discussion on the nature of holiness that men disagree concerning right and wrong, and that

[9] *Crito*, Loeb Classical Library, p. 189.

presumably the gods might do so also.[10] Nevertheless he consistently assumes that the intellect, at least in the case of the philosopher, will always be capable of deciding what is right. This assumption can appear as a foregone conclusion only when it is attached to some such metaphysical safeguard as the doctrine of reminiscence afforded it in the system of Socrates. In the modern world the doctrine of the forms is quite impossible to hold, since it lacks the support of any kind of evidence. The absence of this guarantee leaves the assumption that the intellect can always know the good in any given case in a precarious position. The experience of the modern world tends more to confirm the opposite proposition: that the intellect by no means always knows what the good is.

Rooted in the metaphysic to which Socrates attached his system is another oversimplification of his system: his analysis of the problem of evil. He taught in the *Phaedo* that the sole source of evil is to be found in the body, with its accompanying passions and appetites and its deceptive senses. Though this peculiar metaphysical structure of the doctrine of the forms prevented Socrates from making a very realistic analysis of the problem of evil, he did make one that was to exert a great influence on future ethical thought, since it received quite as wholehearted support from most Christian ethical teachers as it did from the pagan philosophers Plato, Plotinus, and other Neoplatonists. This is not to say that Socrates advocated an extreme asceticism or that he practiced it himself, for if we may believe the picture of him in the *Symposium*, he was pleasant and companionable in society, and in a moderate manner enjoyed the pleasures of good food and good fellowship without any qualms of conscience. However, he did hold a doctrine whose logical fruit was asceticism, as Plotinus saw. The body and its needs, its distracting pleasures and its illusory senses, form the most serious barrier to the pursuit of the ideal virtues, whose seat is solely in the realm of reason and intellect. The philosopher spends his life trying to do the impossible, separate himself from the body, so that he welcomes death which sets him free from this impediment to his pursuit of truth.

[10] *Euthyphro*, Loeb Classical Library, pp. 29, 31.

Even in modern times we have never had an entirely realistic analysis of the exact part played by the flesh in the origin of evil from any ethical teacher, nor has anyone subsequently recognized that the good as well as the evil rests upon and blossoms from an origin that is quite physical, often even fleshly in character. It is a matter of regret that the teaching of Socrates coalesced with certain other trends to produce an overly spiritualized outlook on ethics which rated the flesh as a potential spiritual factor far too low and exaggerated its responsibility for the origin of evil.

What Socrates lacked in his formulation of the doctrine of the forms and of reminiscence was an adequate psychology, an omission natural and pardonable for his time, but it is to be regretted that he transmitted this inadequacy to the ethics of the future. He seems to have had no conception of the complexity of motive, and indeed one might be so unkind as to point out that his own conduct bore witness to this lack. Like the rationalist he was, he oversimplified the problem of the range of motives that underlie any given action and selected as the sole cause of the act one that was in all probability only one out of a number of causes. To take a case in point: the highest and most presentable motive in his disputes with the Athenians was, of course, the one he himself stated in the *Apology*, the desire to find a man wiser than himself. Yet it is impossible to believe that other less respectable motives did not come into these encounters in which he humiliated and devastated his opponents by holding them up to such ridicule as to leave a trail of enemies behind him through all walks of life in Athens. There must have been a strain of sadism obscurely motivating Socrates that he pursued this sport of showing up the Athenians so mercilessly throughout his long career. There is some excuse to be made for his enemies; and to state their case against him in the mildest terms, it may be observed that the gadfly process was not the best pedagogical method by which to instill in his fellow citizens a love of truth similar to the philosopher's own.

As an advocate of self-awareness, Socrates would naturally be supposed to comprehend the involutions of his own motives, and to a certain extent he shows it in the *Apology*, but even there his complete confidence in the rightness of his own position and his consciousness of his own worth do betray a certain self-esteem that verges upon lack of humility. While not a proud man, he did not underestimate himself or feel too keenly his own liability to err. He was no Francis of Assisi by temperament, and even theoretically he did not lay stress upon humility as a cardinal virtue as did Jesus. A thoroughgoing self-knowledge is perhaps the greatest aid to the theory and practice of humility, and this to a certain extent was wanting in the great Athenian.

However, notwithstanding these reservations with regard to Socrates's theory and practice of self-knowledge, his conduct throughout his trial, imprisonment, and martyr's death stamp him as not only a great teacher of ethics but also a great practicer of the same— one fully entitled to be mentioned along with the Buddha and Jesus as one of the greatest and most inspiring of our race. The courage with which Socrates faced death, the charity he displayed toward those who condemned him, as well as his refusal to requite in accordance with less than the best he knew those who had done evil to him, attest his greatness and the perfection of his allegiance to the ideal virtues he taught. His personality, recorded in the four Socratic dialogues of his greatest disciple, is the most priceless legacy to ethics that he has left, and to Plato ethics owes an inestimable debt for preserving that final portrait of his martyred master to posterity.

What a man is personally is surely one of the truest measures of the greatness of his own system; what he bequeaths to posterity in his system is an even greater measure; how much there is in his system that is confirmed as of universal application by history and transplantation is perhaps the highest measure of all.

How does the teaching of Socrates meet this ultimate test of greatness? His teaching has been tested by nearly twenty-four centuries of human experience and has become an integral part of the cultural heritage of the whole Western world. What were the universal elements to which Socrates called attention that made his system, though admittedly designed for philosophers, such a vital influence on the thought and life of the West? His own personality and

example have already been cited. Another element was his democratic optimism in believing that all men are capable of becoming
lovers of wisdom like himself. During his life he had poured out
his wisdom for the rank and file of Athenians quite as freely as for
the aristocratic and the highly educated. That underlying faith in
mankind is a true universal in his system, for it is a conviction of
capacity of all to share in the good life, the democratic view that
the way of wisdom is a highway for all, not a straight and narrow
path for the inner circle of the intellectual elect. Too many of the
philosophers have taught only for the intellectually superior, but
though Socrates was in some respects prone to oversimplify the
problems in the way of the good life, perhaps none of the great
ethical teachers had more courageous faith in the essential goodness
of the human spirit than Socrates, who believed that all men, if they
could be made to know the right way, would unfailingly walk
therein.

From a modern standpoint the metaphysical and epistemological
structure on which Socrates erected his ethical system is wholly untenable; but there is a universal quality in his insistence upon man's
ability to know the right and to do it that completely transcended
and outlasted the metaphysical structure to which he attached it.
Of enduring value, also, was his refusal to believe that ethical
concerns were relative and subject to the same uncertainty and
shifting that occurred in the world of sense. That he went too far
in the direction of underestimating the importance of the world of
nature and sense in the entire scheme of things was merely the
counterside of his emphasis upon the conviction that spiritual values
are the supreme concerns of life. His very exaggerations testify
to the strength of his belief in the ideal virtues of truth, beauty,
and goodness—a faith that he sealed with the martyr's cup.

A particular contribution to the content side of ethics is Socrates's
doctrine of returning good for evil.[11] Although Lao-tze and the
Buddha had formulated this principle for the East, Socrates is the
first ethical teacher to advocate it in the West, and it is beyond all
doubt that this insight was reached independently.

[11] *Crito*, Loeb Classical Library, pp. 179 ff.

Perhaps the greatest single contribution to ethics made by Socrates lies in the realm of method. As has been stated above, Aristotle tells us that Socrates contributed the inductive method to philosophy in general, but of course this method was worked out and employed particularly in ethics. Indeed, it is not too much to say that Socrates contributed to ethics the method that entitled it to a position as a *bona fide* branch of philosophy. For the first time in history ethics received in the hands of Socrates a treatment which is ordered, logical, and consistent. Confucius's treatment is really prephilosophic in its oracular method, its lack of self-consistency and organic unity; and though the Buddha may be called a rationalist in the sense that he used reason to penetrate the delusions of feeling and desire, the reason is but a means to the end of nirvana, and in evolving other parts of his system, the Buddha showed a fine disregard for the laws of logic and correct thinking, of which he seems to have had no inkling at all. Socrates was the first to make a sound methodological attack on the problems of ethics, and that was a contribution to the future of no mean worth. It is lamentable that this promising approach was not extended and corrected by subsequent ethical teachers, since no subject advances beyond its capacity to implement itself well at every step.

CHAPTER V

ARISTOTLE'S NICOMACHEAN ETHICS

Two GENERATIONS later than Socrates another great ethical teacher arose in Greece, Aristotle (born in 384 B.C.; died 322). Aristotle was not an Athenian, and though he passed his youth in that city as a student, then became a tutor in Plato's Academy, he left Athens for a time after his master's death and spent the next few years in various places, principally Mysia, until he was called to the Macedonian court as the tutor of the young Alexander. The death of Philip, the father of Alexander, ended this relationship for Aristotle, and while his youthful pupil embarked upon a career of conquest in the East, the philosopher returned in 334 B.C. to Athens, where he established the Peripatetic School. He remained at the head of that institution, where he lectured, studied, and wrote, until he was exiled from Athens to Chalcis after the death of Alexander. He lived for a year in exile, until his death in 322 B.C.

Unlike Socrates, Aristotle did not devote himself exclusively to ethics. He occupied himself with the whole realm of knowledge as it was at that time. Endowed with one of the master minds of all time, Aristotle is remembered for his contributions to many fields of knowledge, from rhetoric to biology—indeed, biology, psychology, and logic are all sciences created by him. In addition to these varied creations, he wrote one of the world's greatest books on ethics, the treatise known as the *Nicomachean Ethics,* which alone would have been enough to rank him with the immortals. Three works on ethics have come down to us under the name of Aristotle. Of these, the *Magna Moralia* is spurious, written probably by some disciple of Aristotle's a generation or two after his death. The *Eudemian Ethics* is really no more than a brief first draft of the Nicomachean. Since the latter is by far the more important and mature product of Aristotle's thought, the discussion of this chapter is based exclusively upon it.

Aristotle's *Nicomachean Ethics* presents a well-rounded carefully articulated system which covers a wide range of human problems in its discussion—indeed, gives as far-reaching and comprehensive a view of the moral problems of life as any individual living in the small world of the Greek city state could possibly have offered. His is the first completely systematic work on ethics, since Socrates did not write anything and the oriental ethical teachers were not systematic in their approach to the subject. Socrates had already used the inductive method of dialectic in his controversies with the Athenian citizens, but Aristotle gives us the first thoroughgoing and articulated exposition and analysis of the whole field as he saw it. He built upon the ethical thought of Socrates and Plato to some extent, but he not only extended the subject far beyond the scope of anything that they had done but also developed an original and independent system that still stands as one of the great systems of all time.

Aristotle's ethic is a wholly humanistic scheme of morals without any metaphysical or theological orientation. He looks upon virtue as a purely human concern, which does not have any reference to the gods, indeed would be trivial and absurd if applied to them.[1] The moral life as he conceived of it applies only to men. The *summum bonum* of life was the purely earthly goal of happiness throughout as large a part of one's earthly life as possible; and the motivation for the various virtues that contributed to this end was the purely human one of self-respect, or "self-love," as Aristotle called it, and required no supernatural sanctions to reinforce it.[2] Since it is doubtful whether Aristotle believed in any form of personal immortality, these virtues were not referred for their completion or their requital to an afterlife—in marked contrast to the ethic of Socrates, which really constituted a scheme of salvation.[3]

Aristotle defines carefully what he conceives the happiness which is his *summum bonum* to be:

If we declare that the function of man is a certain form of life, and define that form of life as the exercise of the soul's faculties and activities in association with a rational principle, and say that the function of a good man is to perform these activities well and rightly, and if a function is well

[1] Aristotle *Nicomachean Ethics*, Loeb Classical Library, X. viii. 1–8.
[2] *Ibid.*, I. vii. 1–13; IX. viii. 3–5.   [3] *Ibid.*, I. xi. 1–6.

performed when it is performed in accordance with its own proper excellence or virtue,—if then all this be so, the Good of man proves to be the active exercise of his soul's faculties in conformity with excellence or virtue, or if there be several human excellences or virtues, in conformity with the best and most perfect among them.[4]

The hierarchy of virtues which he advocates has a definite social orientation, not a purely individualistic one, for of them the chief is the highly social ideal of justice. He believes the end of the state, as well as that of individuals, is to bring that virtue into society as a working order, and in fact with this aim in view he uses ethics and politics interchangeably. He looks upon justice as the highest and most perfect virtue, the one which comprehends all others in itself.[5] It consists not only of that which is legal, that which is equal, and that which is fair, but it is the virtue which seeks the good of others primarily—in short the description he gives of it suggests that to him it was somewhat equivalent to our modern idea of altruism, though that word was not coined until the nineteenth century.[6]

The formula which Aristotle used to work out the various virtues is his famous "golden mean," a scheme borrowed from the Pythagoreans, who, under the influence of the theory of harmony derived from the musical scale, had applied the analogy of the golden mean to other fields, notably to medicine and physiology, where they supposed health to be attained by a perfect harmony or mean of the four humors in the body, none of which must be present either in excess or deficiency if health is to be maintained. This idea of the golden mean Aristotle applied to the realm of the moral life, where the good, according to his theory, is to be found in the mean between the extremes of excess and deficiency—for example, liberality is the mean between excess of prodigality, or extravagance, upon one hand, and deficiency of meanness, or stinginess, on the other. Courage is the mean between excess of rashness and deficiency of cowardice, modesty between shamelessness and bashfulness, gentleness between irascibility and spiritlessness, and so forth for most of the virtues he discusses. Aristotle admits that his scheme can-

[4] *Ibid.*, I. vii. 14–15.   [5] *Ibid.*, V. i. 15.   [6] *Ibid.*, 15–17.

not be carried through for all the virtues, because things are good in themselves without reference to their contraries.[7]

Aristotle defines virtue itself as neither feeling nor capacity, but a disposition toward the good, which is present as a potentiality in the individual from birth, but whose development is within the power of the individual to control by means of habit, the best technique for bringing the potentiality of the disposition into actuality.[8] The disposition is not entirely under the control of the individual, he concedes, but the actions that strengthen it by the formation of habits of doing right or wrong are entirely under the power of the will; therefore he who would become virtuous has only to act so. He rates as moral only those actions which the individual is free to control, not those which he performs because of some external compulsion, nor does he extend culpability to actions performed by an individual because of ignorance.[9]

The philosopher showed understanding of the fact that the individual is not responsible in a moral sense for some abhorrent vices and perversions that verge upon the psychologically abnormal or arise from some form of insanity, a recognition singularly modern in its tone, but one which by no means all the great ethical teachers were to make. Furthermore, Aristotle recognized the close connection that exists between certain physiological and temperamental factors and the individual's capacity for virtue.[10]

Among the virtues themselves Aristotle distinguished two classes: the intellectual and the moral, corresponding respectively to the rational and the irrational or feeling portions of the soul in accordance with the psychology he himself had formulated. The principal intellectual virtues are prudence and wisdom, but while the philosopher does have a little to say about them in the *Nicomachean Ethics,* he believes that only the virtues of the passions, those of the irrational part of the soul, are the proper concern of ethics.[11] While recognizing the importance of right knowledge in pursuing a course of virtue, Aristotle by no means agreed with Socrates that the two are identical or that the possession of right knowledge

---

[7] *Ibid.,* II. vi. 18–20. 　　　[8] *Ibid.,* II. v. 1–6. 　　　[9] *Ibid.,* III. i.
[10] *Ibid.,* VII. iii. 10–14; v. 　　[11] *Ibid.,* VI. v.

guarantees the presence of virtue. Indeed, he takes issue with this theory of Socrates, which, he says, is plainly at variance with the facts.[12]

Virtue itself is the chief means toward securing the *summum bonum* of happiness, but Aristotle knew full well that it alone did not constitute happiness. He believed that certain other preconditions are very essential to happiness, such as the possession of enough material resources to make possible the practice of such virtues as liberality; a certain basis of health; enough leisure to allow the pursuit of the higher life of the intellect; prosperity and good fortune during enough of a man's life so that happiness may not be destroyed by continual buffeting of fate or dimmed and lost because overtaken by frequent and great tragedies; finally, enough good friends, since no person can enjoy complete happiness alone.[13] All these preconditions of happiness are, however, merely goods in so far as they are means to an end, not the end in itself; for only happiness is that, the good at which all other goods aim: "Every art and every investigation, and likewise every practical pursuit or undertaking, seems to aim at some good: hence it has been well said that the Good is that at which all things aim." [14]

The *summum bonum* of happiness is a form of activity—the highest exercise of the highest faculties, that is, the intellectual ones. It is not to be confused with the mere state of pleasure or avoidance of pain, nor is the life of moral virtue precisely identical with it, since that life can be happy, so Aristotle states, only in the second degree. It is rather the life of contemplation that is the supreme, self-sufficient end, the pursuit of wisdom which aims at nothing beyond itself and partakes of some divine quality, since it is the kind of life the gods enjoy.

In leading up to his discussion of the contemplative life Aristotle makes some fundamental and important qualitative distinctions as to the nature and place of pleasure and pain of various sorts in the ethical realm. He thinks it is foolish to take what a later age has learned to call the "puritanical attitude" toward pleasure—that pleasure is inherently wrong and evil *per se* in all its forms; nor

[12] *Ibid.*, VII. ii. 2.　　　[13] *Ibid.*, VIII. i.　　　[14] *Ibid.*, I. i. 1.

does he take the opposite view, hedonism—that pleasure itself is the aim and end of all things. He draws a distinction between the temporary and the more enduring pleasures, between those of the mind and those of the senses, and he even believes that among the sort which originate in the senses, some are more refined than others. No pleasures of the senses are inherently and *ipso facto* wrong, but only their excesses or perversions are so. This group of pleasures— food, drink, and sex—which we share with the animals, are the lowest form, but they have, when used in moderation, a restorative value for the body that is wholesome and natural, and besides they are the pleasures that can be enjoyed by those not capable of the higher pleasures of the mind. They are bad only if misused or if they impede some higher pleasure. The enjoyment of music or art originates in the senses, but in Aristotle's opinion there is nothing in the least low about these pleasures, indeed they are very refined and exalting. The pleasures originating in the mind are, of course, the highest and purest of all. The inference from the philosopher's discussion of the qualitative differences among pleasures is that both the source and the quality of any pleasure are important in determining its worth, that many pleasures, like amusement, are only means to an end, which in this instance has value in that it recreates us and gets us ready for work again; but the higher pleasures, those of the intellect, are not means, but ends in themselves, since they constitute the contemplative life, happiness. Thus Aristotle advocates a temperate and sane philosophy of the value of pleasure, avoiding the two extremes, asceticism and hedonism.

This judicious appraisal of pleasure is one of the lasting contributions which Aristotle made to the field of ethics. It is unfortunate that it was not adopted as the normative, classic attitude upon the question in all future ethical systems.

The technique or method for the acquisition of virtue which Aristotle put forward was a less felicitous suggestion than his immortal discussion of pleasure and pain. He believed that habit was the means of attaining virtue, and in this he was guilty of oversimplifying the problem. His is not the rationalist's oversimplification, such as that of Socrates, and he shows far more understanding of the part motive plays in conduct than the latter does; yet even in his full appreciation of the conflict between desire and knowledge, he oversimplifies in another direction. Habit alone is not an adequate technique for producing that alignment of good motivation and good external effects which constitutes really good actions. It is clear that Aristotle worked upon the problem chiefly from the standpoint of the external effects of any given action rather than from that of the motive which prompted it. He seems never to have formulated a full solution to problems of motive in conduct, indeed he himself betrays some consciousness of this lack at some points in the *Nicomachean Ethics;* for example, he admits that seemingly sincere conduct might spring either from the presence of some ulterior motive or from pure uprightness of character.[15] On the basis of habit alone the difficulty of the alignment of good motives with good actions from the standpoint of consequences entailed cannot be resolved. Aristotle's advocacy of habit leaves the problem of motive largely untouched, and indeed the process of forming the habit of doing good actions without having the motives in line with the conduct might just as well result in the production of hypocrites as in the production of men whose actions were inwardly good. However, this is a problem of ethics to which no one has yet found the complete answer, the great ethical teachers usually having stressed either motive or consequences as the sole component factor of right conduct and none having given the final answer to how to bring right motives and right consequences together.

The second defect in Aristotle's system is the selection of virtues which he singles out for discussion. It may be granted that sincerity, justice, moderation, honesty, and magnanimity are cardinal virtues, and the inclusion of the subject of friendship in the *Nicomachean Ethics* is surely one of the great merits of the book; but some of the virtues that he discusses at length are of secondary importance, if indeed they really belong to the sphere of ethics at all. He devotes considerable space to such qualities as magnificence, wittiness, and

---

[15] *Ibid.,* IV. vii. 5: "Both Sincerity and Insincerity may be practiced with or without an ulterior motive; but when a man is acting without ulterior motive, his words, his actions, and conduct always reflect his true character."

righteous indignation together with their opposing extremes of excess and deficiency. The inclusion of such matters in a treatise on ethics suggests that Aristotle did not always keep in mind the distinction between manners and morals. Wit and buffoonery, for instance, are surely problems of taste rather than of character. All in all, we are forced to conclude that the virtues which Aristotle stressed are not all of equal worth and that he did not give us a classic list of them in the *Nicomachean Ethics*.

While it is a merit that there is a certain emergence of the social consciousness in Aristotle's ethic, which is a wholesome contrast to the entire absence of perception of any social values which marred Gautama's thinking and the naïve form in which they were apprehended by Confucius, even Aristotle did not go far, according to modern lights, toward seeing the social springs of ethical action. Problems such as the rights of the individual against the group, the conflicts of the various social classes, the moral problems which surround the struggle for existence do not seem to have presented themselves as ethical issues to the mind of Aristotle any more than to the rest of the ancients. Nevertheless, Aristotle's emphasis upon the social virtue of justice as the highest of the virtues demonstrates that his ethic was far more social-minded than that of any of the other ethical teachers of the ancient world, and he did not share the aristocratic prejudices that warped the social thinking of his master, Plato, in the *Republic*.

What were the universals which Aristotle discovered and transmitted to the realm of ethics? First of all, and perhaps most important, his normative appraisal of the quality of pain and pleasure, which has already been discussed. On the side of content a second outstanding norm is to be found in the teleological structure upon which his whole system is built. This dominance of purpose and aim in ethics is an idea which was original with Aristotle. This is an emphasis whose importance for ethics cannot be exaggerated or its significance outlived, a characteristic not peculiar to his ethical teaching, but running throughout his whole philosophy. Teleology is a necessary element of any vital system of ethics, though it may be oriented either to the ends of this life or to the life after death. In Aristotle's case the orientation is decidedly of this world, for it is not likely that he believed in any other kind of immortality except what we are able to achieve here and now through the life of contemplation. The virtues, the activities of life are all focused about this central aim; for nothing in the universe as Aristotle conceived it could be purposeless; all things strive for some higher end, and in the case of mankind, they release their potentiality into the high degree of actuality to be attained in the self-sufficient happiness of the contemplative life.

In this emphasis upon teleology we see in Aristotle an emergence of one of the most distinctive characteristics of the occidental mind in contrast to the oriental. For the Buddha, the only purpose is to be free from the Wheel of Life, loosed from the power of karma. This idea of a central purpose comprehending all the separate and minor purposes is the original contribution of the Western genius of Aristotle, which was not excelled in its teleological character by any of the subsequent systems oriented to this life alone. Bound up as it was with the philosopher's conception of the hierarchy of being, it was one of the elements that gave immortality to his system. "The Good is that at which all things aim."

With regard to method in ethics Aristotle also made some contributions that deserve rank as normative for the future of ethics, though these have not been so widely recognized as his contributions of content. He rendered great service in delimiting the field, marking out boundaries of the properly ethical from those of the psychological and physiological and approaching the subject in a sound, balanced, and systematic way. These distinctions which he was the first to draw were unfortunately lost from sight by many of the ethical teachers who followed him, but there is some prospect that modern thought on the subject will take up his suggestions and extend them further and more scientifically. If this lead of Aristotle's had been followed, it is likely that ethics would be a true science today.

Aristotle himself does not claim the exactitude of a science for his ethic.[16] His own familiarity with the methods of science from his biological and other studies had made him too conscious of the varying degrees of certainty attainable in such subjects to allow him to put himself forward as a purveyor of the sacrosanct canons of an absolute and divinely established code of moral laws. His method of examination is the logical method, but he knew full well that even this did not carry the guarantee of certainty for his findings and that much in the ethical field still lay in the realm of opinion and preference. It would have been well for the future if more of the great ethical teachers had imitated Aristotle's modesty in their claims for their systems. One of the principal factors that has retarded the progress of ethics is the confusion arising from propounding really tentative and controversial opinions or dicta as fixed and immutable moral laws. It is one of the marks of greatness in Aristotle that he avoided this error.

The scheme for the location of the virtue as the mean between the extreme of excess and deficiency is one of Aristotle's most influential methodological contributions. The principle of the mean is an important one indeed, for it regulates all those realms of conduct in which the virtue in question is not absolute in its own right, but a middle ground between the contraries of excess and defect. Aristotle himself does not assert that his mean applies to all the virtues, but not all who used the principle were so careful to bear in mind this limitation. It is absurd, for example, to apply the principle to the pursuit of virtue itself, as Confucius actually did. But within its proper limits the mean is an important regulative principle that governs several different areas of conduct.

The contributions of Aristotle with regard to content, his normative and classic appraisal of pleasure and the teleological orientation of his system, would probably be recognized as two of his outstanding legacies to the ethics of the future; but recognition of the methodological service he rendered to the field has been slower, and there has been far too little attempt to go on with the task from the point where he left off. Yet there is great need of developing the methodology of ethics right at the present time.

[16] *Ibid.*, I. iii. 1–5.

CHAPTER VI

JESUS AND THE JEWISH-CHRISTIAN ETHICAL HERITAGE

JESUS, like Socrates, Gautama, and Confucius, left no written records of his teaching, so that the student must labor with the problems of source criticism. Although the problems of gospel criticism are not so hopelessly involved as those of the Buddhist sutras, nevertheless, they pose some knotty problems which more than a hundred years of historical study of the Gospels have by no means solved. However, it is necessary to wrestle with them, difficult though they may be, since the four canonical Gospels are our only important source of knowledge of Jesus's teaching. Of the four Gospels the three so-called "Synoptics" give us the most important report of Jesus's sayings and doings, because the Gospel of John is generally held by New Testament scholars to be a later interpretation of Jesus's person and work, put into shape about A.D. 100, rather than a report of his *ipsissima verba*. The Synoptics will be the chief source used in the present chapter, but even they did not reach their present form until forty years or more after his death. Mark, the earliest of them, is usually dated about A.D. 70, Matthew comes between A.D. 75 and 80, and Luke perhaps five years after Matthew.

More than a century of criticism of the Gospels has wrought some clarification—as well as considerable confusion—in our knowledge of the authenticity and historicity of the Gospels. To put the results very briefly and generally, the duplications, agreements, differences, and variations among the Gospels are such that the material may be divided into the following three classes: that which the scholars are unanimous in accepting as originating with Jesus; that which scholars agree is secondary accretion; and a certain amount concerning whose genuineness the most competent experts disagree completely. For the discussion which follows the writer has selected only those passages from the Gospels in whose favor there is a goodly presumption of authenticity.

Certain characteristics of the Synoptics must be borne in mind by the student who would really understand their contents aright. The first is the fact that they were not intended to be biographies of Jesus in the modern sense of the word, they were propagandist documents designed for use in conversion and edification, for even the superscription of the Gospel of Mark (1:1) consciously has in mind the purpose of presenting Jesus as the Messiah. Moreover, the Gospels share with other ancient writings a lack of scientific standards of historical and biographical composition: sources are seldom cited by name, often are not indicated at all; quotations are frequently inexact, with the consequence that often it is difficult to distinguish Jesus's own ideas from those held by the evangelists and those traditions about his person which were already accepted as the orthodox belief of the primitive church. However, it is testimony of high order to the honesty and veracity of the Gospels that some facts about Jesus which were not as the early church would have imagined them, some opinions of his which were in direct contradiction to its beliefs are preserved in the Gospels, so that by and large they are good history in comparison to other ancient writings.

Some qualities of the teachings of Jesus fostered good transmission. The sayings seem usually to have been couched in the concise proverbial form which easily stayed in the minds of hearers unaccustomed to dependence upon written records, much of the teaching was in the vivid story form of the parable that remained in the memory for years.

Since such preliminary characteristics of the Gospels as literature must be mentioned before they can be handled by the student, so also certain preliminary observations must be made before Jesus's ethical teaching proper can be seen in its correct historical perspective. The first of these is that Jesus does not give us a complete ethical system, like that of Aristotle. Like Confucius and the Buddha, Jesus did not give a thoroughgoing and systematic exposition of the subject of ethics. He taught in proverbs and parables, which give one central idea more than a complete analysis of the idea in all its ramifications, such as Aristotle would make. Like the Hebrew prophets Jesus taught from the basis of his own experience of God and man, by authority and intuition, by story and picture, rather than by accurate definition, careful scrutiny of premises, and ordered, consecutive presentation of his subject.

Another preliminary observation of vast importance for understanding the ethic of Jesus is that it is a profoundly religious system, resting upon his original apprehension and experience of God. Even in a study strictly confined to ethics it is necessary to go into his religious teaching to some extent in order to understand the chief motivations and impulses that colored his ethics, for the latter cannot be wholly separated from his religious faith. Also, while Jesus touched with the originality of his spirit the whole religious and ethical heritage of Judaism that lay behind him, he nevertheless built upon it and, sifting out the best, perpetuated its highest elements for the future of Christianity. He built upon the ethical monotheism of the Old Testament Prophets, who had insisted that God's foremost requirement of His people was goodness until the nation of Israel ended by believing their word. Jesus's view of the relation between religion and ethics was shaped by this conviction of the Prophets. The finer portions of the Jewish Law, such as the fundamentals of morality expressed in the six moral commands of the Decalogue in Exodus 20, were central to him, so that when the Rich Man asks him what to do to inherit eternal life, the Master repeats these moral precepts from the Decalogue (Mark 10:17-20). The humanitarian emphasis of Jesus's entire ethical and religious system is redolent of that of Israel's most humanitarian law book, Deuteronomy. Coloring all his thought is the Hebrew eschatology, which came to the fore late in the Old Testament period and developed markedly throughout the intertestamental period.

With a sure feeling for the soundest moral and religious values, Jesus worked upon the mass of the religious and moral laws and sundered them from the ceremonial with which they were intermingled. His acceptance of this heritage of his people was therefore critical and judicious, so that he passed on the finest and discarded the less valuable. That which he retained he stamped with the originality of his own religious spirit and moral insight. His system is at once religious and moral, in a combination true to the prophetic tradition. The *summum bonum* of Jesus's whole scheme of ethics is the purely religious one of membership in the Kingdom of God, and that goal also constitutes the reward of the good life as he conceived it.

The fundamental principle of unity between religion and ethics for Jesus was his profound insight that the status of each man in the eyes of God is determined by his status in the eyes of his fellow man. God's chief requirement of men is good will and good conduct towards his fellow man. In his summary of the greatest commandments of the Jewish Law, Jesus coupled love of God and love of neighbor as of equal importance.[1]

Several sections of Jesus's teaching carry out this same theme, that man stands with God as he stands with his fellow men. God's forgiveness of sin is contingent upon man's forgiveness of the offense of his brother man: "And whensoever ye stand praying, forgive, if ye have aught against anyone; that your Father also who is in heaven may forgive you your trespasses" (Mark 11:25, paralleled by the petition in the Lord's Prayer, "And forgive us our sins; for we ourselves also forgive everyone that is indebted to us" Luke 11:4 = Matthew 6:12).

The same teaching is further elaborated in the Parable of the Unforgiving Debtor, peculiar to Matthew, but so characteristic of the thought of Jesus that its genuineness seems assured. It ends: "So shall also my heavenly Father do to you, if ye forgive not everyone his brother from your hearts."

In Matthew's version of the Sermon on the Mount we have the counsel given, "If therefore thou art offering thy gift at the altar, and there rememberest that thy brother hath aught against thee, leave there thy gift before the altar, and go thy way, first be reconciled to thy brother, and then come and offer thy gift" (Matthew 5:23, 24). The plain inference of this counsel is, of course, that

---

[1] It is possible that Luke's report of the summary of the greatest commandment of the Law (10:25–27), is correct where not Jesus, but an unnamed lawyer, makes this summary of the essence of the Law as loving God with one's entire being, and loving one's neighbor as oneself, but at any rate, Jesus approved the summary, and it represents his own view upon the matter.

God will not accept the gift so long as the giver's relations with his fellow men are not right. Finally, the Parable of the Last Judgment (Matthew 25:31–46), though it may have been retouched by the First Evangelist, contains an authentic kernel of the thought of Jesus when it portrays him as saying as the conductor of the Judgment, "Inasmuch as ye have done it unto one of these, my brethren, even these least, ye have done it unto me."

It is possible that the combination Jesus made of religion and ethics sprang largely from his high sense of the worth of the individual man. The ethic is oriented to the view that each individual is infinitely valuable in the sight of God. Jesus teaches that God, a Father Who notices even the fall of a sparrow, cares infinitely more for each man, so that the very hairs of our heads are numbered (Matthew 10:29–31 = Luke 12:5–7). Indeed, on the whole, Jesus held a very high estimate of human nature. Although he did once draw a contrast between men, who, being evil, nevertheless know how to give good gifts to their own children and the absolute goodness of God (Matthew 7:13 = Luke 11:13.), he seems to have intended evil here only in the relative sense of comparison to the absolute goodness of God, since he held human nature in such high esteem that he believed men capable of imitating the Divine Perfection (Matthew 5:49). His treatment of individuals, as well as his express teaching, indicates that he believed he was acting according to the Divine standard of values when he came "to seek and to save that which was lost." Even the publicans and the sinners, outcasts among his fellow Jews, were not too low to be reclaimed, and Jesus laid himself open to the charge of keeping bad company rather than ignore these ostracized members of Jewish society (Matthew 11:19 = Luke 11:34). The Three Parables of lost things—the Lost Sheep, the Lost Coin, and the Lost Son of Luke 15—all illustrate his view that God is supremely interested in every individual, that He cares more about reclaiming the lost one than about the ninety and nine that need no repentance.

Jesus's interest in the individual colors his ethic in other ways also. He thought of moral conduct from the standpoint of the individual rather than the group. It is not so much the social consequences of a deed that interest him as the motives of the man who does that deed: "It is impossible but that occasions of stumbling should come, but woe unto him through whom they come! It were well for him if a millstone were hanged about his neck, and he were thrown into the sea, rather than that he should cause one of these little ones to stumble," he says (Luke 17:1, 2 = Matthew 18:6, 7). According to this individual standard, bad motives are as bad as the deeds they contemplate.

From the section on the subject of motive in the Sermon on the Mount (Matthew 5:21-28), we discover that he believes anger is as bad as killing, that lustful thought in the mind is as bad as adultery—in short, that bad thought is really equivalent to bad action. Jesus's stress upon the importance of motive in conduct is greater than that to be found in the teachings of any of the other ethical teachers. From the social standpoint, which appraises the good or evil character of a deed, as Aristotle did, according to the good or the harm it causes to others, it is impossible to maintain that bad motives are as harmful as bad conduct. Jesus could maintain this view of the matter simply because he viewed the whole ethical transaction from the standpoint of the individual man, not of the consequences to society. The individual who caused the offenses seemed to him to be in a far more deplorable state than those who suffered from them.

Jesus's preoccupation with the individual also accounts for the almost complete absence of any teaching upon social or national concerns. Jesus really did not consider these social problems at any length; we have only a few isolated sayings that bear upon them, such as "Render unto Caesar the things that are Caesar's, and unto God the things that are God's" (Mark 12:17 and Matthew 22:21; Luke 20:25), but out of this single ambiguous saying it is impossible to spin a whole philosophy of government. "They that take the sword shall perish with the sword" (Matthew 26:52), is his only saying which bears directly upon the subject of armed force, and even it is reported by Matthew alone in the dubious context of the scene in the Garden of Gethsemane. Even if it be granted that the logion is genuine, though perhaps recorded in the wrong setting, it is the only one of Jesus's sayings that directly relates to war. The general inference from this and the beatitude "Blessed are the peacemakers" (Matthew 5:9a) is that Jesus advocated peaceful methods, though in the latter verse he seems to have had only the dealings of individual men with each other in mind. At any rate, we have from him no extended and unmistakable denunciation of war as a national and international evil. Very likely this is because he thought that nationality, like other principles governing the present age, would be done away with when the New Age of the Kingdom of God came.

The rigor of his economic teachings reflects the individualistic standpoint of his ethics even more plainly. He views the whole matter of wealth and poverty, not as an economic question of far-reaching social importance, but purely as a concern of the individual man's eschatological destiny. In endeavoring to reach any appraisal of the teaching of Jesus on wealth and poverty one must constantly bear in mind that he believed that the Kingdom of God would come very soon and that then money and all the economic media of the present world order would be abrogated. It is true that the subject of his eschatology is one of the most moot points in the Gospels; but although his utterances upon the time and manner of the coming of the Kingdom were not consistent throughout his whole ministry, and his belief about the part he would play in bringing in the new order probably changed during the latter part of his career, yet it is impossible to maintain that Jesus did not have an eschatological view of these matters, unless one is willing to commit the critical *tour de force* of discarding as secondary all the eschatological passages in the Gospels.

Throughout his ministry Jesus believed that the Kingdom of God was coming very soon. What may well have been his earliest view is represented in the statement of his initial message in Mark 1:15: "The time is fulfilled, and the Kingdom of God is at hand; repent ye and believe the gospel." His later idea on the question of the time of the coming is contained in two verses from Mark (9:1, 2), "Verily I say unto you, there are some here of them that stand by who shall in no wise taste of death, till they see the kingdom of

God come with power"; and his answer to the High Priest at his trial (14:61b), "Ye shall see the Son of man sitting at the right hand of Power, and coming with the clouds of heaven." In other words, up to the end of his life Jesus believed that the Kingdom of God was to come within the lifetime of his own generation, within a span of some thirty years at the utmost. He speaks in several places in the Gospels of the impending doom that will overtake his generation in the Judgment, and from all these passages it is plain that he expects this Judgment which will usher in the New Age to take place *while his generation is still alive*.[2] A further proof that Jesus did expect to return very shortly after his death is furnished by the universal expectation of the primitive church that such would be the fact, as, for example, Paul sets forth in I Thessalonians 4:17.

Seen in the light of his eschatological expectations, the puzzles set by the economic teachings of Jesus vanish. The Kingdom was to come soon; what could the individual man do that would be more wise and foresighted than to prepare himself for that high destiny of entering into it? Hence springs his advice, "Sell that which ye have and give alms; make for yourselves purses which wax not old, a treasure in the heavens that faileth not, where no thief draweth near, neither moth destroyeth. For where your treasure is, there will your heart be also" (Luke 12:33, 34 = Matthew 6:20, 21). The candidate for the Kingdom of God should not, like his pagan neighbors, spend his time in the pursuit of riches or even give much thought to the quest of the necessities of food, clothing, and shelter; hence the admonitions of Matthew (6:23–34 = Luke 12:22–31) not to be anxious for one's life or for the requirements of physical existence. "Yet seek ye first his kingdom and these things shall be added unto you" (Luke 12:31). The primary aim of all should be to seek the Kingdom of God, which could not be combined with the pursuit of money: "Ye cannot serve God and Mammon" (Matthew 6:22c = Luke 16:13c).

That Jesus believed riches to be a serious barrier to the attainment of the good life is further borne out by the story of Jesus and the

[2] Cf. Matthew 11:46 ff. = Luke 10:13 ff.; Luke 11:15–22; Matthew 23:34, 36 = Luke 11:51, 52; Luke 11:29–31 = Matthew 12:39–42.

Rich Man (Mark 10:17–31 = Matthew 19:16–30 = Luke 18:18–30). Their fleeting character is illustrated by the Parable of the Rich Fool, recorded only by Luke (12:13–21), but generally held to be authentic. A man's life, according to Jesus, "consisteth not in the abundance of the things which he possesseth" (verse 15); therefore Jesus's rhetorical question, "For what is a man profiteth if he gain the whole world and forfeit his life?" (Mark 6:36 = Matthew 16:26 = Luke 9:25), urges his conviction that membership in the Kingdom soon to arrive is the one supremely valuable end to which a man can devote himself. The extreme demands that he made of his followers acquire their urgency from the fact that he believed the coming of the new order was imminent. While in the interim his followers might have to make sacrifices, these would be compensated in the New Age, when mammon and all the other principles that held sway in the old order would be superseded. This position underlies his answer to Peter on the point, best preserved in the Gospel of Matthew.

Then Peter answered and said unto him, Lo, we have left all, and followed thee; what then shall we have? And Jesus said unto them, Verily, I say unto you, that ye who have followed me, in the regeneration when the Son of man shall sit on the throne of his glory, ye also shall sit upon twelve thrones, judging the twelve tribes of Israel. And every one that hath left houses, or brethren, or sisters, or father, or mother, or lands, for my sake, shall receive a hundredfold, and shall inherit eternal life" (Matthew 19:27–29).

The *summum bonum* of the good life lay in the eschatological goal of membership in the Kingdom of God, where the good would find their reward in participation in the New Age, and the wicked, on the other hand, would have their punishment meted out to them by being excluded from it. The values which comprise the qualifications for membership in the Kingdom are those values which prepare the way for its coming, and both now and then are those enduring values which in Jesus's own figure withstand any storm, like the house built upon the rock (Matthew 7:25–27 = Luke 6:47–49).

Which were the chief virtues that Jesus deemed essential to the good life? That the cardinal virtue is good will we know from his answer to the question as to what was the greatest commandment, where he places love of one's neighbor immediately after love for God (Mark 12:29–31 = Matthew 22:37–40). In the Lucan variant of this answer (Luke 10:25–27), where the lawyer who is questioning Jesus puts forward the commandment with the approval of Jesus, the Parable of the Good Samaritan, which is told to answer a further question as to who is one's neighbor, defines our neighbor as anyone who needs our help. Good will bulks large in the Sermon on the Mount and its Lucan counterpart, the Sermon on the Plain, where it includes the Golden Rule, the injunction to return good for evil, to refrain from resisting evil, and to go the second mile. The good will that Jesus advocates is not to be confused with the affection of friendship or kinship, it is something far wider, which exceeds the bounds of congeniality and extends impartially to all without thought of recompense or of the merit of the recipient; rather it resembles the Divine Goodness that sends the rain upon the just and the unjust alike (Matthew 5:38–48, 7:12 = Luke 6:27–36).

If good will is the cardinal virtue of Jesus's system, humility ranks next to it in order of importance. In the thought of Jesus humility comprehends gentleness, the absence of all pride and self-righteousness, and also the kind of docility and teachableness which children show. This trait Jesus particularly mentions as an indispensable qualification for all who would be heirs to the Kingdom (Mark 10:13–16). Humility is inculcated by the Parable of the Pharisee and the Publican, where the self-righteous Pharisee is contrasted with the contrite and humble Publican who admits his own unworthiness (Luke 18:9–14). Throughout the pages of the Gospels there echoes like a refrain this oft-repeated maxim: "For everyone that exalteth himself shall be humbled, and whosoever shall humble himself shall be exalted" (Matthew 23:12; Luke 14:11; 18:14b).

The third great virtue in the eyes of Jesus undoubtedly was sincerity. It was the absence of this quality that he condemned most severely in the Pharisees and the other religious leaders of his day, that lack in them which prompted him to say, "Except your right-

eousness shall exceed the righteousness of the scribes and Pharisees,
ye shall in no wise enter into the Kingdom of Heaven" (Matthew
5:20). In his great diatribe against the Pharisees (Matthew 23 =
Luke 11:37–54) it is particularly the hypocrisy and insincerity of
these leaders that he attacks, their outward display of piety and
goodness over against their inner wickedness, their sins of the spirit,
which cause him to term them whited sepulchers. It was this same
regard for sincerity, for purity of motive that underlay his great
stress upon the importance of singleness of aim, his belief that only
the good trees can bring forth good fruit, that only good motives
can produce good conduct.

The purity of heart mentioned in the beatitude of Matthew 5:8,
which has commonly been interpreted to refer only to sex purity
(if it be from Jesus), has a much wider application in his thinking,
it is really a purity of heart that extends to all motives, not just the
restricted group centered about sex. It is of a piece with his saying,
"If, therefore, thine eye be single, thy whole body shall be full of
light, but if thine eye be evil, thy whole body shall be full of
darkness" (Matthew 6:22, 23 = Luke 11:33, 34). Jesus's view of the
problem of motive is a simple one, the sole and sufficient requirement for good conduct being good motives. "The good man, out of
the good treasure of his heart bringeth forth that which is good,
and the evil man out of the evil treasure bringeth forth that which
is evil: for out of the abundance of the heart, the mouth speaketh"
(Luke 6:45, 46 = Matthew 12:34, 35). That a whole range of
motives, high and low, worthy and unworthy, might go into a
single action seems not to have occurred to Jesus, who thought in
quite direct and simple terms.

Beyond the three virtues, good will, humility and sincerity, it is
quite impossible to tell how the other virtues ranked in Jesus's scale
of values, although others are mentioned by him as essential for
membership in the Kingdom of God. In Matthew 23:23, 24 = Luke
11:42 he enumerates as the weightier matters of the Law, justice,
mercy, and faith, though the Lucan variant of this verse has merely
justice and the love of God. In Matthew's version of the beatitudes,
Jesus specifies among the qualifications for membership in the King-

dom, mercy, gentleness, peacefulness, and a genuine desire for righteousness (Matthew 5:6–7, 9). He taught that service was the principle of precedence in the Kingdom of God, rather than power, whose dangers it is one of his contributions to ethics that he saw clearly and pointed out (Mark 10:35–45 = Matthew 20:20–28; Luke 22:25–27).

And Jesus called them unto him, and saith unto them, Ye know that they who are accounted to rule over the Gentiles lord it over them; and their great ones exercise authority over them. But it is not so among you; but whosoever would be great among you shall be your minister, and whosoever would be first among you shall be servant of all (Mark 10: 42, 43).

This service principle is enunciated by Jesus when James and John inquire whether they may sit one upon his right hand, the other on his left, in his Kingdom. It is carried out also as the principle of helpfulness prompted by kindness in the Parable of the Last Judgment (Matthew 25:31–46), where in a large measure it appears to be the standard by which judgment is rendered.

There is one final requirement which Jesus felt was a *sine qua non* of any goodness worthy of the name. It must be a spontaneous expression of the person's whole nature, an unconscious and unstudied sort of goodness that lets not "the left hand know what the right hand doeth." In the Last Judgment scene those who have shown this kind of goodness are surprised when they are commended, and on the counter side, those who are condemned are equally astonished that they should be considered wicked; for Jesus believed that real wickedness was also the kind portrayed in this parable, neglect and carelessness about performing good deeds.

In attempting to form any opinion of the lasting contributions of Jesus to the field of ethics it is necessary to put aside, so far as this is possible for anyone reared in the Christian tradition, all theological preconceptions as to the nature of Jesus's person and work and to view him simply as an ethical teacher, to set him on the same plane as the other great ethical teachers, and to measure his system by the same human standard.

Sometimes in the very encomiums that are heaped upon Jesus

by his followers it is forgotten just what services he rendered to the field of ethics, what permanent contributions he made. What are these? First of all must be mentioned the unfailing emphasis which he placed upon human values, the worth of the individual man, the way in which he never lost sight of the human necessities, even among religious observances and institutions. With a very sound sense of the importance of this human factor, he insisted that religious institutions, even the sacred Jewish Sabbath, existed for man, not man for the Sabbath (Mark 2:27); and that when the Law permitted a man to water the animals or to raise an ox or an ass that had fallen into a pit on that sacred day, surely it was in accordance with the Law to benefit human beings, who were of infinitely more value (Matthew 12:10–13). The act of dedicating gifts to the temple of God could not and should not release a man from the duty of supporting his parents (Mark 7:11, 12).

This sense of the worth of every human being dictates the junction Jesus made between religion and ethics. It is not too much to say that in his thesis that the status of a man in the eyes of God depends upon his status with his fellow men, Jesus made the greatest synthesis between religion and ethics that has been put forward by any of those ethical teachers who have a religious reference to their ethic. This union of religion and ethics is one of the outstanding contributions of the Nazarene to both religion and ethics.

A second contribution of Jesus to both realms is to be found in his infallible sense of proportion, the sureness with which he selected and exalted those ethical attitudes which are primary and fundamental and subordinated those which are secondary and incidental. There are several ways in which his discrimination manifests itself throughout his teaching. He drew the distinction so fundamental for ethics between matters of ceremony, custom, tradition, and manners on the one hand and those which were of truly vital concern to morality on the other. With one stroke he swept aside the whole ceremonial side of the Jewish Law and revealed the moral side in all its purity and power (Mark 7:1–23).

And he saith unto them, Are ye so without understanding also? Perceive ye not, that whatsoever from without goeth into the man, it cannot defile him; because it goeth not into his heart, but into his belly, and goeth out into the draught . . . And he said, That which proceedeth out of a man, that defileth the man. For from within, out of the heart of men, evil thoughts proceed, fornications, thefts, murders, adulteries, covetings, wickednesses, deceit, lasciviousness, an evil eye, railing, pride, foolishness: all these evil things proceed from within, and defile the man [Mark 7: 18–23].

Judaism had long labored under the difficulties of confusion between the moral and the ceremonial, from which Jesus now set it free; and in like manner the ethical structures of such teachers as Confucius, the Buddha, and Aristotle suffered from their failure to draw this fundamental distinction between manners and morals. This is one of the greatest clarifications that had been made in the sphere of ethics by anyone since men had first seriously attacked the problems of moral conduct. It is a sad commentary upon the subsequent history of ethical thought under Christian aegis that this distinction drawn by Jesus, which should have been taken over once for all from him, was frequently lost from sight even by teachers who professed to be his disciples.

Another manifestation of Jesus's moral sense of proportion was the gradation he made, classifying the subtle sins of the spirit as more serious and more defiling than the grosser sins of the flesh. This is not to say that Jesus did not regard the sins of the flesh as serious, but rather that he looked upon the hardening sins of pride and self-righteousness as the more corrosive to personality, as is finely illustrated in the misplaced, but certainly authentic, account of his treatment of the woman taken in adultery (John 7:53–8:11) and by the Parable of the Two Sons, recounted only by Matthew, where Jesus comments, "Verily I say unto you, that the publicans and the harlots go into the kingdom of God before you" (that is, before the scribes and the Pharisees, Matthew 21:28–32).

A third universal of Jesus's teaching is to be found in his exaltation of good will to the position of cardinal virtue in his scheme. His teaching of good will is not new; for Lao-tze had first formulated the principle of returning good for evil, Socrates had propounded it on Greek soil, the Buddha on Indian, and Confucius had stated the Golden Rule in negative form; but the originality of Jesus consists in the central position in which he placed good will.

There are individual insights worthy of mention as contributions of importance. One of these which has rather generally been overlooked is his insight that power constitutes a dangerous barrier to the pursuit of the good life. Much stress has been laid upon his teachings concerning riches as an obstacle to the good life, but little has been said of his discovery of the dangers inherent in power. An original aspect of his ethic is his analysis of the place of motive in conduct, which has the first adequate recognition of the importance of the inner basis of good action. Apparently he took account only of motivation as the determining factor of whether a deed was good or bad, instead of reckoning its consequences as well, but we have already observed that Jesus viewed the ethical transaction purely from the individualistic standpoint, not from the social. If he oversimplified the problem of motive and overemphasized it as against the social consequences, the very overemphasis rendered a service to ethics, for the question of motive had been largely ignored.

Jesus had no scheme of moral discipline to offer as a recipe for the good life. Aside from the practice of prayer and religious devotion, we have from him only the injunction to do the thing commanded and not to do the thing forbidden: in other words, the good life is the result of simple acts of will within the power of every man to make. While, practically speaking, there may be few who find "the way that leadeth unto life," yet the way and the power to follow that good life are open to all who choose to keep the commands of Jesus and share in the happiness of the good life he advocated. The Kingdom of God is, in Jesus's thought, a spiritual democracy.

While Jesus built firmly on the Jewish religio-ethical heritage behind him, in like manner did the primitive Christian church build upon his ethical teaching. However, some supplements to the ethic of its Master, some extensions that the church was forced to make, are to be found even within the pages of the New Testament. Before we leave Jesus's teaching, these New Testament extensions and additions must be considered, since one index to the stature of great moral teachers is to be found in what they inspire.

New Testament additions to the ethics of Jesus.—Aside from the ethics of Jesus, what independent contributions to moral law there are in the New Testament come almost exclusively from the pen of the Apostle Paul. The Epistle to the Hebrews has a great and original theology, but even its hortatory sections add little to the general precepts of the Christian ethic, except perhaps for the injunction to hospitality (Hebrews 13:20), a virtue commended also in I Timothy 2:3, where it is listed as one of the essential qualifications of a bishop. The Epistle of James is deeply imbued with the spirit of the Sermon on the Mount, on which it might almost be said to be a practical commentary, for it applies the Sermon thoroughly and specifically to the situation of the Christian community toward the end of the first century. Its author's sense of social justice compares favorably with that of the Old Testament Prophets. To James religion was principally a matter of ethics, as it was to Micah. Writes the apostle, "Pure religion and undefiled before God and the Father is this, to visit the fatherless and the widows in their affliction, and to keep oneself unspotted from the world" (1:27). Throughout the epistle the necessity for deeds is stressed, but otherwise it adds no new canons to the Christian code.

The three Johannine epistles are virtually commentaries on the Christian law of love, but to it they add no new moral laws; and the Book of Revelation is so exclusively concerned with apocalyptic that it does not enter into the realm of ethics at all.

In order to understand the ethics of Paul, one must realize clearly two facts: first, that the apostle expected the return of the Lord within his own lifetime (I Thessalonians 4:13–18; I Corinthians 15:24 ff.); second, that the letters he addressed to his churches were written distinctly *ad hoc*. He had no idea of the unwinding of a long scroll of history after his own life, when his letters would be read in all churches and held as inspired, canonical writings throughout the Christian world. He wrote his churches in order to give them his advice and guidance upon their local problems, many of which were of purely temporary and local significance, some of which were fundamental moral problems that might come up in any locality in any age.

For the gospel which he preached the apostle believed himself to be directly commissioned by a Divine revelation made especially to him by the Lord Jesus in person (see Galatians 1:11, 12). The general principles of Paul's ethic were those of Jesus; but he conceived some concerns and emphases of the ethical life differently from his Master because of differences in temperament and religious experience. Also, because the apostle had a number of new problems to cope with in the organization of his young churches, he added some new points to the body of Christian ethics as it had come down from Jesus.

In contradistinction to Jesus, Paul considered the ethical life largely the result of the work of the Holy Spirit which produced in the convert what he named the fruits of the Spirit such as love, joy, peace, long suffering, and the rest of the list of Christian attitudes he enumerates in Galatians 5:22. Those in whom the Spirit did not work were largely subject to the domination of evil rooted principally, though not exclusively in the flesh (Galatians 5:19–21; Romans 8:1–9)—a conception more Greek than Jewish. There were a few who were righteous outside the pale of the Christian faith, of the Jews according to the law, and of the Gentiles a few who without the law had the works of the law written in their hearts by the law of nature (Romans 2: 12–16). However, this number was small, and such righteous Jews and Gentiles were alike exceptional. Jews and Gentiles both are saved through faith in Christ alone, not by works. In these men of faith the good life in general is the product of the operation of the Holy Spirit which comes after Christians have died to the flesh along with Christ in baptism. Paul goes into the several gifts of the Spirit extensively in I Corinthians 12–14, where in the course of his discussion he displays great ethical discrimination in singling out faith, hope, and love (Chapter 13) as the three most important gifts of the Spirit. It is notable that such a mystic as Paul should invariably stress the ethical and social gifts of the Spirit against such mystic and ecstatic gifts as

speaking with tongues (I Corinthians 12:13, 14). Even after the
Christian's baptism, however, there was nothing automatic about the
blossoming of the good life; for, while he had supposedly died to
the flesh and its evil works in that experience, it still continued in
some inconsistent but real way to exert its force, to tempt and mislead. The apostle confesses for himself, "For the good which I
would I do not: but the evil which I would not, I practice" (Romans
7:19), and exclaims, "Wretched man that I am, who shall deliver
me out of the body of this death?" (7:24). The Spirit, however,
made intercession for the convert, and gradually, though not completely as long as he remained in the body, the Christian gained the
victory over his flesh, and was able to "walk after the Spirit."

The basis of the Pauline ethic was thus supernatural dependence
on the operation of the Spirit. Some of its extremes at certain points
are due to a second factor: Paul's eschatological expectations which
he held in common with his Master. The extreme character of Paul's
views on marriage and sex dates back to his expectation of the speedy
return of the Lord Jesus; therefore he feels that marriage is a lower
state than celibacy, because the unmarried Christian can devote himself exclusively to the interests of the Kingdom of God; but the
married person is distracted by family cares (I Corinthians 7). The
eschatological framework of his teaching, however, provided the occasion for one of the ethical laws which Paul independently formulated. In Thessalonica some of his converts, hearing from him that
the return of Christ was imminent, decided to give up work in expectation of the end. These persons Paul sternly rebuked with his
law of utility, "If any will not work, neither let him eat" (II Thessalonians 3:10). It is likely also that the eschatological hopes cher-
ished by the Apostle played their part in his advice to the Christians
to be obedient and submissive to the powers that be in the state, for
the last thing contemplated by primitive Christianity was a revolution of the social order, or a serious modification of the framework of
society. Such an upheaval would await the return of the Lord.

The moral law of responsibility Paul formulated is in the hortatory section of the Epistle to the Galatians, where he writes, "Whatsoever a man soweth, that shall he also reap" (Galatians 6:7b).

A final excellency of the Pauline ethic may be mentioned: its sense of social solidarity. To be sure, most of this social sense is confined to the limits of the Christian community itself, as in his famous metaphor of the church as the body of Christ, in I Corinthians 12, where he recommends co-operation in the church similar to that among the members of the human body. In the hortatory section of the Epistle to the Romans he states a truth of social living, "For none of us liveth unto himself, and none of us dieth unto himself" (Romans 14:7, 8). He means this statement exclusively in religious sense, for in the next verse he adds that whether we live or die, it is unto the Lord. Quite apart from its religious setting, however, this formula is an important statement of the social obligations involved in the very process of living. His sense of the social nature of Christian living is also responsible for his apostolic injunctions to the Christians not to do anything to cause the weaker brothers to stumble (Romans 14:21; I Corinthians 8:13; and so forth). This sense of social solidarity—at least within the church—is one of Paul's important legacies to Christian ethics.

SPANNING THE REALMS OF NATURE AND GRACE: SAINT THOMAS AQUINAS

THE FINEST flowering of medieval scholasticism is to be found in the system of Saint Thomas Aquinas, its greatest representative, who is also one of the few thinkers of that period whose teaching still has more than historical significance for the modern world. Not only did Saint Thomas answer the chief questions of the Middle Ages, but as the "Angelic Doctor" of the Roman Catholic Church, his theology is still the official system of that great Christian communion. During the centuries that had elapsed between the death of Jesus and the life of Saint Thomas (1229?–1272) Christian doctrine had been extended into a vast theological structure to which Saint Paul was the first contributor, Saint Augustine the most extensive, and Anselm and Abelard the nearest in time to Saint Thomas. It was left for him to weave the thought of his predecessors into a complete and unified system such as none before him had achieved singlehanded. In ethics as well as theology Christian thought had developed greatly, for as the Church confronted the practical problems of a dying pagan civilization and the birth of a new one after the barbarian hordes had swept the older one away, it added to the nucleus of ethical principles in the New Testament much that was new and some that was quite extraneous to the teaching of Jesus.

Many Christian theologians had written upon ethical problems from the time that Paul wrote his epistles to the time that Saint Thomas began to write his voluminous works; but with the possible exception of Saint Augustine, none of them had formulated an independent Christian ethical system. That was left for Saint Thomas, for while Saint Augustine treated ethical problems, he believed so firmly that the good life was impossible to man without the direct agency of the grace of God to produce even its most elementary forms that his ethics cannot be separated from theology. For him ethics is in no sense autonomous, and his contributions to the field of theology are far more important. The other Christian thinkers largely confined themselves to the extension and interpretation of known Christian values to whatever practical problems confronted the Church in their time and sometimes supplemented the Christian teachings with the ideas of whatever pagan philosophers they deemed valuable, chiefly the Stoics and the Platonists. Like his predecessors, Saint Thomas did not create a wholly original system of ethics in the sense of formulating any new laws for the moral life or of finding a wholly fresh point of departure for the construction of his ethical system, as Spinoza and Kant were to do later on; the essential originality of the Thomist ethic consists in the fact that it was a fusion of Christianity and Aristotelianism.

The sources for the ethical teaching of Saint Thomas consist of the second part of his *Summa contra Gentiles* and the second part of his nine-volume work, the *Summa theologica,* which goes into minute detail in its treatment of all the concerns of the ethical life, beginning with the psychology of the moral life and including two treatises on law, one on the *lex naturalis* and one on the *lex divina.* These three treatises comprise the first part of the second part (*Prima secunda*) of the *Summa theologica.* The second part of the second part (*Secunda secunda*) consists of a very extensive treatise upon various groups of virtues and vices with discussion of many practical problems of the moral life in connection with these.

The method followed by Saint Thomas in the *Summa theologica* is the question and answer procedure, each question being subdivided into articles. The question is raised, objections are stated, then the position the saint means to adopt is given by some authority or by himself, and finally his own analysis of the problem is stated with answers to the objections. Although there are some others, his chief authorities are Aristotle and the Christian teachers.

In the day of Saint Thomas Aristotle was a newcomer to the ranks of the philosophers used to support the structure of Christian doctrine. In the ancient world the Fathers of the Church had— not without reason—looked askance at Aristotle, who, they felt, was no better than avowed materialists, such as the Epicureans and the Atomists and, like Saint Augustine, had in general preferred Plato or the Stoics as buttresses for their Christian systems. However, during the lifetime of Saint Thomas's teacher, Albertus Magnus, the works of Aristotle, many of which had been unknown to the Middle Ages, had come into Europe from the Arabs in Spain. They were at first condemned by the Church and the universities alike, but through the championship of Albertus they had at length been accepted in good standing. It remained only for the work of Saint Thomas to combine the teaching of Aristotle with Christian doctrine in his *Summa theologica* for the latter to appear fully clothed in the garb of a defender of the Christian faith. It is a tribute to both the originality and the ingenuity of Thomas that he was able to combine into a unified whole two systems so divergent and at many points so incompatible as Christianity and Aristotelianism.

The architectural framework upon which Thomas erected this extraordinary structure was the theory of the realms of nature and grace. In the realm of nature, where reason is the directing principle, Aristotle is the supreme authority, to whom Thomas refers for all sorts of facts and premises of a scientific character, including information about biology, psychology, astronomy, and physics. Even in the realm of ethics Aristotle is supreme so far as the moral virtues are concerned, since these, too, lie within the sphere of reason, and the scheme of the *Nicomachean Ethics* governs both the contents and the form of this portion of Thomas's own ethical system. The other sphere, that of grace, was above, but not contrary to, reason, where truths that were beyond the power of the human intellect to discover were made known by Divine revelation. In this realm grace was the operative principle, and the Christian tradition supplied Saint Thomas with his premises. In ethics this sphere was the subject of the theological virtues which could be attained only through the infusion of Divine grace. The scheme uniting these two realms is Aristotle's hierarchy of being. It begins with inanimate objects consisting entirely of matter and potentiality; ascends to the animals, which have a little less potentiality, a little more actuality; proceeds to man, who, as the lowest of the rational creatures, is partly potentiality, partly actuality; and to the astral beings, whom Saint Thomas equated with the angels, beings far more rational and actual than man, but still not of pure actuality, since they need a spiritual body for their expression. The hierarchy of being culminates in God, the highest of all, Who is pure form, pure actuality, a simple and incorporeal spiritual substance containing no potentiality at all.

Since Saint Thomas was a man of the Middle Ages, the subject of his authorities is very important for the appraisal of his ethical teaching; for he, no more than his lesser contemporaries, transcended the characteristic medieval attitude of docile and unquestioning submission to authority, chiefly that of the Church, but more or less also to other kinds of authority, intellectual and political. In the realm of nature the authority of "the Philosopher," as Thomas calls Aristotle, is as complete as that of the Church in doctrine. Along with Aristotle there are a few other pagans, such as Cicero, whom the saint quotes in this realm; but the selection of the authority was about all the liberty that Thomas allowed himself, and once having adopted his authority, he would go to any length to defend the latter's position. It goes without saying that he made no attempt to check the observations or the facts upon which the authority in question based his statement, for in the Middle Ages no one save Roger Bacon was so bold. Consequently Thomas himself is seldom better than his authorities, except that once in a while he argues more ably in defense of their positions than they themselves were capable of doing.

As regards Christian doctrine in the realm of grace, naturally Saint Thomas allowed himself no choice beyond that of the adoption of his authorities. It occasionally happens that he does not choose the strongest authority for the position he is defending; for he made no distinction at all in the relative weight he gave to the several authorities, evidently feeling that a quotation from Gregory the Great was quite as strong support for his view as one from the Apostle Paul or even from Jesus. In the *Summa theologica* Thomas quotes the Bible, Saint Augustine, and Pope Gregory the most frequently among the Christian authorities, though there are some others, such as John of Damascus, Isidore, Macrobius, who are referred to fairly often, and, more rarely, Bede, Anselm, Dionysius, Jerome, and Origen. He also quotes with equal authority the Decretals and the papal encyclicals, and occasionally even the church rituals or its practice. So far as his use of the Bible goes, his exegesis is typically medieval. He uses quotations from the Old and the New Testaments indiscriminately; he takes verses quite out of their context, allegorizes them when it suits his purpose, or even follows some fanciful commentator's explanation, as in the case of Job's children, where he adopts the explanation of Gregory that the three daughters of Job symbolize the three theological virtues, faith, hope, and charity, and the seven sons, the seven gifts of the Holy Ghost.[1] Indeed, where the Bible is concerned Saint Thomas had no more sense of history than the rest of his age, and that lack exerted an unfortunate effect upon his ethic at some points, for he is quite as likely to follow the lower ethic of the Old Testament as the higher one of the New.

The *summum bonum* of Saint Thomas's system is the beatific vision of God, a goal which combines influences from both Aristotelian and Christian thought. He takes the meager suggestions of the conception of the beatific vision set down by Aristotle in the final book of the *Nicomachean Ethics,* but these he vastly enriches with a wealth of content from the experience of the Christian mystics before him and from his own religious experience, for Saint Thomas himself was a mystic *par excellence.* By the beatific vision Saint Thomas means the direct contemplation of God, that immediate and perfect knowledge of Him which is vouchsafed to only a few of the very special saints in this life, but will be enjoyed by all the blessed in the afterlife of heaven. Knowing God is the true and sole end of all rational creatures. Only they can know and love God, and to them He is the sole and complete satisfaction. "God turns all things to Himself as their last end," he quotes from [Pseudo] Dionysius.[2] Man's happiness as a rational creature can

---

[1] The *Summa theologica,* tr. by the Fathers of the English Dominican Province, II,[1] Q. lxviii, art. 1.

[2] *Ibid.,* Q. i, art. 1.

consist only in that which satisfies his intellect completely, and such happiness only God can bestow. Happiness, therefore, cannot consist in wealth; for wealth is only a means to the satisfaction of bodily needs, not an end in itself. Physical pleasures cannot compose man's happiness, for they are neither happiness itself nor proper accidents of happiness. It cannot consist in power or glory, since these things are no end in themselves, nor is it honor which is merely a tribute paid to a man because of some quality in himself. Even moral virtue does not provide that perfect happiness which God alone can give; for happiness the saint defines as an intellective operation. The virtues are a means to this happiness, but not the happiness itself. Only this immediate knowledge of God gives the perfect knowledge of all that will satisfy the intellect and at the same time all other desires.[3]

Merit, delight, and rectitude of will are necessary for this true happiness, though in themselves not sufficient to give it, for God alone can do this; the contemplation of Him brings with it eternal life, which the saint thinks of as simultaneity rather than sequence.[4] They are the roads or the accompaniments of happiness, but not happiness itself, which is the satisfaction of all desires. Only this immediate and complete knowledge of God is happiness, not the partial knowledge of Him possible in this life by intellectual demonstration, or by the indirect means of causality, or by faith can suffice.

The *summum bonum* of human life is thus a purely religious one, toward which the moral life builds up merit to prepare the way, but which man cannot attain by his unaided powers, since only the lower reaches of the good life are possible to him in his natural state without the agency of Divine grace. To merit eternal life he needs the coming of the Divine grace in forgiveness, atonement through the work of Christ, and the continuance of the Holy Spirit to perfect the higher virtues infused by grace. This *summum bonum* of the beatific vision in heaven is Thomas's interpretation of Jesus's ideal of the Kingdom of God, which for centuries before the time of Aquinas had been equated with the enjoyment of eternal bliss in heaven.

---

[3] *Ibid.*, QQ. ii–iv.   [4] *Summa contra Gentiles*, III. lxi.

How, then, did Saint Thomas conceive of the good life which was to fit and prepare man for the reward of eternal life and the happiness of the beatific vision? The preparation for it spans the two realms of nature and grace, and in both it rests in the last analysis upon the authority of the Divine commands, those of reason in the realm of nature and the direct precepts of the Divine Law in the realm of grace. His view of the *lex naturalis* and the *lex divina* the saint sets forth in the *Summa theologica* (II[1], QQ. xc-cxiv). There is, he believes, in all men the law of nature, resting upon the light of reason which is implanted in them by God and serves as the foundation for virtue, inasmuch as it is uniform, timeless, unchangeable, and common to all.[5] Since the natural law rests upon Divine authority, its commands are beyond question.

In addition to the natural law, which is implanted in all men of God, there is the Divine Law, which consists of revealed commandments of God, the two dispensations of which are the Old Law and the New Law, corresponding to the Old and the New Covenants, respectively. There is nothing particularly original in his statement of the functions of the Old and the New Laws, rather he follows the accepted theory of it which begins with Paul and goes on down through Christian theology to Thomas's own time. The Old Law contained three kinds of precepts: moral, ceremonial, and judicial. The Decalogue, which is the most important moral section of it, was given directly by God to Moses on Mount Sinai, the rest was revealed indirectly through the agency of the angels, but the whole of it was given to the Jews alone as tutor and pedagogue to lead them to Christ.[6] The Old Law was good, but it relates to the New Law as the imperfect to the perfect. It has been superseded by the New Law, for the Old Law did not have the power to justify, that is, its moral precepts did not cause justice.[7] The ceremonial side, which had served the purpose of mirroring heavenly things and weaning the Jews from idolatry, was entirely abrogated by the New Law, so that it would constitute a mortal sin for Christians to keep these provisions since the coming of Christ.

[5] The *Summa theologica*, II[1], Q. xciv. [6] *Ibid.*, Q. xciv.
[7] *Ibid.*, Q. xcvii, art. 3.

The New Law differs from the Old in several fundamental respects. Instead of being written, it is unwritten and in the heart. It fulfills the Old Law, as the perfect does the imperfect, for the Old is contained in the New as a wheel within a wheel, a figure which Thomas borrows from Gregory.[8] It is less burdensome than the Old and at the same time a deeper inner law which deals with purity of motive as well as with outer acts, though it also commands or prohibits some of these as requisite for those who live after the Spirit. However, grace is necessary to the fulfilling of the New Law, which commands charity and the avoidance of mortal sin; neither of these is possible to the natural man unaided by the infusion of grace. Grace is the gift of God which comes prior to the beginning of the theological virtues; it justifies from sin, gives the soul peace with God, moves the free will toward Him, enables the soul to love Him more perfectly than it can do in its natural state, and finally, prepares it to merit the reward of eternal life.[9]

The entire moral life of man thus falls within the two realms: in its lower aspects, its beginnings and predispositions, it belongs to the realm of nature and is governed by the law of reason; in its higher aspects it lies within the realm of grace, and is directed by the Divine precepts of the Old and the New Law. For the psychological analysis of the basis and habits of the good life Thomas follows very closely that of Aristotle in the *Nicomachean Ethics,* namely, that the virtues are habits, and strangely enough, applies the analysis not only to the moral virtues but to the great theological virtues of faith, hope, and charity as well. For, whereas the latter cannot be obtained without the operation of grace, the saint thinks they are habits that intensify under the guidance of the Holy Spirit working through grace. The only psychological difference from the moral virtues is that the theological ones are not habits that man with his unaided powers can cultivate, and, also, since they are infused by grace they cease at once if grace is withdrawn.[10]

Since virtue is a matter of habit, it follows that Thomas believed that the two most important subjects of it in the human soul were

---

[8] *Ibid.,* Q. xcvii, art. 3. [9] *Ibid.,* Q. cix, cxiii, cxiv.
[10] *Ibid.,* II[1], QQ. xlix, lxxxix, xlix, lxii, lxiii.

the will and the intellect, and of these two the intellect was primary. Such virtues as prudence and wisdom are seated directly in the intellect; but the strictly moral virtues are located in the will.[11] The function of the intellect in the operation of the virtues is primary to that of the will, however, because in all moral acts prudence, an intellectual virtue, has to determine the means and the ends for the others to follow. The will functions afterward to direct toward the end and the means that prudence dictates to it. The proof of this primacy of the intellect Thomas finds in the fact that the will can move in several directions, both as to means and to end; hence the intellect is the sovereign causal agent, because it dictates both choices to the will.[12]

Saint Thomas's psychological analysis of the basis of the moral transaction is an elaborate reproduction of the psychology set forth in Aristotle's *De anima*. Reduced to its simplest terms, this psychology runs thus: The soul has four powers: the vegetal or nutritive, the sensitive, the appetitive and the intellective. The first two, and to some extent the third, are common to man and the lower animals; the intellective is possessed only by man and the other rational creatures. This last power is the most divine part of the rational creatures, for the intellect constitutes their likeness to God.

The will may properly be spoken of as the appetition of the intellect. In any moral transaction it is the goodness or badness of the end which determines its character, but the goodness or badness of the will which motivates the action is not the responsibility of the will itself, but of the intellect whose servant it is. Below the level of the intellect and the will lies passion, which is in the sensitive appetite and is common to men and the lower animals; therefore it is an irrational faculty which in man is only partly subject to the direction of the will and the intellect. There are two types of passion, the irascible and the concupiscible. Love, joy, hatred, and sorrow are concupiscible passions; anger, fear, hope, and daring are irascible. These are concerned in moral action insofar as they are subject to the control of the will and the intellect. None of them

---

[11] *Ibid.*, Q. lvi.   [12] *Ibid.*, Q. x, art. 1.

is good or evil in itself, but they partake of good or evil according as they are directed to an end dictated by a good or evil love. Below the passions lie those impulses and actions which are not subject to volition and reason; these are the only ones that do not signify in the ethical realm. They are the lower sensitive appetites and the properties of the nutritive or vegetal power.

The psychology of Saint Thomas is important today only as background for the understanding of his ethical system, and it is largely outmoded in the modern world; the great debate of the Middle Ages, which he opened, as to whether the will or the intellect is primary in the moral realm has little meaning for the problems of ethics today. More interesting and vital from the modern standpoint is his analysis of what constitutes moral action from the viewpoint of subject and object, cause and effects.

Deeply imbued, as he was, with Christian ethical tradition, Saint Thomas does not neglect the importance of motive in moral action, but, unlike Jesus, he does not place the whole weight of the character of an action upon it alone. In the *Summa contra Gentiles* he states four canons for determining whether an action is good or bad: (1) executive power to do the will's command; (2) apprehensive power; (3) judgment; (4) motive.[13] The most important cause of bad action, he goes on to say in this connection, is lack of order in the reason, and, indeed, throughout the lengthy treatise on ethics that forms the second part of the *Summa theologica* also, the most important standard for good action is conformity to the ordinateness of reason.[14] He also ranks actions as sinful in proportion to the amount of harm that they cause. Of all the sins those directed against God, such as heresy, blasphemy, sacrilege, and unbelief, are the most serious. Next in seriousness, strangely enough, are not those against our fellow men, but those against ourselves; hence Thomas argues that suicide, being directed against the self, is more grievous than murder.

This extraordinary point of view is partially an adoption of Aristotle's emphasis upon self-love and self-respect as a major founda-

---

[13] *Summa contra Gentiles*, III[1], x.
[14] The *Summa theologica*, II[1], QQ. xlviii, lxxxix, lxxii, *et passim*.

tion of virtue in the *Nicomachean Ethics;* but Thomas also buttressed his argument with the Christian commandment, "Love thy neighbor as thyself." From this he reasons that since we are commanded to love our neighbor as ourselves, we are therewith commanded to love ourselves more, on the ground that the model is greater than the copy.[15]

Sins against our neighbor are rated in seriousness according to the amount of injury that they cause to the victim and the amount of disorder they produce in their perpetrator, and Thomas classifies all sins as mortal or venial, not on the basis of the amount of punishment they receive, but according to whether their consequences are irreparable or reparable.[16] The inordinate character of sin is to be measured in two ways. For the moral virtues, which are always the mean, the corresponding sins are its contraries of excess and deficiency. Either excess is inordinate. For the theological virtues, the seriousness of the corresponding sin is determined by its being the logical opposite of these great virtues, and of this class of sins, those opposed to charity (the greatest virtue) are the most serious.

Saint Thomas enumerates a number of other considerations which must be taken into account in estimating the gravity of a sin, such as the circumstances surrounding the act, whether or not it was done in ignorance, which in some instances is an extenuating circumstance, whether it was done through passion or through what he calls certain malice (malice prepense), and whether or not the sin was committed under the stress of great temptation.[17]

For Saint Thomas all forms of evil and vice fall into the category of sin, since the inordinateness of all such conduct makes it contrary either to some precept of the law of reason or of the Divine Law. Besides the two varieties of actual sin, mortal and venial, the inheritance of all mankind has been tainted with original sin since Adam's fall. Saint Thomas quotes the opinion of Saint Augustine that original sin is concupiscence. Though original sin is inherited through the flesh by every member of the human race and entails

---

[15] *Ibid.,* II², Q. xxvi, art. 4.
[16] *Ibid.,* II¹, Q. lxxii, arts. 8–9; Q. lxxii, art. 8; II², Q. xxviii, art. 1.
[17] *Ibid.,* II¹, Q. lxxvii, arts. 4–8; Q. lxxviii.

death as its punishment, nonetheless it does not utterly corrupt freedom of will and is disposed of by the sacrament of baptism, which removes its taint.

Saint Thomas discusses various mortal sins at considerable length, enumerating them along with the seven deadly sins that the Church had recognized since the time of Gregory the Great: vainglory (or pride), envy, anger, sloth, covetousness—the five spiritual sins; and lust and gluttony—the two carnal ones.[18] The sins that he deems serious enough to be called mortal are indeed so numerous that the list is far too long to reproduce, but it includes about every grave offense he knew of. Saint Thomas defends the traditional list of the seven deadly sins that the Church had worked out, though if he had been a more critical man living in a bolder age he might have challenged some on the list. For example, it is difficult to see why gluttony should be reckoned as a mortal sin: for though it is unwholesome from a physiological standpoint, it hardly seems to be productive of serious enough consequences to be in the same class with murder and adultery. It is difficult also to see why the saint should reckon despair as a mortal sin, for though this attitude is likely to paralyze effort, it scarcely seems disastrous enough to warrant the name of mortal sin. In this instance, however, the saint so classifies it upon the strictly logical basis, which accounts for a number of his strange classifications. Despair has to be a mortal sin, because it is the logical opposite of the theological virtue of hope; therefore, since it is opposed to a theological virtue, it must perforce be reckoned as a mortal sin.[19]

Saint Thomas's analysis of the virtues is just as elaborate as his treatment of the vices, but the former follow somewhat different lines. Though he did not believe that all the sins could be found in even the most hardened sinner, since some of them would be logical contradictories, he did believe that all the virtues grew together and that each of the great virtues brought in its wake a train of subsidiary or satellite virtues which are annexed to it. For example, the cardinal virtue of justice has five subsidiary virtues annexed to it: religion, [filial] piety, revenge, observance, and truth, a list he

18 *Ibid.*, II², QQ. xxxv, xxxvi, cxlviii.   19 *Ibid.*, QQ. xvii, xx.

takes from Cicero.[20] The subsidiaries of temperance are continence, mildness, and modesty; [21] those of fortitude are magnificence, confidence, patience, and perseverance; [22] those of prudence are solicitude, memory, docility, foresight, caution, and counsel.[23] The four cardinal virtues are thus the foundations of all the other moral and intellectual virtues which they bring with them and prepare the way for the three theological virtues which are the work of the Holy Spirit. The three theological virtues also have each a train of the subsidiary virtues which are the possession of all whom the Spirit inspires.

These good habits, the virtues, continue throughout life if a man possessed of them remains in a state of grace until death, and some of them go over to the next life also, but only a few, since most of them are valid only for the conditions of this world. The four cardinal virtues, of which the greatest is justice, a virtue "perpetual and immortal," remain in the next world, an opinion that Saint Thomas takes from Saint Augustine.[24] The intellectual virtues, inasmuch as they consist of knowledge of universals, survive after death; but of the three theological virtues, only charity remains in the next world, because faith becomes knowledge there, and hope is fulfilled.

During this life the virtues require each other in order to come to completion, and according to the logic of the saint, unlike the vices, the virtues can all exist together without any incompatibility, because since they are all good, they cannot be either contraries or contradictories of each other.[25] Throughout this discussion Thomas fails to recognize any relation between temperament and virtue.

Those virtues which Thomas rates as most important—indeed those he singles out for comment at all—are selected according to the valuation placed upon them by one or the other of his authorities. The four cardinal virtues are the choice of Gregory and Ambrose, who in turn had taken them over from the pagan philosophers before them. Paul, of course, is responsible for the three theological

[20] *Ibid.*, Q. lxxx, art. 1.
[21] *Ibid.*, Q. cxliii, art. 1.
[22] *Ibid.*, Q. cxxxviii, art. 1.
[23] *Ibid.*, Q. xlix.
[24] *Ibid.*, Q. lviii, art. 1.
[25] *Ibid.*, II[1], Q. lxv.

virtues which he gives in I Corinthians 13 and for the choice of some others, the fruits of the Spirit in Galatians 5:22 and those which he names as gifts of the Spirit in I Corinthians 12:28. The seven gifts of the Spirit which Thomas includes in his discussion of the virtues are taken from the list of the qualities of the Messiah in Isaiah 11:2. They are: wisdom, understanding, counsel, fortitude, knowledge, piety, fear (reverence).[26] These are genuine habits bestowed by the Spirit; therefore they fall into the class of virtues, while the gifts of the Spirit are rather effects or accompaniments of its operation, such as love, joy, peace, and all the rest. The fruits are virtuous deeds in which the individual delights after the Spirit has begun to work in him.[27]

The moral virtues other than the cardinal virtues which Thomas discusses are largely those which Aristotle singled out in his *Nicomachean Ethics,* such as liberality, magnificence, and other minor virtues. Aristotle's original list was not good, since he selected a number of virtues that were really rather trivial. Saint Thomas improves upon him only because the Christian teaching provided him with a far more fundamental and normative list of virtues, so that Aristotle's catalogue is only one part of the whole for Thomas.

The seeds or bases of the lower moral virtues are in us by nature, from the very nature of reason. A virtue such as prudence is the result of experience and training. The higher life of virtue is founded upon the four cardinal virtues, which are greatly aided by the coming of the Holy Spirit; they, in turn, form the basis for the operation of the three theological virtues, which the Spirit infuses. Thus it is to be observed that Saint Thomas did not follow Saint Augustine in believing that the natural man is incapable of any virtue at all; but he did not believe that unaided by grace man is able to progress beyond the lower ranges of the good life, since grace is necessary both in order to avoid mortal sin and for the coming of all the higher virtues. Thus the good life as he viewed it was a kind of joint production of the two realms of nature and grace.

It is to be observed that on the one hand Saint Thomas thinks

[26] *Ibid.,* Q. lxviii. [27] *Ibid.,* Q. lxx.

of the virtues and on the other of the vices, which all fall into the class of either mortal or venial sins, never of faults or other ethical classifications, such as unsocial traits which are not included within the limits of sin: to him the term "sin" was coextensive with all bad habits and dispositions and spanned the wrong side of all the relationships possible to man in the two realms of nature and grace. Good and bad, in fact, were categories that not only included the relationship of man to God, his fellows, and himself but extended to the angels and demons as well. Consequently some of the classifications he makes of the virtues and vices are poor, because to him all was either virtue or vice or because he simply took over the poor classifications of his authorities.

It has already been remarked that it is hard to justify classifying despair as a mortal sin; on the other hand, hope would hardly seem to be a virtue. Paul himself possibly did not intend the latter as such in his statement in I Corinthians 13, for that chapter forms part of his discussion of the gifts of the Spirit, not a catalogue of virtues. Thomas himself, in his treatise on the passions, names hope among them, but, after stating in the rest of that same section [28] that the passions are not in themselves either good or evil, but are so only according to the nature of the object toward which the direction of the reason and the will attaches them, he forgets about that admission through the remainder of the Second Part of the *Summa theologica,* and consistently treats hope as one of the three great theological virtues. That his first classification of hope as a passion is the correct one is clear; for hope is not a virtue at all, inasmuch as it can equally well be directed toward the evil as toward the good and also toward ends that are quite neutral from the ethical standpoint.

This proneness to follow the classifications of his authorities leads Thomas into one serious misclassification from the standpoint of the Christian ethic, when he follows Cicero in saying that vengeance is a virtue annexed to justice. From the teaching of Jesus it is clear that he regarded vengeance as a vice; but Thomas maintains

[28] *Ibid.,* II^1, Q. xxiii, art. 1, and II^1, Q. xxiv, art. 7.

that it is a virtue both from the Christian standpoint and from the Aristotelian standpoint. On religious grounds he argues that vengeance cannot be unlawful, because it is written in the Scripture, "Vengeance is mine." Instead of stating that vengeance is a prerogative belonging exclusively to God according to the plain sense of this verse, Thomas asserts that it must be a virtue, since whatever God does is good. Moreover, though he concedes that we ought to take vengeance more for the wrongs of God than for our own, he does feel that vengeance is a virtue for man as well as for God. The saint buttresses his argument by the further contention that vengeance is a moral virtue because it conforms to the scheme of the golden mean. It is the mean between the excess of brutality on the one hand and the deficiency of remissness in punishing on the other. It should be wrought upon those who have willfully sinned by depriving them by due legal process of whatever they hold dear.[29]

This argument is simply a defense of the *lex talionis*, but it is difficult to see how a great Christian teacher could advocate a view of vengeance in such glaring contradiction to the ethics of the Sermon on the Mount. But Thomas is occasionally carried away with his own logic, and here is one glaring instance when he ranks vengeance as a virtue instead of a vice and carries his argument out consistently.

In connection with his discussion of the virtues and their opposing vices, the saint goes into some practical problems concerned in their application; for example, the discussion on war comes into the section on charity and its opposites, hatred, strife, and the like. To conclude the discussion of his ethics, it will be necessary to notice some of his teachings on such enduring practical problems of life as wealth, power, war, and peace, and the general nature of evil, especially when he takes an original view or makes a contribution to Christian ethics on these points. Although Saint Thomas was a monk, one cannot but feel from reading these practical discussions that he had observed human life with a discerning and sympathetic

[29] *Ibid.*, II², Q. cviii.

eye and that he had forged a philosophy from his own experience and reflection as well as from what he read about the problems of life in the works of the ancients.

On the question of wealth Saint Thomas did not attempt to apply literally the economic teachings of Jesus, except for those who had made a profession of religion—the clergy and those in monastic orders.[30] For them alone such counsels of perfection as celibacy and poverty hold good. For those "in the world" the saint advocates an "ethic of service" with regard to wealth, that in no way forbids the possession of it or looks upon its right use as constituting any barrier to the spiritual life. To be sure, he condemns covetousness and greed and advocates almsgiving in proportion to another's need and one's own ability to give without impoverishing one's self, and he feels that all those "in the world" should be self-supporting; [31] but beyond these limits there are no restrictions upon the accumulation of money and other forms of wealth.

Wealth is to be regarded as a means, not an end, and it cannot in itself constitute happiness, since it contributes to that end only through securing the means of physical subsistence and comfort and, of course, is a means that might be put to bad as well as good uses. The saint expressly condemned taking interest on loans, on the ground that wealth, like food or drink, was a good only when it was consumed; therefore, if a man possesses more money than he needs, he should not expect any interest for lending it to someone who needs its use.[32] He argues ably and ingeniously for his stand on interest, but it would seem that the analogy to food or wine is not entirely sound, since money is not a perishable commodity. However, his views with regard to trade were wholesome, for he set his face rigidly against fraud, cheating, and all sharp practices of the market place and stood for fair dealing and honest trade on the basis of mutual advantage to seller and buyer, with a fair profit to compensate the seller for his labor.

Saint Thomas showed little awareness of the dangers of power,

[30] *Ibid.*, II², QQ. cxxviii, clxxvi, clxxvii.　　[31] *Ibid.*, Q. xxxii.
[32] *Ibid.*, Q. lxxviii.

of which he says merely that it cannot be an end, since it may be used either for good or evil and does not in itself constitute happiness.

The saint discusses the problem of war as part of a discussion on the taking of life in general. He finds that feuds and killing between private individuals are sinful, indeed, murder; but he does not feel that depriving a wrongdoer of life when he has been found guilty by a properly constituted tribunal of justice is wrong. He advocates the customary medieval course with heretics and schismatics, who should first be excommunicated, then delivered to the secular authorities for execution.[33] He also endorses the execution of witches and wizards, on the ground that the Old Testament commands it.[34]

War is not always sinful, but Christians should engage only in just wars. He sets the following qualifications to define what constitutes a "just war": (1) it must be waged by the authorization of the sovereign of the state; (2) it must be waged on behalf of a just cause, namely, that those who are attacked deserve to be attacked because of some fault; (3) the belligerents should have as their aim the avoidance of evil or the bringing to pass of some good, so that their intentions are the furtherance of peace, not opposition to it.[35] Only those in holy orders are forbidden to fight, since warlike pursuits do not comport with their sacred office. It is plain to be seen that the real sources of Thomas's teaching on war are the mores of his time and the Old Testament sanction of holy wars rather than inferences from the spirit of the teachings of Jesus.

The treatment of the subject of sex is more extensive than in most of the great ethical systems; but the quality of it in Thomas's case is somewhat vitiated by the fact that women were considered inferior by medieval monasticism, because of the influence of the Garden of Eden story and the misogyny of Saint Paul. To these reasons Thomas added an argument for the inferiority of women erected upon Aristotelian ideas of matter and form, activity and passivity, so that he went to the length of declaring that a man should love his father better than his mother, because the father

[33] *Ibid.*, QQ. xi, xxxix.   [34] *Ibid.*, Q. lxiv, arts. 1–3.   [35] *Ibid.*, Q. xl.

is the active, formative agent in generation and in consequence more worthy than the mother, who is merely the passive, material principle in the same.[36]

He takes for granted the inferiority of the intellect of women and their subordinate position to that of man because of Eve's part in the fall; and indeed he thinks a man should love his parents more than his wife. That position he arrives at by the following somewhat tortuous process of reasoning: Saint Paul wrote in Ephesians 5:38, "Men ought to love their wives as their own bodies." Now, the saint reasons, a man ought to love his neighbor more than his own body, and among his neighbors, he should love his parents most; therefore he should love his parents more than his wife.[37]

Saint Thomas goes into the whole subject of sex relations, including sex crimes and perversions, in his commentary on temperance; for since continence is a subsidiary virtue of temperance, he discusses it here together with its opposing vices. In this connection, his theory of sexual intercourse is that it is ordinate and right only when it takes place between two married persons for the purpose of begetting offspring; all other forms are in excess of this, the order of reason, and consequently wrong. Fornication is the least serious of the sex crimes, though it is a mortal sin, since the Decretals prescribe the same penance for it as for adultery. However, the saint finds the wrong involved to be that it is an injustice to the child, who needs two parents to rear it properly. Reparation should be made by the marriage of the parties.[38]

Adultery is more serious, since it is wrong on several counts: it is an offense against chastity; it runs contrary to the good of the children procreated through such a union and to that of any other lawful children of either or both of the guilty parties; finally, it is disloyalty to God and to the wedded mate.[39] Incest is wrong on three grounds: it is a violation of filial respect; it tends to keep the mind constantly inflamed with lust, because near relatives live in such close proximity to each other, hence is highly inordinate; and

[36] *Ibid.*, Q. xxvi, art. 10.   [37] *Ibid.*, art. 2.
[38] *Ibid.*, Q. cliv, arts. 2–3.   [39] *Ibid.*, art. 8.

finally, it hinders a man from making friends outside his own family circle.[40]

The unnatural vices are sinful because they are inordinate and contrary to the design of reason and nature, which is, after all, the true and intrinsic reason against such perversions as sodomy, bestiality, and self-abuse. Thomas also comments upon seduction and rape, which are wrong because inordinate. They can be amended by the marriage of the parties.[41]

Virginity and continence, which the saint esteems highly, belong to the counsels of perfection for those in religious orders and the clergy, in whose case he advocates them on the basis that they enable those who practice them to set their minds more fully upon the pursuits of religion than the married can do.

On the philosophic rather than the practical side, perhaps one of the most interesting of Saint Thomas's ideas is his theory of the nature of evil, though it is not entirely original with him, since he took over the broad outlines of his theory from the conception of Saint Augustine. It is, of course, an inconsistency in Thomism to find such a thoroughly Neoplatonic idea in a system substantially Aristotelian, but the saint was evidently not conscious of the inconsistency. Like Saint Augustine (at least most of the time), Saint Thomas did not believe that evil was a reality, an essence in the sense of being a self-subsistent real; for it could not be a cause and was itself caused accidentally by good. God is in no sense the author of evil, even though He knows it and foreknows it, as He does all other things; and the fact that God permits evil is to the saint but one more evidence of His goodness, since He allows it in order that good may come out of it. Evil is in no sense a full reality, but merely a kind of parasitical growth on the good, a contingent and fortuitous result of some defect in the cause. Evil is privation of being, for the saint asserts that goodness and being are convertible terms.[42]

The essential incompatibility of this conception of evil with the rest of Thomas's system lies in the fact that any ethical theism such as his demands the recognition of the reality of evil, and this in fact

[40] *Ibid.*, art. 9.   [41] *Ibid.*, arts. 6–7, 9–10.
[42] *Summa contra Gentiles*, III[2], iv, xiv.

the saint's practical treatment of evil elsewhere throughout his works presupposes, whatever he may have held philosophically and theoretically. Logically as well as practically the idea that goodness and being are convertible terms is weak; for both good and evil are attributes of some existent subject, so that logically as well as factually it is no more correct to maintain that goodness and being are convertible terms than to say that evil and being are such. Such a theory of the nonreality of evil is the logical concomitant of a pantheism or a monism, not of the essentially dualistic philosophy predicated by an ethical theism.

It has long been fashionable to criticize the Schoolmen of whom Thomas is the greatest for the hairsplitting and pedantic lengths to which they carried their logical method. As has been indicated at individual points all the way through this chapter, the writer believes that the limitations of Thomas as an ethical teacher are in general not those of the pedantic logician, but of the subservient authoritarian. In a few instances his logic does go astray, but usually these are the times when he feels compelled to stretch logic to its elastic limit in defense of some extreme stand of one of his authorities, and usually even the errors in classification are initially mistakes of his authorities rather than his own. A striking instance of such misclassification as has already been noticed is his adoption of Cicero's assertion that religion is a moral virtue annexed to justice, in defense of which Thomas spins his logic out very thin.[43]

Another place where he seems to be carried away with his own logic is in treating the virtues and the vices as such simply on the ground of their logical opposition. Granted that wisdom is a virtue, does it follow that folly, its logical contrary, is necessarily a sin, as Thomas strains his logic to argue? [44]

The mistakes that Thomas makes as an ethical teacher are usually those, not of logic, but of fact, such as adopting certain premises as true without sufficient examination, a mistake far more pardonable in his age than in ours. In common with his less gifted contemporaries, Thomas makes no epistemological distinction between facts and value judgments and in consequence treats as facts whose truth

---

[43] *The Summa theologica*, II², Q. lxxx, art. 1.   [44] *Ibid.*, Q. xlvi, arts. 1–2.

is guaranteed by revelation or by the mere assertion of some revered figure of tradition many propositions that are at best highly controversial opinions, at worst completely erroneous. This error proved all the more serious because Thomas covered such a wide area in his ethics, in trying to span the two realms of nature and grace and include all the moral problems of man within the embrace of his systems. Like the Jewish Law which had earlier tried to do likewise, he confused with well-established moral laws and Divine commands all sorts of extraneous elements: traditions, customs, opinions, and judgments ranging in degree of certainty from a fair degree of probability to patent falsity, with no distinction among them. The fault was not entirely that of Thomas, but of the credulous age in which he lived, that he, its greatest son, did not transcend its limitations at this point. Had he done so, it is unlikely that his own age would have understood him, and he might have fallen into immediate oblivion. However, this defect did vitiate for later times much of his far-flung ethical synthesis. Since his originality was so inhibited by his authoritarianism, he falls short of the creative stature of those ethical teachers such as Jesus and the Buddha who were able to pierce the illusions of their time, to re-examine its mores, and from the scrutiny to discover new moral laws, define new aims, and attack the problems in a fresh light.

Thomas's synthesis is vast and glorious in its range, for he has a definite answer to give to every conceivable problem of his time, but later generations have discovered that many of his answers are wrong. It is surprising also that while he treated moral problems so extensively, he did not formulate any new moral principles or even revive many neglected ones of first importance from the systems of his authorities. Indeed, his true greatness in that synthesis lies more in the mysticism which dominates it than in his ethical sense, for Thomas was one of the world's great mystics. His philosophy has in many respects the same golden mysticism that Dante caught from him and cast into the poetry of his *Divine Comedy,* and it is in the mysticism rather than the logic or the ethics that Thomas's greatest claim to universalism lies.

What were his positive contributions to the future of ethics? Not so many as one would suppose from his vast system, but there are, besides the individual solutions he gave, a few general principles that were of lasting value. The most important seems to be his revival of the criterion of the ordinate, that which accords with the *raison d'être* of a thing and with reason as the index of goodness and rightness. This standard was not original with Thomas, in fact it came into Christian thinking with the writings of Origen (*ca.* A.D. 250), but it had not been prominent as a main index of the good until Thomas revived it. For some classes of action there can be no better standard of goodness than that the actor involved shall fulfill the order of his own *raison d'être.* The second standard, which Thomas never mentions explicitly and as such, is that of progress toward some higher form. But this canon is implicit in much of Thomas's thinking, from two roots: the Aristotelian theory of the hierarchy of being, with its progress from potentiality toward actuality, from matter toward form; and the Christian scheme in which all rational creatures progress toward God. Thus Thomas had, in many respects, a dynamic rather than a static teleology, but he himself is not fully aware of that fact. The ordinate is, however, the fulfillment of the highest purpose for which the thing is designed; the inordinate is a regression from its higher form and design to some lower state, so that there is a certain element of progress inherent in the index of the ordinate itself.

In most cases Thomas identifies the ordinate with the mean, which the moral virtues follow, and the inordinate with the extremes of excess or deficiency: temperance, for instance, is the mean, drunkenness and gluttony are excesses.[45] In the matter of sex, all the forms of lust are perversions and abnormalities, excesses of departure from the natural and the ordinate. This standard, being intrinsic and factual, is really final for large areas of morals.

It is the life achievement of Thomas to successfully combine Aristotelianism and Christianity in his original synthesis. On the surface the combination does not appear to be logical or even desirable, but it is the great merit of Aquinas that he was able to produce a combi-

[45] *Ibid.,* II^2, QQ. cxlvi–cl.

nation so harmonious and so fertile for both. In the main the concept
of the two realms, nature and grace, helped to tone down the conflicts
between the Aristotelian ethic of the mean, and the Christian ethic
of absolutes, each of which was supreme in its own sphere. Other
difficulties were smoothed out by the saint's ingenuity in defending
his thesis that reason and revelation, the two directing principles of
each realm, could never conflict—a position more easily maintained
in Thomas's day than at later times, when science became dominant.
But in spite of the fine skill with which Thomas fused the two divergent systems, there were some places where the junction was not
perfect; indeed, in some cases the teachings of the two conflicted so
glaringly that he was obliged to make a choice. Which did he choose?
Sometimes the one; sometimes the other.

The postulate of the realm of grace admitted many values into
Thomism that were quite unknown to Aristotelianism, so that this,
the most ingenious part of the system, worked smoothly; but there
are also areas where it would seem that the saint unconsciously chose
Aristotle against Jesus, who is not by any means always the prime
mover of Thomas's thought. Somewhat questionable from the Christian standpoint is the ethical importance which Thomas attached to
self-love, where his teaching accords more nearly with that of Aristotle than that of Jesus. Indeed, though the saint attempts to defend
this idea of his from the Christian standpoint, he gives no more than
an ingenious misinterpretation of the commandment to love our
neighbors as ourselves, for the plain intention of that command is
not to erect love of self to a higher position than that of neighbor, as
Thomas argues, but to have us love our neighbors as much as ourselves, which has been the general understanding of the precept
within the Christian church.[46] From the standpoint of the facts in
the case it is hardly necessary or desirable to enjoin with ethical sanctions self-love, to which the human animal is only too prone, and
most of the trends in ethics have rightly been to mitigate rather than
to increase and emphasize self-love. It is likely that Thomas, who
went beyond Aristotle himself in this respect, did so because he felt

[46] *Ibid.*, Q. xxv, arts. 4, 7, 12.

that there was something unnatural in not loving oneself first and foremost. But he misunderstood the intention of the Christian teaching in exalting love of self over that of neighbor.

In other particulars as well, it is not unfair to say that Thomas displayed a tendency to tone down and to moderate the heroic character of the ethic of Jesus. While it is perhaps well that he did so in the case of Jesus's teachings on wealth and poverty (for these ideas of Jesus were intended as an interim ethic until the Kingdom should come), there are other instances in which the moderation of the Christian absolutes is not so happy. The saint is very halfhearted and compromising when he treats love of enemies. He says it is more meritorious to love a friend than an enemy, for the friend who loves you is a better man than the enemy who hates you.[47] This dictum reflects the teaching of Aristotle on the high value of friendship between the good. The only obligations entailed by Christian love of enemies, according to Thomas's exegesis, are that we should love them because Christ commands it; that we should, if necessity arises, love them individually, but we do so primarily for the sake of God, Whose children they also are. He goes on to say that it is not necessary for salvation that we should show our enemies the signs and effects of love, for this is a counsel of perfection.[48]

That the ethic of Thomas is not more faithful to the teachings of Jesus is not wholly because Thomas was so true to Aristotle, whose teachings are rich and worthy of the restoration that the Angelic Doctor gave them. The fault was partly in the view that Thomas took of the Old Testament, which accorded more with the mores of his time than did the Sermon on the Mount. Bound as he was by his authorities, Thomas could not view the Old Testament in a historical light any more than he could scrutinize the worthies he accepted from antiquity with detachment. Such a critical approach in ethics was left for a different age, when science had broken down the authoritarianism of the Middle Ages and prepared the way for a more factual approach to the problems of man and his corporate life. The system of Thomas, shot through with the golden rays of his mysticism, is the finest flowering of all that the Middle Ages had to give

[47] *Ibid.*, Q. xxvii, art. 7.   [48] *Ibid.*, Q. xxv, art. 8–9.

to the world. He was as great as his time allowed him to be, he transcended it in a few respects such as his wide-hearted belief that man is by nature capable of some goodness; but he did not transcend his world enough to pierce through its illusions and to give it a new ethical synthesis. He could only give a synthesis of past and present that provided an answer to the multifarious problems that was final for his day, but not for the future.

CHAPTER VIII

PANTHEISM AND DETERMINISM IN THE ETHIC OF BENEDICT DE SPINOZA

FOUR CENTURIES elapsed between the lifetime of Saint Thomas Aquinas and that of Baruch, or Benedict, de Spinoza, who was born into a Jewish family in Amsterdam in 1632, and died in 1677. These centuries had brought in their course the great changes of the Renaissance and the Reformation and, most important of all for the thought of Spinoza, the rise of modern science. Thomas was the son of the Middle Ages, but Spinoza is a typically modern figure, though he brought to bear upon the problems of his age a mind among the most original of those who essayed to work upon ethics in the Western world. By the time that Spinoza began to formulate his system, the work of Copernicus, Kepler, and Galileo had been accomplished in physics, astronomy, and mathematics. The invention of the telescope had made possible many of these revolutionary discoveries, and the technique of lens-making was rapidly perfecting instruments for extending the scope of science. Mathematics also was advancing with rapid strides, and in physiology Harvey had discovered the circulation of the blood just a few years before the birth of Spinoza.

In the progress of all these sciences Spinoza took the keenest interest. He himself was a mathematician of no mean order, and his appreciation of the importance of the new instruments is reflected in the fact that he became a lens-maker. The new currents of thought that science had set in motion had already begun to react upon philosophy. Giordano Bruno and Descartes on the Continent and Francis Bacon and Hobbes in England had erected new philosophic systems on the foundation of the implications of the recent cosmology. Spinoza, influenced especially by Descartes, on whose system he wrote a treatise, set himself the task of drawing inferences from the new science for theology and ethics.

Gone was the old anthropocentric world view and the Ptolemaic cosmology that had nurtured it, and gone with it, as Spinoza viewed the matter, were the theism and teleology of orthodox religion. Not only had the new cosmology revealed that the earth revolved about the sun, but also, to his mind, all the new sciences agreed in revealing a world of nature impersonal and mechanistic, operating upon the necessity of the laws of its own structure instead of upon the Will of a Supreme Being whose central concern was the welfare and redemption of man, the crown of His creation. In theology, for the first time in the Western world, Spinoza put forward a full-blown pantheism, which he set forth together with his views upon the relation of the Bible to the new world in his *Tractatus theologico-politicus* in 1665. Spinoza was excommunicated from the Jewish Synagogue for the publication of this work, which outraged equally the Jews and the Christians, Catholics and Protestants alike, by all of whom he was viewed as an atheist of the most shocking sort. It is not the concern of the present chapter to deal with the theology of Spinoza except in so far as it relates to his ethic; therefore, the discussion will be confined to his two important works on that subject, the *Short Treatise,* which he wrote at about the same time as the *Tractatus,* and the *Ethic,* which he withheld from publication during his lifetime, because of the furor the *Tractatus* had caused. The *Ethic* appeared among the *Opera posthuma* which were published soon after his death, in 1677.

Misunderstood as his ideas upon the nature of God were by his orthodox contemporaries, Spinoza is now recognized as a profoundly religious spirit, and indeed his "heresies" were only a revolt from orthodox and anthropomorphic theism. They were more theological and philosophic than ethical and religious, for he retains both moral fervor and ardent mysticism. Pantheism was his substitute for theism; and this pantheism, with its matrix of mechanistic determinism and unalterable necessity, forms the background and framework for his new and highly original analysis and reconstruction of the groundwork and problems of ethics.

The very method which Spinoza used in treating the problems of ethics reflects his strong mathematical interest, for he wrote the *Ethic* in the form of a geometrical system, with axioms, postulates, demonstrations of the propositions, and finally, corollaries and scholia drawn from the propositions he had proved with the same deductive reasoning employed in mathematics. The axioms are the assumptions about ethics which he deemed fundamental and self-evident, the propositions represent his ideas on the subject, which he believed he had demonstrated to be true by the same incontrovertible and necessary deduction that a mathematician employs. This is the only attempt ever made by anyone to apply the exact form of mathematics to ethics, and while the idea that ethics could be as exact as mathematics persisted for some time, even in the thinking of the great Kant, no one after Spinoza followed his form, which, it is to be conceded at once, was neither a felicitous nor a successful mode of treatment for the subject.

While Spinoza's deductions were in the main carefully and well reasoned, the same trouble haunted his attempt that had vitiated the logical analysis of the Scholastics, namely, the insecurity of the premises. Of course, this is not to say that he duplicated the authoritarian errors of the latter, for Spinoza does not take the dicta of others as his premises, rather he originates his own. However, the difficulty lay in the fact that Spinoza, using deduction instead of induction, made in the realm of ethics the kind of a priori assumptions that are characteristic of mathematics, which it is not possible to do on any large scale in an empirical science such as ethics must be, if it is to be a science at all. Only if these axioms and postulates which underlie his propositions rest upon fact is the system of Spinoza sound, and unfortunately Spinoza drew many of these from intuition, which he believed to be the most certain form of knowledge.[1]

Spinoza proceeded upon the theory that there are three kinds of knowledge: (1) opinion, which consists of confused ideas containing some fact, but mingled with conjecture and error; (2) belief, which rests upon facts assorted and worked over into conviction by the reason; (3) intuitive knowledge, which is always clear, simple and certain, inasmuch as it comes directly from God.[2] The last kind of knowledge is the highest sort. In fact, all our ideas are true and ade-

[1] *"Kurzgefasste Abhandlung"* (*Short Treatise*), Part 2, chap. ii.
[2] *Ibid.*

quate only as they are in God, but the third sort alone is entirely un-
mixed with confusion and falsehood, therefore entirely reliable.
This intuitive, direct knowledge, of course, Spinoza looked upon as
the source of his propositions concerning the nature and essence of
God.

Thus Spinoza's conception of God was thoroughly a priori in its
fundamental roots. He held, in contradistinction to the Aristotelian
theory of a plurality of substances in which the Schoolmen had believed, that God is the sole existent substance, eternal in His essence,
infinite in His attributes, self-caused and free in the sense that He
alone acts according to the necessities of His own nature.[3] The Being
of God is perfect, and perfection, by its very definition, necessarily
implies existence, since inability to exist would mean impotence,
which is an imperfection.[4] As there can be only one substance, God, it
follows that all there is in nature is but this one substance, with its
infinite attributes manifested under two principal modes—mind and
body, or extension. All nature is, moreover, perfect, for perfection is
synonymous with existence. Since all reality is but the sum of the
attributes of this one substance, God, it further follows that nothing
in nature could be other than it is, for all that happens in it follows
from the necessity of the nature of God.[5]

From this conception of God follow several important consequences for the construction of the philosopher's system. First of all,
with regard to God Himself, it is, in Spinoza's opinion, an absurd
anthropomorphism to attribute to God such human characteristics
as will and purpose, as has been done by the orthodox theism of
Judaism and Christianity. It is equally inappropriate to speak of purposes or a final cause in a universe in which all things come to pass
according to the necessity of the nature of God, since the achievement of purpose would also imply an imperfection out of keeping
with a reality that is perfection.[6] A third important consequence is
that there can be no chance events in nature, where all moves according to necessity, whether it happens to be for the good of man or not:

[3] Spinoza, *Ethic*, tr. 1930, Part 1, prop. xvii.   [4] *Ibid.*, props. vii, xi.
[5] *Ibid.*, props. v, vii, xiii, xvii, xxix.   [6] *Ibid.*, Part 1, Appendix, pp. 39 ff.

The attempt, however, to show that nature does nothing in vain (that is to say, nothing which is not profitable to man) seems to end in showing that nature, the gods and man are alike mad.

Do but see, I pray, to what all this has led. Amidst so much in nature that is beneficial, not a few things must have been observed which are injurious, such as storms, earthquakes, diseases, and it was affirmed that these things happened either because the gods were angry because of wrongs which had been inflicted on them by man, or because of sins committed in the method of worshipping them; and although experience daily contradicted this, and showed by an infinity of examples that both the beneficial and the injurious were indiscriminately bestowed on the pious and the impious, the inveterate prejudices on this point have not therefore been abandoned. For it was much easier for a man to place these things aside with others, of the use of which he is ignorant, and thus retain his present and inborn state of ignorance, than to destroy the whole superstructure and think out a new one. Hence it was looked upon as indisputable that the judgments of the gods far surpass our comprehension; and this opinion alone would have been sufficient to keep the human race in darkness to all eternity, if mathematics, which does not deal with ends but with the essences and properties of forms, had not placed before us another rule of truth. In addition to mathematics, other causes also might be assigned, which it is superfluous here to enumerate, tending to make men reflect upon these universal prejudices, and leading them to a true knowledge of things.[7]

Now, of nature man himself is but a part, and as such he is no more free than any other part; therefore it seemed incontrovertible to Spinoza that man, in common with the rest of nature, is completely determined. That freedom of the will, which former ethicians had regarded as fundamental to any sort of ethics, he believed to be completely illusory. Only God is free, that is to say, can act in accordance with the necessities of His own nature, uncompelled and undetermined by any exterior cause. God Himself cannot act otherwise than in accordance with His nature. Thus, from the orthodox standpoint at least, it would seem that Spinoza's God is hardly free in the sense that He might do what He wills, but in accordance with Spinoza's somewhat contradictory definition, freedom consists in the ability to

---

[7] Spinoza, *Ethic*, Part 1, Appendix, pp. 40–41.

act according to the necessity of one's own nature, not as one wishes or wills.

Most fundamental of all the consequences of Spinoza's conception of God for ethics is that he looks upon good and evil as simply human modes of thought, since they cannot be otherwise when all that exists is perfect. Perfection, as Spinoza uses the word, is therefore an ontological, not an ethical, term. Since no divine plan governs the universe or human life, the distinctions between good and evil represent only man's preferences in the matter. The good is what is useful to man; the evil is what is not useful to him.[8] Such a denial of ontological reality to evil is common to all types of pantheism, but that of Spinoza is unique in that he makes a place for ethics in the human realm in spite of it; and the ethical struggle is real for man, even though evil does not have absolute, objective reality. This point thus brings us to the subject of Spinoza's anthropology.

It has been stated that man is a part of nature, that is to say, he is compounded of attributes of God, and in him these appear in their two main modes, as thought, or mind, and extension, or body. His mind, as that of a thinking being, is part of the infinite mind of God. His body, as extension, is one with the rest of nature and subject to the same laws. There is nothing in the essence of man which necessarily involves existence, and indeed the power of man to persist in existence is very limited, because its strength is surpassed by that of external causes. In so far as he has a limited capacity to act from reason or necessity, man is said to possess the power of action; but in so far as he is acted upon by external causes, he suffers, or is passive, subject to passions. Since man is to such a large extent determined by nature, that is, by external causes, he suffers many changes which cannot be understood from his own nature. He also experiences passions which are the source of much confusion and difficulty to him. However, since his mind is part of the infinite mind of God, he possesses some true and adequate ideas which correspond with facts, while the passions are confused ideas that contain error, arising from the deprivation of complete knowledge.[9] All ideas, however, are true and adequate in so far as they are related to God. Those ideas

[8] *Ibid.*, Part 4, Preface.   [9] *Ibid.*, props. ii–iv.

which are directly derived from God, or most fully related to Him, are the very ones which are clear, simple, and definite in our minds. Now the scheme of salvation, if the phrase may appropriately be used of such an impersonal system as Spinoza's, consists of the reduction of all our ideas by the intellect to clarity by relating them to God.

Only when we apprehend that we act from necessity can we hope to understand the true causes of our actions, and only when we relate our ideas to God can we see that we act from necessity—never while we imagine ourselves to be creatures acting from free will. However, as we understand ourselves to act from necessity, we do the will of God. The free man, the one who understands that he acts from necessity, is the one who truly does the will of God and is in communion with His infinite mind. The way by which this end comes about is the suppression of the wrong passions or affects and the substitution of what he names the intellectual love of God.

The most famous section of Spinoza's *Ethic* is the fourth part, entitled "Of Human Bondage," in which he deals with the bondage of man to the passions and affects. In the third part he dealt with the nature and the kinds of affects, and in the final section, called "Of the Power of the Intellect, or of Human Liberty," he finishes the work of the fourth part by describing how he believes that the reason can emancipate man from the passions. He was the first of the great Western ethical teachers to appreciate the role played by the emotions or affects as obstacles and barriers to the good life and to work out a mode of dealing with them. Saint Thomas had given an extensive discussion of passions based upon the psychology of Aristotle, but psychological treatment of them in Spinoza's work is a great advance upon that of the Angelic Doctor, both in treatment and in firsthand psychological observation.

In so far as the mind possesses adequate ideas, it has the power to act; in so far as it has inadequate ones, it suffers, that is, is subject to passions.[10] Through the ideas of both itself and the body which it has through its affects, the mind tends to imagine those things which will foster its own action and that of the body. Affects either help or hinder the power of the action of the mind and the body. Spinoza

[10] *Ethic*, Part 3, prop. i and corollary.

gives an elaborate analysis of the affects and their power to help or to hinder the power of action of both the mind and the body. In general, affects that cause joy are those which the mind tends to imagine, because they increase its capacity for action; those which cause sorrow impede its power of action, hence the mind tends to exclude the imagination of these. Spinoza divides all the affects that he covers into one or the other of these two groupings and defines them all in terms of either joy or sorrow, connected with some external cause. Love, for example, he defines as joy connected with some external cause; hatred, as sorrow connected with one.[11] In his discussion of this subject of the affects we find some remarkable anticipations of the findings of modern psychology, such as his anticipation of the law of association. He states that if the mind has been simultaneously affected by two objects at once, whenever one of these appears, the other will be experienced also.[12] Moreover, he continues, anything may accidentally be the cause of either joy or sorrow. The same object may cause sorrow to one person, joy to another, or it may at different times cause joy and sorrow to the same person.[13]

Objects affecting the mind in the present do so more vividly than those experienced in the past or anticipated in the future, and those which we imagine to be necessary and inevitable cause a stronger affect than those which are contingent or remote possibilities.[14] We tend to extend our own affects to objects we love or hate, affirming everything which causes joy to the beloved object just as we do for ourselves, and denying everything which causes sorrow to the beloved object; and toward an object of hatred, we tend to affirm everything which causes it sorrow and to deny everything which causes it joy.[15] If we experience contrary affects toward the same object, we are in a state of vacillation. The only way, however, to displace one affect is to substitute another for it.[16]

It is not necessary to reproduce here all Spinoza's definitions of the affects, such as fear, confidence, hope, shame, self-esteem, and pride, since most of them do not differ essentially from the use of the

---

[11] *Ibid.*, prop. xiii, scholium.   [12] *Ibid.*, prop. xiv.
[13] *Ibid.*, props. xv, li.   [14] *Ibid.*, Part 4, props. ix–xiii.
[15] *Ibid.*, Part 3, props. xxviii–xlix.   [16] *Ibid.*, Part 4, def. v.

terms in popular parlance. However, it is desirable to comment upon the valuation that he gives to a few of these, since in some cases it is not in agreement with the estimate of other ethicians. According to Spinoza, only those affects which spring from reason instead of external causes are good; therefore humility, which does not spring from reason, is not a virtue. In like manner, repentance, which the philosopher limits to repentance for what we have done when we imagine ourselves to be free agents, is no virtue, but a sign of impotence.[17] He does go on to concede in the scholium following these two propositions that humility and repentance are less dangerous than some of the other harmful affects, because if a man sins, it is better for him to repent than to be shameless. Others, he asserts, have praised the humble only because they are easily led, especially by good influences. However, he thinks that the repentance and the humility of such people eventuate well only if these men become converts to the way of reason, when they will abandon both these affects. This position of Spinoza's is in decided contrast to the usual religio-ethical glorifications of humility as one of the foundation stones of the moral life.

Pity is another affect which Spinoza feels is out of place in the man of reason, since it is sorrow for another's lot. The man of reason should strive as much as possible to avoid being touched by it.[18] Pride and despondency are the two affects which indicate the greatest impotence of mind. The first is contrary to reason, because it ascribes to the self virtues which it does not in fact possess; the second, because it ascribes to the self limitations and weaknesses which are not there. Hence both alike reveal a lack of self-knowledge and are out of conformity with reason.[19] Of all the affects, the most harmful is hatred, which cannot under any circumstances be a good; and the affects that follow in its train, such as envy, contempt, mockery, anger, and revenge, are all very wrong and hurtful. The man of reason will strive to eradicate them by treating with love and generosity those who have shown hatred to him.[20] In his teaching on returning

[17] *Ibid.*, props. liii, liv.
[18] *Ibid.*, prop. l.
[19] *Ibid.*, prop. lvi.
[20] *Ibid.*, prop. xlv.

good for evil, Spinoza is in full agreement with Jesus and a number of the other great teachers, such as the Buddha and Socrates.

The standard by which Spinoza evaluates the various affects is the one by which he measures all good and evil, namely, what is useful to man. On the basis of this same standard of utility he argues that the greatest good of everyone is his own self-preservation, and that no one who does not want to live can be happy. Thus he affirms life as man's supreme good. He states that the man of wisdom does not think about death, tries not to fear it, and out of his wisdom makes life rather than death the subject of his meditation. On the other hand, anyone who commits suicide, he believes, is impotent in mind and thoroughly overcome with external causes.[21]

The most virtuous man is the man that preserves his own being the most, but Spinoza does not intend this merely in a selfish sense, for the being of each man is better preserved by social living in the state than in solitude.[22] Such a man is not selfish, on the contrary he recognizes his duty to be helpful to others and to meet their failings with the tolerance that comes from understanding their causes. He meets life as a whole with equanimity, because he realizes that all things happen of necessity. There is harmony among men of reason, for people differ only because they are agitated by varying affects. When they live according to reason, they agree, for they all have the same goal and the same nature.[23]

The road to perfection for man is to make reason the source of his desires rather than the affects. This is effected only by bringing the affects under the scrutiny of reason in such a manner that the confused and inadequate ideas which form them become clear and plain. Evil itself is only inadequate knowledge, and if we lived according to reason all our lives, we should have no knowledge of evil at all.[24] In order to be really evil, that is, harmful to us, an object must be like ourselves, for one totally different from us in nature cannot do us real harm.[25] The evil comes from the passions, which, in

[21] *Ibid.*, prop. xviii, scholium.   [22] *Ibid.*, prop. lxxiii.
[23] *Ibid.*, prop. xxxiii–xxxv.   [24] *Ibid.*, prop. lxiv and corollary.
[25] *Ibid.*, props. xxix–xxx.

turn, arise from the inadequate ideas, and many of them cause sorrow, which constitutes the injurious element in them. The reason,
which has a considerable, though not an absolute, power of ordering
the affects, turns them into clear and adequate ideas by relating them
to their true causes and to God. The man who understands that all
follows from the Divine Nature will not be subject to these harmful
affects; rather, his desires will spring from reason, in which no desire
can be in excess.[26]

Other characteristics of the desires arising from reason are: everything being conceived *sub specie aeternitatis* and all being perceived
to happen of necessity, such a desire will exert equal effect over the
mind, whether it relates to the past, the present, or the future. The
mind will be influenced to endure some present evil for the sake of
a future good, instead of choosing some fleeting good of the moment
against the higher value of the future.[27] Thus, the man of reason
seeks the more lasting good; but he does not eschew all pleasures,
only those excessive ones which spring from lust and other passions.
His pleasures are different and qualitatively finer than those of persons who are not free men. The free man strives to avoid the errors
of the ignorant, indeed, he retreats from and shuns temptations
which might lead him into succumbing to evil, and, so far as in him
lies, he tries to remove evils from his path.[28]

The temper of Spinoza's ethic is indicated by its avoidance of all
that is immoderate and excessive, even to the excess of pleasurable
excitement, which may be partly bad. The virtues which it inculcates
are those of equanimity and serenity in the face of all the vicissitudes
of fortune, but he does not go to the extreme of lumping together as
bad all the pleasures and the joys of life. The selection is made on the
principle of pleasure and pain in its highest sense; for Spinoza
thought that the highest pleasures were the cool, tempered sort that
relate to the mind. Furthermore, these desires that come from the
mind are not accompanied by any sorrow at all. Characteristic, also,
is his caution to avoid pity as being out of conformity with reason.

The mind is the chief instrument for eradicating the passions and

---

[26] *Ibid.*, prop. 1, scholium, prop. lxi.   [27] *Ibid.*, prop. lxii.
[28] *Ibid.*, prop. lxix.

turning them into adequate ideas, desires that originate from the reason, not from external causes. Deceit, for example, is not in accord with reason; therefore the man of reason shuns it. Here speaks the rationalist *par excellence*. Even the *summum bonum* of Spinoza's system, the intellectual love of God, is a rather cool and moderate goal; for he does not conceive this love of God in the ardent terms of love that the mystics frequently employ in describing union with Him. For him it is an affair of the intellect, and the communion with God that it brings can scarcely be called a fellowship with Him. He explains carefully what he means by the intellectual love of God in the fifth part of the *Ethic*.

This *summum bonum* is reached when the mind causes all the affections of the body and of particular things to be related to God.[29] When this takes place, one understands one's self and all one's affects clearly and at the same time loves and understands God better than one does one's self. This love for God, which is the highest kind of knowledge, thenceforth occupies the mind above everything else. Nevertheless, since God is free of all passions He is not possessed of such anthropomorphic attributes as will and intellect in the ordinary sense. He cannot be properly said either to love or to hate anyone; hence he who loves God should not strive to have God love him in return.[30] The logic of this position of Spinoza's would, of course, be to state that God is absolutely indifferent and unresponsive to the intellectual love of the free man; but this Spinoza cannot quite bring himself to affirm. Instead, he declares that the intellectual love of God is eternal. Out of this thesis he draws two important conclusions for the duration of the relation between man and God.

Having asserted that the free man's intellectual love of God is eternal, Spinoza therewith raises the problem of human immortality, which he resolves in the following manner. In God there is an eternal idea of the essence of the individual human body.[31] Now the human mind, which is more important than the body, has some eternal quality about it which will not allow it to perish with the human body; something of the mind must remain that is eternal, and this eternal

---

[29] *Ibid.*, Part 5, props. xiv–xv.   [30] *Ibid.*, props. xvi–xvii, xix.
[31] *Ibid.*, prop. xxii.

element is the idea of the essence of the individual mind in God.[32]
Herewith Spinoza evolves a conception of immortality which is neither quite a theory of personal survival nor quite an immortality of
influence. The theory is also a singular variation from the usual pantheistic form of immortality through absorption into the Being of
God. It is, however, nearer to the pantheistic than the personal conceptions of survival, for it is a survival of the idea of the essence of
both our minds and our bodies in the mind of God. In fact, it may be
truly said that here Spinoza has found the excluded middle between
to be and *not to be* and rested his theory squarely upon it.

The persistence of the idea of the essence of the individual mind in
God is the only response that man receives from God. Of it, Spinoza
has this to say:

The intellectual love of the mind towards God is the very love with
which He loves Himself, not in so far as He is infinite, but in so far as He
can be manifested through the essence of the human mind; considered
under the form of eternity; that is to say, the intellectual love of the mind
towards God is part of the infinite love with which God loves Himself.

Hence it follows that God, in so far as He loves Himself, loves men,
and consequently, that love of God towards men and the intellectual love
of the mind towards God are one and the same thing.[33]

This *summum bonum* of the intellectual love of God is not the
reward of virtue, for to Spinoza the idea of being good for the sake
of reward or of avoiding evil for fear of punishment was repug-
nant. "Blessedness is not the reward of virtue, but it is virtue itself; nor do we delight in blessedness because we restrain our lusts;
but, on the contrary, because we delight in it, therefore we are able
to restrain them." [34]

The intellectual love of God constitutes salvation, in which we
ought to persist even if we have no assurance that our mind is
eternal. The intellectual love of God is not only the highest knowledge and state of perfection for man but also a state which all may
share; for there is no room for any jealousy in the love of God,

---

[32] *Ibid.*, prop. xxiii.   [33] *Ibid.*, props. xxxvi and corollary.
[34] *Ibid.*, prop. xlii.

rather, all are united by it and mutually strengthened by their common love of Him. There is no affect contrary to the love of God, since no one can hate God; and this most adequate of all ideas cannot turn into hatred, because in it there is no sorrow at all.

Such, in brief outline, is the ethical system of Benedict de Spinoza. Its originality in the Western world sets it apart from all the Western systems; and though its pantheism has some features in common with the Indian pantheisms, its ethical emphasis makes it distinct from them, and its mysticism is far more intellectual. Indeed, it is the combination of pantheism and determinism that together constitute the uniqueness of his teaching, either in the East or in the West.

Theoretically, it would be possible to detach the ethic of Spinoza from the pantheistic matrix in which he implants it; but to him this seemed essential to the ethic, both as the means and the end. Yet his ethic could be detached from pantheism, because the mind itself might so work over the illusions of the passions and the affects as to evolve a state identical with that which Spinoza describes, and the goal itself would be about the same condition if he had elected merely to call it intellectual love of the necessary laws of the universe. Unfortunately for the finality of his pantheism, Spinoza rests the existence of his God upon some assumptions whose insecurity he himself did not perceive. He believed that he had established a priori the existence of God by defining Him as a perfect, infinite substance, Whose existence was necessarily involved in His perfection, since inability to exist is an imperfection, a sign of impotence.

Kant was later to show the falsity of assuming that existence is an attribute of perfection, as Spinoza, in common with Anselm and Descartes before him, had done. It is strange that Spinoza, whose thinking was so original and so critical of orthodoxy at many points, should have believed as heartily as did his predecessors that the existence of God could be established in this way. But the fact is that he did, and the shift from theism to pantheism did not make his case any more valid than theirs. The natural universe, to be sure, exists, but what right have we to call it the sole, perfect, infinite substance, God, as Spinoza does? For perfection itself has no meaning as he employs the term. If it is simply identical with the finished, in its ontological sense, then he is right that it is simply a synonym for the existent. However, he is not consistent, but is simply transferring some of the connotations of the word from orthodox ontological arguments for the existence of God when he talks about the inability to exist as an imperfection, a sign of impotence. His argument for the existence of his perfect, infinite substance is no more valid than the orthodox arguments for the existence of a perfect, infinite Being. The difference is merely verbal.

A second invalid assumption vitiates Spinoza's pantheistic arguments, because to a certain extent the *summum bonum* of his ethic and a part of his ethical process depend upon the validity of this second assumption. This is his confidence that all clear, simple, and definite ideas are necessarily true. Locke and Kant were later to show the error of this assumption. The validity of Spinoza's intuitive knowledge depends entirely upon the truth of this assumption, and since we cannot grant it to him, the truth of this third kind of knowledge is no longer guaranteed.

Even had this second assumption proved perfectly true, however, there is still another difficulty with the ethic of Spinoza, namely, that it is much too intellectualistic. The human mind is not powerful enough to assure the good life by merely reducing all the passions and affects to clear ideas. It is not true that the individual always follows the reasonable and right course, even when he intellectually recognizes it as such. Of this difficulty Spinoza himself sporadically displays some awareness; but by and large throughout his ethical treatises he goes on the assumption that if all the passions and the affects were but reduced to the status of clear ideas, the ethical battle would be won and the *summum bonum* of the intellectual love of God would be attained. Indeed, the use of the intellect for this reduction of the passions and affects to clarity is the sole technique for the good life which he advocates.

However, his reliance upon the intellect for the transformation of the affects is not so radical as that of the Buddha, who believed that it was the most powerful means of eradicating all desires. Spinoza wished only the eradication of the desires that did not spring

from reason. In fact he believes that all the joyful affects are wholesome and build up the character of man in his pursuit of the good
life. This recognition that there is a qualitative distinction among
the desires was much needed, and it is a contribution of Spinoza's
to the subject that he made the distinction. "Cheerfulness can never
be excessive, but is always good; melancholy, on the contrary, is
always evil." [35]

The most valuable emphasis of Spinoza's was his insistence that
life is the supreme value and that the good is all that aids man in
living for his own best preservation and development. Ethics is
simply the discovery of what is good and useful to man, a wholesome corrective for the other-worldly orientation of ethics which the
Middle Ages had inherited, chiefly from Saint Augustine. Probably Spinoza thought that a pantheistic orientation of his ethic was
essential to this important conception, but this affirmation of life is
really the foundation stone of any wholesome and properly conceived ethic, whether theistic, pantheistic, or even atheistic.

"Of Human Bondage," the fourth part of the *Ethic*, is deservedly
the most famous part of Spinoza's work, for it contains a truly masterly discussion of the relations of the passions and affects to moral
problems; and if we had nothing else from his hand, this section
alone would be sufficient to place his name among those of the
greatest ethical teachers. Several of Spinoza's anticipations of the
discoveries of modern psychology, such as the law of association
and the principle that one affect can be displaced only by another
affect, have been noted earlier. Hatred can be conquered only by
love, and so each of the undesirable affects, according to Spinoza's
scheme, can be replaced by a desire that springs from reason, each
inadequate idea with an adequate one. Of course, modern psychology
does not substantiate Spinoza's general position that the affects are
merely confused, inadequate ideas; for in maintaining this he did
not understand the physiological basis of emotions, which was first
elucidated after the beginning of the twentieth century and has been
further illuminated by present-day medical work on the endocrine
glands. While Spinoza did take into consideration the mind-body

[35] *Ibid.*, Part 4, def. ii, prop. xlii.

problem more than the traditional ethicians before him, the physiology of his day was not such that he could present a complete solution; even today this problem is still somewhat obscure. That limitation does not alter the fact that he is really the pioneer in dealing with the problem of emotions and ethics or the fact that he made signal contributions to it.

Whatever Spinoza himself thought was the source of his treatment of the emotions and affects, the real source was not intuition, but keen and careful psychological observation of the way the mind of the human animal operates in its emotional complications. This portion of his work, which is definitely empirical, seems to rest on a much surer foundation than the sections which avowedly are a priori and intuitional, though the data on which the former rest were not invariably compiled and compared with sufficient care to earn his method the name "scientific."

Indeed, it may fairly be said that the parts of his *Ethic* which are the most empirical are the soundest and most valid. Unfortunately for the finality of the whole, it labors under the handicap of the mathematical method, the form into which he cast the whole of the *Ethic*, which is also the governing pattern, though not the form, of the *Short Treatise*. The form of a geometrical treatise is not a felicitous one for the handling of ethical problems, which are definitely empirical and a posteriori, instead of abstract and a priori. Since the source of some of his propositions was intuitional and a priori and his conclusions are reached by the deductive reasoning of mathematics, it is all the more remarkable that so much of his work is really empirical. The standard of good and evil itself is purely empirical. In fact all the best parts of his system are far more factual and empirical than he himself seemed to realize.

In one respect Spinoza made a signal epistemological advance over his predecessors, for he came nearer than any of them to stating that many of our standards of good and evil rest upon value judgments.

With regard to good and evil, these terms indicate nothing positive in things considered in themselves, nor are they anything else than modes of thought, or notions which we form from the comparison of one thing with another. For one and the same thing may at the same time be both good and evil or indifferent. Music, for example, is good for a melancholy person, bad to one mourning, while to a deaf man it is neither good nor bad. But although things are so, we must retain these words. For since we desire to form for ourselves an idea of man upon which we may look as a model of human nature, it will be of service to us to retain these expressions in the sense I have mentioned. By *good*, therefore, I understand in the following pages everything which we are certain is a means by which we may approach nearer and nearer to the model of human nature we set before us. By *evil*, on the contrary, I understand everything which we are certain hinders us from reaching that model.[36]

Although he does not use the term "value judgment," it is clear that Spinoza recognizes this type of moral standard—a distinct advance over the earlier ethical teachers, who regarded all moral dicta as eternal and necessary laws. This clarification of the problem was carried further by later investigators; but there is an important anticipation of their work in Spinoza, who, however, did not go on to mark off the values and the laws clearly from each other.

It is not to be inferred, however, that Spinoza looked upon the moral life as a relative matter; for he believed these judgments to be certain, and furthermore, the determinism of his system precluded any such relativism. To him the essence of the life of reason was just the recognition of the necessity of all things. The reasonable man is the one who, understanding the causes of all things, perceives that even his own actions are completely determined and does not delude himself with the notion that he is a free agent in his conduct. He makes this submission to necessity with tranquillity and is poised and calm in the face of all the vicissitudes of fortune and of any injustices he suffers from his fellow men. He views with equanimity the world without and within, for he sees neither freedom in man nor contingency in nature, but in both, alike, the eternal necessity of the nature of God. Fixed in the intellectual love of God, this man is the perfect man that Spinoza holds up as a model for humanity—an ideal high, but cool and attainable only by the philosopher.

[36] *Ibid.*, Part 4, Preface, p. 179.

CHAPTER IX

KANT'S CONSTRUCTION: THE CATEGORICAL IMPERATIVE OF DUTY

SINCE THE FIRST impact of the new science upon ethics is to be found in the seventeenth-century construction of Spinoza, in like manner, the science of the eighteenth century, dominated as it was by the commanding figure of Sir Isaac Newton, forms the background and sets the problems for not only the ethical construction of Immanuel Kant (1724–1804) but also his entire philosophic system. This imposing philosophic structure is contained principally in his three critiques: *Kritik der reinen Vernunft* (*Critique of Pure Reason*), 1781; *Kritik der praktischen Vernunft* (*Critique of Practical Reason*), 1788; *Kritik der Urtheilskraft* (*Critique of Judgment*), 1790. Of these three, the *Critique of Practical Reason* alone treats exclusively of ethics, and he further expands and modifies the ethical construction laid out in the second critique in his minor ethical treatises: *Grundlegung zur Metaphysik der Sitten* (*Foundation of the Metaphysic of Morals*), 1785; *Metaphysische Anfangsgründe der Sittenlehre* (*Metaphysical Elements of Moral Philosophy*), 1797; *Metaphysische Anfangsgründe der Tugendlehre* (*Metaphysical Elements of Ethics*), 1797; the first section of *Die Religion innerhalb der Grenzen der blossen Vernunft* (*Religion within the Limits of Pure Reason*), 1792; and finally two fragments of the work left incomplete by Kant at his death, which were pieced together and published with commentary under the title *Opus Postumum* by the German scholar Erich Adickes, in 1920.[1]

The reason for Kant's writing of the *Critique of Practical Reason* was that the novel view of knowledge which he had set forth in the *Critique of Pure Reason* called for a complete reconstruction of ethics. This he gives in the second of the trilogy of critiques and the minor ethical treatises. Although he gave to the discipline of

[1] Kant, *Opus postumum*, dargestellt und beurteilt von Erich Adickes, Berlin, Reuter und Reichard, 1920.

ethics a construction original and novel in its entire approach and structure, he was never satisfied with his answers to its problems, and even at the very end of his life he was searching for a new and better solution to the problems he himself had raised, as is evidenced by the *Opus postumum*. Although the two segments relating to ethics are very fragmentary in character, they cannot be ignored, for they contain some startling modifications of his earlier positions as presented in the second critique. It is unfortunate that his eyesight and then his memory failed before he was able to finish this latest work. However, as he left it, it is merely a composite of small fragments, composed between 1799 and 1803, and the two ethical sections, scarcely more than notes, come from the very latest of these years, when he no longer possessed the mental vigor to work out a consecutive discussion on any point.[2] However, we shall refer to the *Opus postumum* whenever it gives one of these important modifications or reversals of his earlier position.

In certain respects Kant was a typical son of the eighteenth century, for in his thought we see reflected a number of the characteristic trends of the Age of Reason, such as faith in reason, which gave the period its name, fear of sentiment, humanistic interest in history and ethics, which relegated religion to a position secondary to that of morality, and confidence in the mechanistic world view of the Newtonian physics. Although Kant's philosophy embodied to a greater or lesser extent all these rationalistic trends of the age to which he belonged, he was saved from the complete sterility of some forms of eighteenth-century rationalism by his own genius and his curious admiration for Rousseau. If Kant believed in reason along with the rest of his generation, he nevertheless fixed definite bounds over which the reason could not pass. The spell of the Newtonian science dominated his thinking throughout his entire life, but, unlike his less gifted contemporaries, he gave a new philosophic interpretation to that enthusiasm, and his sure ethical sense caused him to assert the freedom of man as a moral being over against the mechanism of the world of nature which Newton de-

---

[2] I and VII *Konvolute* (bundles), as Adickes designates them, deal with ethics and religion.

lineated. Thus, like most great men, Kant embodied his century, but he also transcended it, even as he transcended his own experience, to produce the most original ethical structure that the world had seen since ancient times.

Although he lived a very quiet and circumscribed life in the small university town of Königsberg and although, in consequence, his experience was narrow, these limitations do not show at many points in his ethics. For the genius has a true sense for the universal that enables him to transcend his own horizon and sets him apart from ordinary men, who need exceptional experiences if they are to rise above their fellows.

In order to understand the structure of Kant's ethic, it is necessary to indicate some of the background in the *Critique of Pure Reason* out of which it arises and to state some of the characteristic elements of his general philosophic position which carry over into the *Critique of Practical Reason*. Starting, as he does in the first critique, with the question "How are a priori synthetic judgments possible?" he answers that they are possible because all our knowledge, which rests upon sense perceptions, is received under the forms of time and space, which are a priori epistemological forms in the mind of man. These perceptions, in turn, are apprehended by the mind through certain categories, also a priori. Because of the fact that both time and space, as well as the categories, are pure forms antecedent to all experience, they can provide no knowledge in themselves, until the sense perceptions are received by the mind from without. Consequently, since all our knowledge comes to us through the forms of time and space, we cannot know anything outside the phenomenal world which the sense impressions bring to our minds. Furthermore, we can never know even these as things in themselves (*Dinge an sich*), but merely our sense impressions of them. Now, above and beyond this world of phenomena, the world of nature, where the principle of mechanical causation operates in an unbroken chain throughout and to which man, also as a part of nature, is subject, there is also another world, the intelligible, or noumenal, world, to which man as a soul, or noumenon, belongs. Of this world—the term "intelligible" notwithstanding

—we can know nothing by means of the pure, or theoretical, reason, because the noumenal realities lie beyond the ken of time and space. We cannot therefore establish by the pure reason even so much as the existence of such noumenal realities as God, freedom, and immortality.

Having taken this position as to the knowledge of the "intelligible" world, Kant proceeds to demolish the traditional rational arguments for the existence of God: the ontological, the cosmological, and the physico-theological, or teleological, proofs. It is not agreed that he completely destroyed the latter two; but there can be no question but that he demolished the ontological argument which had been originated by Anselm of Canterbury, revised by Descartes, and, in the Cartesian form, employed by Spinoza.

Kant pointed out that the whole ontological argument hinged upon the mistake of supposing that existence is an "attribute" of perfection. He argued that the existence of a subject can never be established by means of any of its attributes or predicates, such as perfection; for the subject, together with its predicates, either does or does not exist, and the existence of all or any of the attributes depends wholly upon the existence of the subject itself. Being is not a predicate or a concept which can be added to the concept of anything. Take away the thing itself and all its predicates vanish with it. Nor does the mere presence of any idea in the mind prove the existence of an object corresponding to that idea, since the mind is capable of forming synthetical concepts without any corresponding realities, as we know from the existence of concepts of imaginary creatures, such as fairies and dragons. Being is never a predicate or a concept which can be deduced from the concept of the subject itself, for it is a category which refers to the whole subject and is the admission of the thing itself with all its predicates. Take away the thing itself, and all the predicates go with it. The mere presence of the concept in the mind is not sufficient to establish the reality of a thing, since logically all that the concept can do is, provided that it be free from inner contradiction, *to establish the possibility of the existence of the corresponding thing*. Hence the concept of God, if free from self-contradiction, establishes no more than the logical possibility of His existence, not the fact of that existence.[3]

By this demonstration Kant demolished the ontological argument for God. He himself was convinced that he had destroyed the cosmological and physico-theological arguments along with it, for he believed that in the last analysis both of these revert to the ontological argument: the cosmological because it argued that the existence of the universe called for the concept of a necessary Being as First Cause; the physico-theological because it inferred that the presence of order and ends in the universe points to the existence of a Supreme and Unconditioned Author of its existence. Thus, according to him, these two proofs revert to the ontological argument to establish the existence of the Divine Architect.[4] This reversion is not so inevitable as Kant supposed, for both can rest their case on the inference of His existence from the data to which they point; but this Kant did not grant. However, Kant himself was so firmly convinced that in the first critique he had destroyed all the old rational proofs for the existence of God, that he tried in the second to replace them with a new proof for the existence of God, the so-called "moral argument," the formulation of which is one of the important objectives of the *Critique of Practical Reason.*

The *Critique of Practical Reason* carries out the same philosophic pattern that the *Critique of Pure Reason* had set and endeavors to provide answers to the moral problems the latter had raised; for the new ethical structure is erected on the epistemological foundation laid by the first of the trilogy. The minor ethical works are chiefly expansions and clarifications of points worked out in the *Critique of Practical Reason;* only the *Opus postumum* contains any significant departures from it.

Over against and aside from the pure, or theoretical, reason, in his second critique Kant postulates the existence of the so-called "practical reason," which operates in the realm of moral experience; and, while not furnishing the exact knowledge of the theoretical reason, nevertheless provides sufficient knowledge to assure a right basis for making moral decisions. In short, though the pure reason never

[3] Kant, *Kritik der reinen Vernunft,* pp. 561 ff.   [4] *Ibid.,* pp. 575–96.

affords us knowledge of any realities outside of the a priori forms of time and space, such things in themselves in the phenomenal world, or any of the noumenal realities, the practical reason finds it necessary to assume certain postulates concerning the noumena which are essential to the operation of the moral life.

To demonstrate that the practical reason exists is the first aim of the *Critique of Practical Reason,* and its existence thereafter is assumed in the other ethical writings. That such a realm did exist the philosopher believed to be fully demonstrated by the fact of freedom, which is not only the causal principle but also the foundation stone of the whole structure of morality—a fact known to us a priori, because it is the condition of the fulfillment of the moral law, which, in turn, we also know a priori through its demands upon us. Having demonstrated to his own satisfaction in the first part of the *Critique of Practical Reason* the existence of the practical reason itself, Kant addresses himself in the second part to the task of criticizing its powers.[5]

What, then, is this moral law which Kant so confidently affirms that we all know? The moral law is the categorical imperative of duty,[6] the a priori form of the practical reason, possessed by all rational creatures, men and any others there may be. It is the "Thou shalt" (*du sollst*), an imperative originating in the practical reason and objectivity valid in determining the will to moral action in answer to its demands. It is a pure form whose content is supplied by the concrete situations which arise from experience. Moreover, all men have at all times the power to fulfill the demands of this categorical imperative, duty. Kant is careful to distinguish the categorical imperative from the older belief in innate ideas; for he insists that it is but a form, not a moral sense, and, at least in the earlier writings, he does not equate it with conscience. Until the writing of the *Opus postumum* he held that the belief in some particular moral sense is a misconception which arises from the view

[5] Kant, *Kritik der praktischen Vernunft* (seventh edition), Preface, pp. 1–2.

[6] Kant uses the expression "categorical imperative" in two senses: as here in reference to the demand of duty, and also as the imperative involved in his great precept to act at all times as though the maxim of one's will were to become a universal law.

that morality is a combination of duty and inclination,[7] but in the *Opus postumum* he seems to look upon the demand of duty as not only conscience but also the voice of God, and upon its commandments as direct from the voice of God within the soul.[8] This consciousness of duty cannot be explained upon the grounds of the theoretical reason, but it is nonetheless a priori, necessary, and universally valid.[9] It appears to be distinct from conscience, which is the subjective necessity of obeying the moral law or the sense of guilt which arises from failure to heed its commands.[10]

Such is Kant's definition of the moral law. Necessary for its operation is freedom, the causal principle of moral action, without which true morality would be impossible. However, freedom is itself a principle of causality which can operate only in the intelligible realm, of which the self as a noumenon is a part; for in the world of nature, to which man as a phenomenon is subject, everything is determined by an endless and uninterrupted chain of mechanical causation throughout, with no break, no margin open for the operation of freedom. Freedom, therefore, is an important and valuable possession which sets man apart from and above the world of nature to which he is physically, but not spiritually, subject.[11]

Since the principle of causality in the moral realm is, then, that freedom which raises man as a moral being above the rest of nature, man, if he would act morally, must act according to its operation upon his will through the dictates of the practical reason, not according to some heteronomous principle from the world of nature. As Kant phrased it, the will must be governed solely by the maxims of the moral law, not by some hedonistic consideration, such as the desire for happiness, well-being, preference, inclination, or feeling. The maxims of the will come wholly from the practical reason, whereas these eudaemonistic considerations have their source in feeling, desire, or emotion, which are all a part of man's nature

[7] Kant, *Theory of Ethics*, pp. 311–12.   [8] Kant, *Opus postumum*, pp. 825–26.
[9] Kant, *Kritik der praktischen Vernunft*, pp. 36–43.   [10] Cf. Note 7 above.
[11] Kant, *Kritik der praktischen Vernunft*, pp. 37–39.

as a physical rather than a rational being. The mark of true moral action is, then, the autonomy of the will.[12]

These maxims are principles dictated to the will by the practical reason and are regulative prescriptions covering specific applications of the moral law to the situations which arise from experience. Unlike the moral law itself, these are not objective, but subjective in character. It is to be emphasized that they must arise from the moral law, from duty, or from preference, or else the action they inspire cannot be regarded as moral. Only that action inspired solely and directly by the categorical imperative has the right to be termed moral. Even a mixture of other impulses makes the action submoral, because they are dictated from the world of nature rather than the intelligible world of freedom. Such motivations as self-preservation, comfort, happiness, desire, inclination are all submoral, for they arise from experience or from nature and cause heteronomy of the will. These motives all are empirical instead of a priori and can yield no more than general rules of action, never universal laws, as moral laws must be. The moral law has a right to command the will, but maxims dictated by these heteronomous considerations can do no more than advise. The object at which they aim is happiness, to which they can lead only occasionally; for Kant believed that the empirical conditions necessary for happiness can seldom be fulfilled, whereas the moral law can be fulfilled at all times.[13]

The maxims of the practical reason, on the other hand, are pure and genuine, and as prescriptions of the moral law they carry along with them a sense of guilt if the dictates of the latter are not fulfilled. The fulfillment will generally lead to a truly exalting sense of satisfaction; but this state is by no means to be identified with the happiness that constitutes the *summum bonum* of some of the older ethical systems, particularly those of the Stoics and the Epicureans, who Kant thinks were alike at fault in believing that happiness was bound to be the result of virtue. The Epicureans asserted that one should follow virtue in order to be happy, and the Stoics contended that virtue, their *summum bonum*, would

[12] *Ibid.*, p. 39.   [13] *Ibid.*, pp. 47–48.

bring happiness. Kant believes that happiness and virtue rarely coincide, and that when they do, it is purely accidental, since the two have no necessary relation to each other. Indeed, he insists repeatedly that true morality must be independent of the heteronomous drive to happiness.[14]

Kant distinguishes between the maxims which are subjective and specific prescriptions given to the will by the practical reason and certain imperatives of the practical reason which are universal, necessary, and objective in character. He states only two of these, the great categorical imperative [15] and another regarding the treatment of human personality, which he believes is identical with the first. The categorical imperative is a general prescription for all kinds of moral action, which differs both in kind and in importance from the specific maxims, and indeed is an inclusive principle which comprehends them all. This imperative is stated several times, with slight variations in wording, by Kant in the *Critique of Practical Reason* and in *Fundamental Principles of the Metaphysic of Morals*. The simplest statement of it reads, "So act that the maxim of thy will may at all times serve as a universal law." [16] A more elaborate statement is, "Act only on that maxim whereby thou canst at the same time will that it should become a universal law." The latter statement comes from *Fundamental Principles of the Metaphysics of Morals*, and a little later on in that same treatise he states that the categorical imperative may well read, "Act as if the maxim of thy action were to become by thy will a universal law of nature." [17]

The categorical imperative covers all kinds of moral action and comprehends within itself the specific maxims of the will. He cites the maxim, "Thou shalt not lie," as a case in point. We could never will that a lie should become a universal law; therefore we should never under any circumstance lie.[18] The same reasoning applies in the matter of suicide; again we could never will to have such a

[14] *Ibid.*, p. 143.
[15] This is the second sense in which Kant uses the phrase "categorical imperative."
[16] Kant, *Kritik der praktischen Vernunft*, p. 39, tr. by the writer.
[17] Abbott, *Kant's Theory of Ethics*, pp. 38–39.
[18] Kant, *Kritik der praktischen Vernunft*, p. 25, also *Kant's Theory of Ethics*, pp. 18, 38.

principle of action become a universal law.[19] The categorical imperative, then, may be seen from these illustrations to be an apodictic principle, objectively valid, formal, and binding, without regard to the effect of the action, but referring directly to the motive of the action, to the will behind it. Indeed Kant makes a point of the idea that moral action is necessary in itself, without reference to the effects of that action, and he looks upon the whole question of what constitutes the moral from the standpoint of the motive behind it, that is, that the action shall simply be dictated as necessary by the practical reason. The categorical imperative is a law of moral action, in the same sense that gravitation is a law of physics, for it is universal, necessary, and a priori valid. Although the categorical imperative is really a regulative principle, Kant certainly thought of it as an operative principle as well.[20]

Kant maintains that the authoritative position of the categorical imperative is unique; and though it is clear that he places a second imperative along the side of it, for the sake of consistency he asserts that the two imperatives are really identical. The second imperative is, "So act as to treat humanity, whether in thine own person or in that of any other, in every case as an end withal, never as a means only." [21] Man as a rational creature, with the endowments of reason and a legislative will, belongs, according to Kant, to a Kingdom of Ends, in which he is both sovereign and subject inasmuch as his moral decisions affect all other members of the kingdom and he, in turn, is affected by those of all his fellow members. Now, each human individual has the right to be considered as an end in himself, not merely as a means to this or that will. This insistence on the worth of each human being as an independent member of the Kingdom of Ends is a great merit of the philosophy of Kant, a sound human emphasis in the midst of his rationalism.

Kant then proceeds to argue—none too cogently, in the opinion of the writer—that this second imperative is really identical with the categorical imperative. He tries to prove their identity by showing that in a number of concrete cases, such as suicide, one would

---

[19] *Kant's Theory of Ethics*, pp. 47 ff.   [20] *Ibid.*, pp. 14–18.
[21] *Ibid.*, p. 47.

violate both imperatives; for one could not will that suicide should become a universal law, and also in it one is misusing his own person by treating it as a means rather than as an end.[22] Now it is to be granted that in this instance the course dictated by the two imperatives would undoubtedly be the same; but it does not follow that the two imperatives are identical, for the motivation which each dictates is quite a different one. Thus, what Kant really shows is not that the two imperatives are identical, but that they frequently come together and dictate the same course. It is quite conceivable, however, that in some situations the two might conflict, but that is a possibility that Kant, who believed that duties never could conflict, rejects on the face of it. Perhaps what Kant should have maintained was not that the two imperatives were identical, but rather that the second was a special case subsumed under the first, the maxim governing all moral situations involving questions of the relation of human personalities to each other.

These two major imperatives govern the formulation of the maxims which are more or less hypothetical and particular, since the latter refer to special classes of actions and have imperative force upon the will only when the particular situations they cover arise. The imperatives have categorical force; the maxims only hypothetical.[23]

The dominance of the categorical imperative of duty in the mind of Kant leads him to some surprising conclusions concerning what constitutes morality, the relation between desire or preference and the following of the imperatives in the path of moral action. He goes so far as to state that service done to our fellow men out of love for them is not strictly moral action, for its wellspring is inclination, rather than duty.[24]

Out of this last dictum that only action performed from a sense of duty can constitute morality comes a peculiar interpretation of the Gospel commandments to love God with all our heart, soul, strength, and mind and to love our neighbor as ourselves. The im-

[22] *Ibid.*, pp. 47 ff.   [23] *Ibid.*, p. 31.
[24] Kant, *Kritik der praktischen Vernunft*, p. 106, also "Fundamental Principles of the Metaphysic of Morals," in his *Theory of Ethics*, pp. 14 ff.

perative form of these commands Kant takes to be a plain indication
that only duty is the mode of their fulfillment. He argues that they
could not be based upon preference, which is no substitute for obedience to a command. Love of God he interprets to mean only that
we should reverence God and gladly obey His commands; for,
he explains, we cannot love God in the ordinary meaning of that
word, which implies an attachment or affection such as we can entertain only for objects of sense, and God is no object of sense. Duty
can be commanded, but not feeling; *ergo,* the Great Command
could not refer to anything but duty. This interpretation not only
rules out all mystical love for God, all obedience to Him on the
ground of devotion to Him, but also, following a similar line of
reasoning, Kant is able to rule out all preferences and inclination
from the command to love our neighbor as ourselves. He believes
we are commanded only to do our duty by our neighbor, to maintain an attitude of readiness to serve him in need, and to cherish
good will, not affection, toward him.[25]

The divine laws generally, like the Ten Commandments and the
Gospel precepts, are considered by Kant imperatives which one
must fulfill; but in addition he takes the position that every command of duty is a divine command. The argument by which he
supported this contention differs in the earlier works, such as the
second critique, from the position he took in the *Opus postumum.*
In the latter he affirms simply that the voice of duty is the voice
of God, Who speaks to us directly from within through the voice
of conscience.[26] The position by which he justified it in the earlier
writings is more elaborate. It runs thus: To obey the divine commands gladly demands of the finite human being a state of holiness
which is nothing short of perfection, and this perfection he does
not in fact possess.[27] This assertion leads him to make certain postulates of the practical reason which are not only a part of his ethical
construction, but also contain his answer (for the most of his life)
to the problem of the relation between religion and ethics.

---

[25] *Kant's Theory of Ethics*, pp. 106–8.
[26] Kant, *Opus postumum*, pp. 822–26.
[27] Kant, *Kritik der praktischen Vernunft*, pp. 106–8.

Since the moral law makes absolute and unequivocal demands upon us, we must have the ability to fulfill its "Thou shalt." This necessity of the moral law entails the a priori assumption of freedom as the first postulate of the practical reason, because if we are commanded to fulfill demands, we must have the ability to do so. The second postulate of the practical reason is immortality, for it is not possible for the will of a finite creature to become perfectly conformed to the Divine will except within an infinitely long time. Otherwise men cannot perfectly fulfill the demands of the moral law; for the holiness required to keep the Divine commands gladly involves the assumption of immortality, which thus becomes the second postulate of the practical reason.

Now we have the right to postulate that freedom to keep the moral law exists in the intelligible world alone, not in the world of nature, where we are subject to the same kind of determinism which Kant believed runs through all nature. Freedom is the principle of causality in moral action, however, inasmuch as it operates in the intelligible world and is a priori possible in that realm. Now, through the moral law we belong to that intelligible realm, and the fact of freedom for moral action exalts us above the whole natural world. The pure or theoretical reason can know only our impressions of the phenomenal world, never the things in themselves, and in the intelligible world it cannot even establish the existence of the noumena, nor can it bring together the two worlds. It is in bridging the gap between the noumenal and phenomenal world that Kant comes to the third postulate of the practical reason, the existence of God.

Kant does not use the term "Kingdom of God" in any orthodox Christian sense. Though he gives it a religious frame of reference, this by no means includes what Jesus intended the phrase to cover, nor has it any of the usual interpretations given it in Jewish-Christian theology. Kant uses the expression "Kingdom of God" simply to denote the object of any will that is directed by the moral law, for the Kingdom of God is the object of the moral law itself.[28] That end is holiness, the order of the intelligible realm, the Kingdom of God, where all His commands are obeyed. Men are creatures of both

[28] Kant, *Kritik der praktischen Vernunft*, p. 147.

réalms; but since they are finite, therefore participants of the world of nature, it requires an infinitely long time to conform their wills to holiness; hence the assumption of the second postulate of the practical reason, immortality. Through progressive conformity of our wills to the moral law over an infinitely long period, we come eventually to the state in which we are worthy of happiness, because we make the realization of the *summum bonum* instead of any thought of reward or punishment our aim. But now the order of nature in which our human lives are passed promises no such necessary connection between virtue and happiness as is to be found in the Kingdom of God. Since through freedom we can act as moral beings even in this world, we have the right to assume that God is the Cause of the world of phenomena as well as that of noumena. Thus the third postulate assumes that God is the Creator of both worlds, Who has created them in order to bring them together in the Kingdom of God, an ultimate state of holiness in which the phenomenal and the noumenal worlds achieve a harmony and happiness foreign to them both. The finite creature can partake of this holiness only after that infinite progress toward holiness has prepared it to find that combination of happiness and virtue in the Kingdom of God.[29]

According to Kant's view, the conception of the Kingdom of God as *summum bonum* of an ethical system remedies one of the chief defects of the ethical constructions of antiquity. The Epicureans were wrong, according to him, in supposing that the quest of happiness would ever lead to virtue, and the Stoics were equally wrong in asserting that the pursuit of virtue would be bound to end in happiness for the finite creature. In Christianity alone the combination of the two is possible through the introduction of the religious ideas of God and immortality to provide the culmination and *summum bonum* of its ethic in the Kingdom of God. In other words, the Greek moralists failed because they never went on from the existence of the human spirit to the existence of God.[30] The latter, as Cause of both nature and of the intelligible world of freedom, is able to effect this very harmony of the two which is seen as the goal of creation, the coming of the Kingdom of God.

[29] *Ibid.*, pp. 141, 161.   [30] *Ibid.*, pp. 162–65.

In the assumption of the three postulates of the practical reason we have Kant's answer to the problem of the relation between religion and morality, at least the one he gave for a long period of his philosophic career. This construction is his famous moral argument for the existence of God, which he offers as a substitute for the three traditional proofs which he was convinced that he had demolished in the first critique. That he himself was never quite satisfied with the moral argument is clear from his attempts to modify it in the *Opus postumum*. Several observations must be made upon the success of the moral argument in the form in which it appears in the second critique.

The assumption of the three postulates God, freedom, and immortality is made solely because Kant considers them to be necessary to the fulfillment of the moral law, which is an a priori form of the practical reason. The postulates are, he explicitly states, by no means to be considered as theoretical proofs of these, all three of which are paralogisms of the pure reason and are valid only for the practical reason, since they are noumenal realities not accessible to the forms of time and space. Even their existence is established, or rather assumed, by the practical reason only and is not susceptible of proof through the theoretical reason. The practical reason itself furnishes no further or more precise knowledge of their nature, since it has no categories by which to interpret them. Thus the practical reason does not really extend our knowledge of the noumenal realities much beyond that of the pure reason.[31] That is to say, in the realm of practical reason the existence of these noumena is given as a bare assertory judgment, not as a perception which makes further predication possible. Kant believes that this absence of further knowledge of the realities of the intelligible world is all for the best. It is well that we should know no more of God than the bare inference of His perfection from the fact of His creation of the world, because to know more of His attributes would lead only to the emotional excesses of mysticism and religious *Schwärmerei*.[32]

However, it might not be unfair to ask whether we really have any more knowledge about these noumena from the practical reason than

[31] *Ibid.*, pp. 169–71.   [32] *Ibid.*, pp. 181–88.

from the pure. In the light of modern psychological advances we have no right to divide the mind into these two realms of the pure and the practical reason, in which case the whole argument built up on that distinction falls to the ground. What we really have is only a practical hypothesis that God, freedom, and immortality exist, not any real proof that they do, for the mere introduction of the phrase "a priori" by no means takes the place of genuine proof of their existence.

As to the relation of religion and morality that Kant sets forth in this argument, it is obvious that in his construction religion is not an independent end, but subordinate to morality, for which it serves as the supernatural sanction by guaranteeing the perpetuity of the individual through the infinite period needed for his will to conform to the demands of the moral law. God serves the purpose of bridging the gap between the two realms of noumena and phenomena and preparing both for the state of holiness and harmony which constitutes Kant's *summum bonum,* the Kingdom of God. Indeed, the subsidiary role of religion is so decided that Kant goes so far as to state that if obedience to the will of God were the motivating consideration in moral action, that would be a heteronomous principle, and, as actuated by such, the action would, of course, not be strictly moral.[33] This Kantian construction of the relation between religion and morality, with its subordination of religion, has been frequently and justly criticized by many theologians. It is at once a failure on the part of Kant to understand the autonomy of religion as an independent concern of man and at the same time involves his peculiar misconception of the Christian Kingdom of God. It is a singular shift from the emphasis of Jesus, who taught that our status in the eyes of our fellow men establishes our status in the eyes of God, and is understandable only against the background of eighteenth-century deism, out of which Kant comes, and the personal prejudice he held against all the feeling side of religion as smacking of pietism and mystical excesses.

Now that some account of the actual construction of Kant's ethic has been given, it is clear how strikingly it diverges from any of the

[33] *Ibid.,* p. 165.

ethical systems which preceded it; and in forming any estimate
of his permanent contributions to the field the first comment to make
is to call attention to the sheer brilliance of a system so novel, so
original in its entire construction. The construction is largely a formal
one, but in erecting his framework he has given us some lasting and
valuable suggestions as to method and content as well.

In forming any estimate of his system one of the first questions to
arise is that of the value of the a priori of the practical reason upon
which so much of his ethic rests. The interest which he intended the
a priori of duty to serve was to assure that morality should be a universally valid absolute, transcending all dependence upon such a
fluctuating and variable element as experience. Experience, he thinks,
can never yield absolutes and universals, but at best mere generalizations which would form no sure basis on which to rest an absolute like
the moral law. Instead of basing his system on any empirical factors,
he thus resorts to regarding duty as an a priori form in the mind,
possessed by all rational creatures, even the simplest of men.[34]

Kant's great emphasis on duty, on the formal and a priori nature of
its "Thou shalt," is new to ethics, for the ethicians before him, while
laying down plenty of precepts of all sorts, really had surprisingly
little to say about duty itself. It is strange that so important a foundation stone in any ethical structure could have been almost overlooked
until Kant pointed it out as central to all morality. However, while
admitting the merit of his pointing out that duty is a cardinal principle of morality, we must qualify our admiration somewhat by add-
ing that Kant certainly overemphasized duty by regarding it as the
sole key and index of all moral action and that the a priori construction he gave to it is not an analysis which was to bear scrutiny for
long after his day. The work of the nineteenth century was to show
that from an anthropological and historical standpoint the conception
of duty turned out to be empirical and a posteriori in demonstrable
ways of which no one in Kant's day could have dreamed. Even Kant
himself had moments when he was not altogether consistent about
the a priori character of duty. While asserting repeatedly that it is
wholly a priori and cannot be learned from experience, he nonethe-

[34] *Ibid.*, pp. 193–95.

less advocates the study of biography in order to see the operation of the moral law, which would appear to contradict its absolutely a priori character.[35] However, he insists many times that moral law would not be valid at all if it were not universal, as, for example, in the following quotation:

These [moral laws] are valid only so far as they have *a priori* basis and can be seen to be necessary; nay, the concepts and judgments about ourselves and our actions and omissions have no moral significance at all, if they contain only what can be learned from experience; and should one be so misled as to make into a moral principle anything derived from this source, he would be in danger of the grossest and most pernicious errors.[36]

The refutation of the a priori nature of moral ideas in general and duty among them is to be found in the nineteenth-century advances in anthropology, history, and sociology, by which it was discovered that the development of these ideas, duty among them, is very largely due to the influence of quite empirical factors in the life of the group and of the individual. Conscience and the sense of duty are not only empirically directed toward certain objects to which they attach, but even their imperative character is in no small measure the product of group opinion, herd instinct, parental discipline, and numerous other social and environmental factors.

Indeed, the Kantian a priori of the practical reason is only a slight advance over the older belief in innate ideas of God, freedom, and immortality, all of which were supposed to be implanted in all men by the Creator. The only way in which the a priori of the practical reason does improve upon innate ideas or Spinoza's "intuitions" is that Kant wisely construed it as a pure form which could function actively only when provided with content from experience. That Kant feared experience as relative and unsure and trusted reason so much is to be accounted for by his own rather circumscribed life on the one hand and the *Zeitgeist* of his century, the Age of Reason, on the other. Much of Kant's ethical construction shows how remarkably his great mind transcended the limitations of his age, but

---

[35] *Ibid.*, pp. 193–95.
[36] Kant, *Theory of Ethics*, "Introduction to the Metaphysic of Morals," p. 270.

insistence upon the a priori character of his categorical imperative and the oversimplification of morality which made him single out duty as the sole moral law dates back to his own innocence and lack of acquaintance with the great temptations and complex motivations of those in the thick of life's battle.

A further criticism of Kant's emphasis upon duty as the sole spring of moral action is his denial that any conduct not motivated completely by duty deserves the name "moral." He will not allow that any admixture of inclination can enter into moral action. This is, in the first place, an oversimplification of the problem of motive. He does admit occasionally that it is hard to find such simon pure obedience to the moral law from sheer duty as he demands, and that it is hard to discern our own motives sufficiently well to make sure that they are free from all taint of preference; but he concludes that this is possible, though difficult, and cites several instances of motives which pass current as moral, but are not really so, because they are a mixture of duty and inclination.[37] He believes that it is no mark of moral conduct to serve people because we love them and enjoy doing kind things for them; this is moral only when for the sake of obeying the commandment to love our neighbor we promote their welfare because *it is our duty to do so.* In like manner, it is a duty to preserve our own lives—a proposition in which Kant agrees partially with Spinoza—but we cannot be said to act morally in so doing unless we are preserving ourselves in existence at a time when we would rather not live.[38] In fact Kant's idea is that no action is really moral unless it runs counter to all our inclinations. It was this item of his philosophy that Schiller satirized in his couplet:

> Gerne dien' ich den Freunden
> > doch tu' ich es leider mit Neigung
> Und so wurmt es mir oft
> > dass ich nicht recht tugendhaft bin.

It is interesting to contrast this dislike of Kant's for all kinds of hedonism and pleasurable feeling in morality with the theory of

[37] *Ibid.*, p. 23.
[38] *Ibid.*, pp. 280 ff., and Kant, *Kritik der praktischen Vernunft*, pp. 104–6.

Jesus that an action done otherwise than as an expression of a man's true nature and disposition is submoral.

It is scarcely possible to exaggerate the lengths to which Kant goes in insisting that morality is purely a process of reason and duty, not one of feeling or desire. Reverence for the moral law is rooted entirely in esteem for duty. It is not enthusiasm for virtue, but a sober willingness to obey the commands of duty without regard to one's own happiness or desires, manifested in the highest form in suffering. Such is the stern and serious view of Kant, who, denied the poetic gift to celebrate duty in an ode such as Wordsworth's, nevertheless waxes almost lyrical in praise of her as law when he writes in the famous conclusion to the second critique:

Two things fill the mind with ever new and increasing admiration and awe, the oftener and more steadily we reflect on them: *the starry heavens above and the moral law within*. I have not to search for them and conjecture them as though they were veiled in darkness or were in the transcendent region beyond my horizon; I see them before me and connect them directly with the consciousness of my existence. The former begins from the place I occupy in the external world of sense, and enlarges my connexion therein to an unbounded extent with worlds upon worlds, and systems of systems, and, moreover, into the limitless times of their periodic motion, its beginning and continuance. The second begins from my invisible self, my personality, and exhibits me in a world which has true infinity, but which is traceable only by the understanding, and with which I discern that I am not merely in a contingent but in a universal and necessary connexion, as I am also thereby with all those visible worlds. The former view of a countless multitude of worlds annihilates, as it were, my importance as an *animal creature*, which after it has been for a short time provided with vital power, one knows not how, must again give back the matter of which it was formed to the planet it inhabits (a mere speck in the universe). The second, on the contrary, infinitely elevates my worth as an *intelligence* by my personality, in which the moral law reveals to me a life dependent on animality and even on the whole sensible world—at least so far as may be inferred from the destination assigned to my existence by this law, a destination not restricted to conditions and limits of this life, but reaching into the infinite.[39]

[39] Abbott, *Kant's Theory of Ethics*, p. 260.

That Kant made duty the center of the moral life, that he looks upon the imperative of its "Thou shalt" as *the* moral law, accords with the soberly rational and scientific exactitude which impelled him as a lifelong student of science and mathematics to view life in terms of universal and necessary laws. That he excluded the feeling side almost completely is natural to this highly rational temper, especially to one whose experience was confined to the academic life of the small university town of Königsberg. The emphasis on duty, extreme as it was, was a service in that it called attention for the first time to the importance of duty in the ethical life.

Less felicitous, however, was his contention that the moral life is solely an affair of reason and obedience to the law of duty, to the exclusion of all affective elements. As someone once said, "Though we need the reason to steer the ship, we need the emotions to propel it." That the feeling side could be anything but a hindrance seems not to have occurred to this child of the Age of Reason. In this respect Kant's construction is inferior to that of Spinoza, whose outstanding merit was the analysis of the part played in "human bondage" by the affects. It is unfortunate that Kant scorned this valuable legacy from Spinoza. The only feelings whose values Kant is willing to admit are that high reverence which the moral law inspires and the tempered self-esteem that obedience to the moral law invokes in those who have heeded its commands.

However, one modicum of truth underlies this extreme position of Kant's that duty alone, not inclination, makes for the strenuous moral life. A large part of moral effort does run counter to feeling and is necessarily undertaken only through imperatives, not preferences. Kant put the point negatively, instead of positively, when he declared that morality cannot rest upon preference or desire, because it is a matter of obedience to law. Now, no law is needed to command what we like to do, nor can a command control or produce in us a desire in accord with itself. However, it does not necessarily follow from this fact, as Kant infers, that an action cannot be moral because some elements of preference enter into it. The good is not always the unpleasant surgical operation to which Kant liked to compare it.[40]

[40] Kant, *Kritik der praktischen Vernunft*, p. 79.

In spite of the limits of puritanism and rationalism which Kant set upon some parts of his work, he is one of our greatest ethical teachers, not only because of the novelty of his approach, but also because he made some perpetually significant methodological suggestions for the pursuit of ethics and some formulations of moral laws that are of universal significance. To speak first of the methodological suggestions: Two contributions of Kant's on the side of method are of prime importance: his suggestions for materials in which to study the operation of the moral law and his designation of freedom as the principle of causality of the moral life. Kant's treatment of freedom as the causal principle of the moral life has a permanent value far beyond and above the categories of the eighteenth century in which he discussed the question and apart from the Newtonian *Weltanschauung* within which he found a place for its operation. It is, of course, possible to construct an ethic on the basis of either freedom or determinism, and the great ethical systems in fact afford examples of both; but ethics can be autonomous only in the systems which recognize the reality of freedom.

Valuable in Kant's construction is his recognition that the very presence of the moral demand upon man implies that he has the strength and the ability to fulfill it, and that this sense of freedom is not an illusion. Perhaps Kant went too far in oversimplifying moral problems, he may have been wrong in believing that duties never could conflict; but there was a soundness of insight in his pointing out freedom as the principle of causality in the moral life which none of these shortcomings could mar. Indeed, conceived though it was in the terms of rationalism, there is a certain democratic quality in his belief that all men are free and that all can fulfill the demands of the categorical imperative, which was a great service to the future.

It has been noticed earlier in this chapter that Kant was convinced that the moral life was wholly rooted in the a priori of the practical reason and that it was his belief that ethics was an a priori instead of an empirical science. In spite of this firm conviction, it is likely that his own study of it was far more empirical than he knew, for he recommends in the second critique [41] the study of biography

[41] *Ibid.*, pp. 193–203.

as an important source for moral analysis. Quite properly, too, he believed that the study of moral law from such sources is the right and duty of every person. He thinks that even very simple people, such as women (*sic!*) and children, are not only interested in the moral life but also have pure and excellent moral perception. Biography can serve these and all other students of the moral life as valuable material in which they may learn by comparison of similar actions in various circumstances to waken in young people admiration for the moral law and a wish to imitate the virtuous man. He concludes this recommendation with the opinion that virtue is so easy to discern that a ten-year-old child is perfectly capable of understanding it, and adds that it is only the philosophers who have succeeded in making the whole subject difficult.[42] Kant's advice about biography as a source for moral study was not followed through by subsequent ethicians, but it has possibilities worthy of modern consideration.

However, in the last analysis the claim of Kant to a place among the greatest of the Western ethical teachers rests upon his discovery and formulation of the two great imperatives: the categorical imperative so to act that the maxim of the will may at all times serve as a universal law; and the second, to treat humanity as an end withal, never as a means. These two regulative principles cover a very wide range of moral actions and are among the few generalizations in the realm of ethics which have the right to be pointed to as laws. If Kant had done nothing else in the field but to formulate these two laws, it would be enough to rank him among the very greatest ethicians of all time. These are the two most important moral laws discovered since the time of Jesus; and indeed the little philosopher of Königsberg, their discoverer, thereby became to modern ethics what his master, Newton, was to modern science.

[42] *Ibid.*, p. 196.

Chapter X

THE IMPACT OF THE NINETEENTH AND TWENTIETH CENTURIES ON ETHICS

With the death of Kant the era of the great classical systems in ethics came to a close, for since then there has not arisen any other ethical teacher who approaches his stature or that of the long line of his predecessors in the field. Although the nineteenth century was to see many changes in ethics, these came as a result of influences that reacted upon it from without, and while many competent ethicians occupied themselves with its problems, none of them proved to be a creative thinker of the foremost rank. The same observation applies to as much of the twentieth century as has already elapsed. Thus, for the first time the center of the quest for moral law shifts from the consciousness of the individual thinker to the currents of his time; for the systems that arise within these two centuries are distinctly the creations of the *Zeitgeist* rather than the originative productions of single minds, as the older systems had almost invariably been.

Because the advances in the sciences and many other branches of knowledge were so enormous during the period, it will be impossible to consider any but the main currents and these only in the briefest fashion. Also, inasmuch as there were many ethical thinkers during this time, it will be possible to notice only those whose contributions to content or method were important for the subsequent development of ethics into a science, and the selection has been determined accordingly.

The Nineteenth Century

Before turning to the various schools of ethics in the nineteenth century, certain influences that shaped their thinking must be noticed briefly. The first of these to come to full fruition in the new century was that of economics, or political economy, as it was then called. Even before the end of the eighteenth century this influence on ethics began to manifest itself. Adam Smith, the originator of economics, was sufficiently interested in ethical problems to write a treatise on morals entitled the *Theory of Moral Sentiments,* and among the utilitarians Jeremy Bentham (1748–1832) is notable as a writer who combined both interests, as did also the elder Mill.

The forging of a truly scientific historical method is generally credited to the German historian, Leopold von Ranke, who first exemplified it in his brief work, *Geschichten der romanischen und germanischen Völker,* Leipzig, 1824, in which he announced his intention of presenting history "wie es eigentlich gewesen ist" (as it actually was). [1] The scientific and accurate composition of history was of significance for ethics in several different ways. First of all, it cleared up the facts about the historical development of morals and made such mythological conceptions as the Golden Age, toward which some of the ethical teachers had wistfully looked back, forever impossible. The new method also prepared the way for a number of important historical researches on the history of morality, such as Lecky's monumental *History of European Morals.* Finally, as the methods of historical criticism were turned upon the Biblical books they clarified the manner in which these sacred writings were composed so that the older theories about the origin of moral law in the Old Testament became untenable.

Another social science which came into being early in the nineteenth century is sociology. The French philosopher Auguste Comte (1798–1857) originated and named this new science, upon which he wrote extensively in the social section of his philosophy of Positivism. Although Comte was greatly interested in ethics and one of the first to insist that it ought to be a science in its own right, it cannot be said that his thought on that subject was of lasting importance, since he attacked the problem principally from the angle of its sanctions rather than the formulation of its independent principles. Spencer is the first thinker to make a fruitful combination between ethics and sociology.

While the nineteenth century saw much progress in both the natural and the physical sciences, perhaps the outstanding scientific event

[1] Quoted by Johnson, *The Teaching of History,* p. 12.

of the century was the publication of Darwin's *Origin of Species* in 1859. After that date ethics, as well as other branches of knowledge, set about to reorient itself in the light of the new facts and problems with which the theory of evolution confronted it. Ethicians of the second half of the century are not only influenced but really governed by it in their thinking. Combining this biological interest with his knowledge of sociology and psychology, Herbert Spencer exemplifies this trend in ethics *par excellence*.

ETHICAL SCHOOLS

THE ECONOMIC UTILITARIANS

The school of ethicians known as "utilitarians" share in common the general theory that the good is the pleasant, the useful to man, the evil the unpleasant and useless, the harmful to him. They differ upon many other points; but this thesis they all hold in some form or other, and the additional one, that the *summum bonum* of ethics is the happiness of man, though they differ among themselves as to whether the noun "man" should be used in the individual or the generic sense. The group spans a period of more than two centuries, for though utilitarians of one type or other dominate the whole nineteenth century, they go back through the eighteenth into the seventeenth century. In the course of that period they included within their ranks Locke, Hutcheson, Hume, Paley, and Butler— all of whom are more or less important exponents of this type of ethic. As far as Locke is concerned, however, his main philosophic contributions were epistemological, and with him ethics was but a side line. Hutcheson, Butler, and Paley are not first-rate ethicians; therefore they will not be considered at all. Hume wrote one ethical treatise, his *Enquiry concerning the Principles of Morals*, which is an able exposition of and argument for the main tenet of utilitarianism, namely, that the good is the pleasant and useful, the bad the opposite. But, as in the case of Locke, ethics was really only a secondary interest with Hume, and the *Enquiry* really adds nothing of paramount worth to the sum of our ethical knowledge.

The early nineteenth century utilitarians, the economic utilitarians as one may call them, to distinguish them from the later group, include Bentham, James Mill, and his son John Stuart Mill. On the whole, this group holds to the egoistic interpretation of the characteristically utilitarian hedonism, namely, that the happiness of the individual is the highest good, though John Stuart Mill is not consistent about this, but frequently inclines to an altruistic or universalistic interpretation of the *summum bonum*. He represents the transition between the economic utilitarians and the later altruistic group who believe that the *summum bonum* consists in the greatest good of the greatest number.

For the method of this earlier wing, it is not too much to say that the new science of economics set the model for their construction of morality. They hold in common with the economists of their day the individualism expressed in the laissez-faire theory. They believed firmly that ethically speaking, as well as economically, the interest of each individual, if but left free to take its natural course, would automatically adjust itself to that of other individuals and of the group as a whole. Although this idea was not so much the center of contemporary attacks on utilitarianism as the theory that the good is the useful, today the former seems the most patently false of their tenets. Nevertheless, it took less time to discover its falsity here than in the sphere of economics in which it originated, so that by the end of the century the utilitarians had already discarded the notion in favor of a more altruistic hedonism. From some standpoints, however, the analogy between ethics and economics was sound, for the regulative principles of both are derived in a similar manner, and the tests of validity for each set are comparable. The most helpful insight of this group was that ethics, like economics, is an empirical science.

Neither the individual contributions of Bentham or of John Stuart Mill are considerable enough to call for extensive discussion. Bentham's are more negative than positive, for he is at his best in holding up to ridicule the dour systems of the ethical ascetics, rather than in originating new and significant principles of his own. He refutes very convincingly the implied premise of all these ascetic schools, which, he asserts, is really that only the unpleasant can be the good.[2] A second criticism of his concerns all types of intuitional ethics: namely, that their judgments of good and evil rest upon no more secure basis than what he names the theory of sympathy and antipathy. This means that a thing is good or bad only because one feels it to be so, without any objective and extrinsic grounds for moral approval or disapproval.[3]

Against the sympathy-antipathy theory Bentham argues with considerable acuteness that effects rather than motives are the sole index of whether or not an action is moral. He believes that using motive as the sole index is a mistake incidental to all intuitional (sympathy-antipathy) theories; and that utilitarianism should avoid this error.[4] Since the Kantian morality had so resolutely ignored effects in its emphasis on the importance of fulfilling the demands of the categorical imperative by actions necessary in themselves without regard to consequences, Bentham provided a restoration of balance by his insistence upon the importance of consequences. It may, of course, be contended with some justice that he and the rest of the utilitarians went to the opposite extreme in overemphasizing consequences to the exclusion of motives. However, it has long been one of the vexing problems of ethics to determine the proper weighting of motives and consequences in reference to each other in moral action —but at least effects are more tangible and enduring.

Somewhat different from Bentham's approach to utilitarianism is that of John Stuart Mill. He, like the others, holds that essentially the good and the pleasant, the evil and the unpleasant, are synonymous; but he maintains that this identity is at the same time the widest social, as well as individual, basis for morality. To him, to deny the possibility of happiness is to deny that life itself is a good, and in consequence he affirms that the greatest right of both the individual and the group is the pursuit of happiness.[5] Even those schools which disclaim with the greatest vehemence that their systems in any respect work upon a basis of happiness instead of duty (for example, Kant's) merely affirm, according to Mill, the happiness principle by disguising it under the name "bliss" or some

---

[2] Bentham, *Principles of Morals and Legislation*, pp. 8–10.   [3] *Ibid.*, pp. 15 ff.
[4] *Ibid.*, pp. 23 ff.   [5] Mill, *Dissertations and Discussions*, III, 308 ff.

similar euphemism. He goes so far as to declare: "In the Golden Rule of Jesus of Nazareth, we read the complete spirit of the ethics of utility." [6]

The *summum bonum* of utilitarianism, Mill believes, is the greatest good of the greatest number, a simple matter of the multiplication of the happiness of the individuals, which he calculates in the following manner:

No reason can be given why the general happiness is desirable, except that each person, so far as he believes it to be attainable, desires his own happiness. This, however, being a fact, we have not only all the proof which the case admits of, but all which it is possible to require, that happiness is a good; that each person's happiness is a good to that person; and the general happiness, therefore, a good to the aggregate of all persons. [7]

By stating the *summum bonum* of his own form of utilitarianism in these social terms Mill escaped one of the main charges frequently leveled against the school, namely, that its morality was merely prudential, a matter of self-interest and egoism; but, in so doing, he lays himself open to another objection, that the happiness of the group is not easier, but far more difficult to define concretely than the happiness of the individual. Besides, the classic criticism of this statement of Mill's is that in his computation of the happiness of the whole group by simple multiplication of the happiness of the individuals comprising it, he commits a notorious fallacy of composition.

Mill successfully demonstrates that the *summum bonum* of even those systems of ethics which exalt the pursuit of virtue or duty as their *summa* and despise the quest of happiness as a low motivation to the good life ultimately revert to some form of the realization of the desire for happiness in the conception of the *summum bonum*. Kant's own ethic of duty required for its completion the bliss of an eternity which the finite creature would enjoy after the expiration of the infinitely long time required to bring his will into perfect conformity with the moral law. The ascetic systems which renounce earthly happiness, Mill declares, one and all do so in the hope of

---

[6] *Ibid.*, p. 323.   [7] *Ibid.*, p. 349.

gaining some form of happiness in the life to come, for it is mere quibbling to maintain that the bliss of which they talk is anything but a form of happiness.

However, it is one thing to agree that in the last analysis all ethical systems revert to the realization of some form of happiness as their highest good and quite another to admit the utilitarian contention that all acts of the moral life are dictated by the desire to gain some form of happiness, some pleasure, or to avoid some evil. Bentham especially, but the other members of the school, including Mill, also, champion this theory, and on this point their intuitionalist opponents justly pounced. Perhaps none of the latter ever put the case against the former more trenchantly than did William Lecky in the introductory chapter to his *History of European Morals:*

In all nations and in all ages, the ideas of interest and utility on the one hand and of virtue on the other, have been regarded by the multitude as perfectly distinct, and all languages recognise the distinction. The terms honour, justice, rectitude or virtue, and their equivalents in every language, present to the mind ideas essentially and broadly differing from the terms prudence, sagacity or interest. The two lines of conduct may coincide, but they are never confused, and we have not the slightest difficulty in imagining them antagonistic. . . . In the exact proportion as we believe a desire for personal enjoyment to be the motive of a good act is the merit of the agent diminished. If we believe the motive to be wholly selfish the merit is altogether destroyed. If we believe it to be wholly disinterested the merit is altogether unalloyed.[8]

The latter group of utilitarians shifted from egoism to altruism with the happiness of the group instead of the individual as their *summum bonum,* but the problem of adjusting the interest of the individual to that of the group remained with them, as it did with Mill. As for the thesis that the good and the pleasant are identical, this also carried over to the later exponents of the theory, but they defended it differently. Since the trends of later utilitarianism combine with other currents of the nineteenth century, perhaps the discussion of the earlier group may best be brought to a conclusion with

[8] Lecky, *History of European Morals,* Vol. I, pp. 34–35.

an estimate of the simon pure tenets of utilitarianism, which are better exemplified in the earlier than in the later representatives of the school.

The service utilitarianism rendered by insisting upon the empirical character of ethics has already been noticed and likewise the fact that however faulty Mill's formulation of the altruistic *summum bonum* of their ethic, its social character represented a considerable advance over the earlier prudentialism of the school. It remains to evaluate the most characteristic tenet of the school, the theory that the good equals the pleasant, the useful; the evil, the unpleasant, the hurtful. Seen in the perspective of nearly a century that has elapsed since then, the debates that raged about the idea seem something of a tempest in a teapot. However, viewed against the contemporary background of the Kantian insistence that action could not really be virtuous if pleasurable, the emphasis of the economic utilitarians appears as a useful and wholesome counterpoise. In an absolute sense, however, neither side saw the matter in its full breadth, for the good is something deeper and more fundamental than a feeling tone, such as either the pleasant or the unpleasant. There are times when the good and the pleasant do coincide, as the utilitarians contended; and there are also times when the good is the unpleasant, when in fact it may actually be the surgical operation to which Kant liked to compare it. There are also numerous instances which both sides overlooked, when the good is neutral and consists in routine performance of duty and fulfillment of obligations that are useful and necessary, but without strong emotional coloration either of pleasure or of pain.

LATER UTILITARIANS: INTUITIONALISTS AND EVOLUTIONISTS

Henry Sidgwick, Intuitional Utilitarian.—Contemporary with the later group of utilitarians and agreeing with them sufficiently to count himself one of them is Henry Sidgwick (1838–1900), sometime professor of philosophy at Cambridge University. While sharing the universalistic hedonism of the later members of the school, he also presents some affinities with their opponents the intuitionalists, inasmuch as he was influenced by the a priori rationalism of

Kant's method. In short, Sidgwick's position among the utilitarians is unique, because he alone among them attempted a compromise with intuitionalism. With the altruistic wing of the utilitarians he affirmed the belief that the happiness of the group is the proper *summum bonum* for ethics and that self-interest is not an unworthy motivation in moral conduct. In the last book of his most important work, *The Methods of Ethics*, he declares also his general allegiance to their empirical method,[9] yet at a number of points he employs the a priori rationalism, or "intuitionalism," as he prefers to call it, which he had learned at the feet of Kant. On this account he was at times rather sharply criticized by his fellow utilitarians.

More modest in his claims than his contemporary Herbert Spencer, Sidgwick does not seek to make ethics into a science, but merely calls it a "study." [10] The term is accurate, for he does not pretend to use the exact method of a science, but only the critical analysis and reflection of a philosopher, though often this is indeed supported by no inconsiderable observation of the facts of the moral life. As the title of his book indicates, he confines the work to the investigation of methods in ethics and surveys those of the intuition-alists, as well as of the two branches of utilitarianism, which he calls egoistic and universalistic hedonism. He states that his aim is merely to develop a consistent method in ethics, not to attempt a historical, comparative, or originative study of the subject.[11] Thus, although the book does not make a contribution to ethical method beyond this aim, he not only has a fresh attack upon the problem in his comparison of the morality of common sense with that of the three schools of formal ethics; but also presents some new insights into the content of the subject and gives some classic discussions of certain long-standing controversies between the opposing schools of thought.

First he surveys the general methods of the two types of hedonism and that of intuitionalism, then assembles and investigates the moral-ity of common sense, which he compares point by point with that of universalistic hedonism. He gives an excellent and judicious presentation of common-sense morality on both formal and informal

[9] *The Methods of Ethics*, 6th ed., p. 477.   [10] *Ibid.*, p. 1.   [11] *Ibid.*, p. 12.

obligations and upon the duties arising from various human relationships such as parenthood, filial respect, the rights of spouse and
friends—indeed, all the main items of the code of the average man.
This code of common sense he finds to be lacking in precision at
many points, and his judgment is that in spite of its familiarity, it
fails to strike the reflective investigator with the force of self-
evidence. Upon analysis, many of these axioms of common sense
prove to be tautological (for example, "It is right to act rationally";
and "It is right to consider that the lower parts of our nature should
be governed by the higher"); hence, they are quite meaningless.[12]
Others of these supposed axioms are inconsistent with each other
when the scattered items of the code are assembled, and a number
of them require justification by rational argument before the
thoughtful investigator is willing to accept them as moral imperatives.[13]

In order to arrive at genuine axioms of morality, furnished by
the practical reason and capable of meeting the test of reflection,
the rules must, according to Sidgwick, meet four conditions:

I. The terms of the proposition must be clear and precise.

II. The self-evidence of the proposition must be ascertained by careful reflection.

III. The propositions accepted as self-evident must be mutually
consistent.

IV. Since it is implied in the very notion of Truth that it is essentially
the same for all minds, the denial by another of a proposition that I have
affirmed has a tendency to impair my confidence in its validity.[14]

Having set up these four canons of self-evidence, he formulates
a set of rules which, he believes, conform to them and therefore
have the right to be called "moral axioms." He considers that the
Golden Rule is lacking in precision of statement in the New Testament formulation, for which he substitutes a negative paraphrase
which he thinks obviates the difficulty:

It cannot be right for *A* to treat *B* in a manner in which it would be wrong
for *B* to treat *A*, merely on the ground that they are two different in-

[12] *Ibid.*, p. 374.   [13] *Ibid.*, p. 379.   [14] *Ibid.*, pp. 338–41.

dividuals, and without there being any difference between the nature or circumstances of the two which can be stated as a reasonable ground for difference of treatment.[15]

This statement of the Golden Rule is somewhat cumbersome, but it meets the qualifications which Sidgwick considered requisite for attaining the status of a moral axiom. As a kind of special case under this rule, he adds the law of justice, which states that moral as well as civil laws must apply to all alike under the same circumstances.[16] His second law he calls the "Maxim of Benevolence": "Each one is morally bound to regard the good of any other individual as much as his own, except in so far as he judges it to be less, when impartially viewed, or less certainly knowable or attainable by him." [17] Two other maxims he classes as full moral axioms: "I ought not to prefer a present lesser good to a future greater good," and "I ought not to prefer my own lesser good to the greater good of another." [18]

These four rules are the only ones that Sidgwick is willing to admit to the status of full moral axioms conforming to all four of his canons of self-evidence. Even these four did not commend themselves as indubitable moral axioms to other ethicians, so that they failed to meet the requirement of that modified *consensus gentium* stipulated by his fourth canon. Objections on the grounds of the four canons of self-evidence may be raised to the individual maxims. Over and above the infelicitous form in which he states the Golden Rule, a further difficulty with Sidgwick's statement is that his paraphrase does not necessarily commend itself to everyone as a complete and self-evident principle of moral action any more than the New Testament form, which has the advantage of being more concise, if not more precise. His law about preferring a future greater good to a present lesser good is by no means a self-evident moral axiom. At first sight it strikes the observer as being merely a general prudential maxim, which requires further definition before it can be accepted as a specifically moral precept at all. The maxim concerning self-interest has been criticized on the ground that the word

[15] *Ibid.*, p. 380.
[16] *Ibid.*, pp. 266, 380.
[17] *Ibid.*, p. 382.
[18] *Ibid.*, p. 383.

"interest" introduces certain intangibles that are so difficult to determine that they invalidate the law. However, this is the one of
the four which seems to the writer to have genuine claims to the
status of a moral law, though not on the grounds of self-evidence.
In spite of the fact that the term "interest" is a variable, to the
agent in a particular situation his own interest is sufficiently apparent
so that no blanket definition is needed; each person supplies his
own.

Whether one agrees or disagrees with Sidgwick's selection of
any or all of these four maxims, however, a fundamental objection
to his whole method of selection remains. If ever agreement about
the items of the moral code is reached, it will certainly not be on
the precarious ground of their self-authenticating cogency. Sidgwick
himself admits in the course of this very discussion the difficulty
of distinguishing genuine axioms from propositions which merely
appear to be self-evident because they are familiar and pass un-
challenged in some particular circle where it is taken for granted
that they are such.[19] On reflection, it is not clear why the four
rules that Sidgwick accepts are truly axiomatic when the maxims
he rejects, "I ought to speak the truth," and "I ought to keep my
promises," are "in need of considerable rational justification" before they can be received by the analytic observer as moral imperatives. While to Sidgwick his four seemed self-evident, someone else might argue with equal cogency that the two he rejects
are so. In a day when the whole conception of axioms has changed
radically—including those of mathematics, which were formerly
held to be unassailable—we see that neither in the realm of morals
nor anywhere else can we derive laws by this a priori method. If
any one of these "axioms" does turn out to be a true moral law,
that fact is accidental, and the intuition must have been validated
by some other means.

At individual points Sidgwick's book is a real classic in the field.
It makes a number of valuable contributions to the content of ethics
and furnishes new insights in the course of the discussion of some

[19] *Ibid.*, p. 379.

long-standing controversies in the field. Of these, only the two in which Sidgwick gives a classic solution to the problem need be mentioned.

He draws a useful distinction between motive and intention in judging the moral quality of an action. Having understood the complexity of motive in a manner that few of the earlier ethicians did, Sidgwick correctly points out that it is much easier to fix the major intention of an act as either good or bad than to ascertain and weigh correctly the whole range of motives that may actuate it.[20] Classic, also, is his discussion of exceptions to the maxim "Do not lie." These include the case concerning the telling of an untruth to an invalid whose life would be endangered by the shock of some piece of bad news; to children when it is not expedient for them to know the facts; and to those who ask unwarranted questions to which even silence would constitute a reply equivalent to revealing the truth.[21] These exceptions Sidgwick admits as legitimate, but he makes one important qualification about all of them. Whatever special cases are permitted as exceptions to the rule against lying, for the sake of preserving some more important value, should be allowed only with the understanding that they *are* and *remain* exceptions and that the example will not be widely imitated. He uses the analogy of celibacy. A few persons live in celibacy, but everybody understands that their example could not be followed by any considerable number without bringing about the extinction of the race.[22]

Some of the weaknesses of Sidgwick's book were incidental to the form of utilitarianism that he held, others were peculiar to the mode in which he attempted to combine it with intuitionalism. Naturally, the other members of the school found it an inconsistency in him that he trusted intuitionalism in any form, while they themselves believed so firmly that the empirical method alone was the correct one in ethics. On the other hand, he himself devoted considerable space in *The Methods of Ethics* to the refutation of egoistic hedonism (which even Spencer held in a modified form and

---

[20] *Ibid.*, p. 204. [21] *Ibid.*, p. 316. [22] *Ibid.*, pp. 483 f.

reconciled ingeniously with altruistic) by showing the impossibility of measuring various pains and pleasures against each other.[23] Furthermore, Sidgwick regarded the happiness of the individual as too trivial an end for the ultimate of any ethical system, but thought that he escaped from this difficulty by advocating universalistic hedonism instead. However, as for all altruistic forms of utilitarianism, this substitution of the happiness of the group for that of the individual did not obviate the difficulty. Like others of that wing, he merely proceeded from the less incommensurable to the more incommensurable.

Herbert Spencer: Evolution, Sociology, and Utilitarianism.—Sociology was not the creation of Herbert Spencer (1820–1903), but of Comte. However, Spencer did much to extend the study and to make it into a real social science. To him also belongs the credit for the first fruitful application of the method of sociology to ethics, for Comte's attempt had been centered chiefly on the problem of sanctions rather than the transformation of ethics into an independent science.

Spencer is at once a utilitarian, an evolutionist, and a sociologist. His system is the first ethical construction (unless one counts Nietzsche's as an ethic) to wrestle with the problems set by the theory of evolution and to face the readjustments necessitated in the fields of morals by the publication of Darwin's *Origin of Species*, in 1859. Spencer himself acknowledged the affinities between his thinking and that of the other utilitarians,[24] but his biological and sociological studies greatly enriched his thought, so that he was able to reshape and improve upon the systems of earlier members of the school by means of the data supplied by these new sciences. He discarded entirely the economic model that the earlier utilitarians had used and substituted for it the new one of organic evolution.

Spencer definitely set out to make ethics a science, but his attempt was pioneer instead of final. There were points at which he

[23] *Ibid.*, pp. 123 ff.
[24] Spencer, "Morals and Moral Sentiments," in *Recent Discussions in Science, Philosophy and Morals*, pp. 11 f.

himself felt doubtful about the possibility of reducing the material of ethics to an exact enough basis to entitle it to the name "science." The method he employed was to apply to the moral data the conceptions of evolution gleaned from the biological realm and in the light of these to review the facts about the genesis of morals revealed by the new studies of sociology and anthropology. In *The Data of Ethics* he traces moral development from the simple to the complex in a manner which parallels that of biological evolution. According to him, ethics has a biological, a psychological, and a social aspect,[25] and in all three of these areas the development is analogous to that of the organic. Man's nature has changed by adaptation to new conditions, and those individuals who lack the capacity for this change become retarded or lose out in the upward struggle.[26]

The points Spencer particularly emphasizes in his ethic are those which naturally stand out for a biologist or a sociologist. At the beginning of *The Data of Ethics* he lays down some general principles for construing ethics into a science after the manner of the biology and sociology of his day. To be made into such a science he considers the most urgent need of ethics in his time. There had been no such formulation of the principles of right conduct previously, he explains, because of the assumption in the past that the moral code was of divine origin.[27] The chief failure of all the schools of traditional ethics (including the utilitarian) is their failure to establish a principle of causality in morals and to ascertain the relations between cause and effect in the precise manner necessary to any science.[28] When and if the latter should be done, moralists would then be in a position to formulate general principles of right and wrong which would be permanently valid: "Every science begins by accumulating observations, and presently generalizes these empirically; but only when it reaches the stage at which its empirical generalizations are included in a rational generalization, does it become developed science." [29]

The evolution of an ethical method involves ascertaining such relations between cause and effect as shall make possible the formula-

[25] Spencer, *The Data of Ethics*, pp. 62–63.　　　　[26] *Ibid.*, chap. viii.
[27] *Ibid.*, p. vi.　　　　[28] *Ibid.*, p. 49.　　　　[29] *Ibid.*, p. 61.

tion of general rules from which the rules of conduct can be deduced. He believes that moral conduct, which to him is self-restrained conduct, does exhibit such relationships between antecedent and consequent as can be anticipated and reduced to statements that would form a proper scientific basis for ethics.[30] The moral law, however, would be the law of the perfect man in this absolute sense, but this we are not yet in a position to state.[31]

Similarly, then, is it with the relation between absolute morality, or the law of perfect right in human conduct, and relative morality which, recognizing wrong in human conduct, has to decide in what way the wrong deviates from the right, and how the right is to be most nearly approached. When, formulating normal conduct in an ideal society, we have reached a science of absolute ethics, we have simultaneously reached a science which, when used to interpret the phenomena of real societies in their transitional states, full of the miseries due to non-adaptation (which we may call pathological states) enables us to form approximately true conclusions respecting the nature of the abnormalities, and the courses which tend most in the direction of the normal.[32]

Having indicated the method by which he believes ethics could be reduced to the status of a science, he goes on to study its structure after the mode of organic evolution. He finds that moral evolution, like organic, proceeds from the simple to the complex; that in both realms the test of any action is, "Does it tend to complete life for the time being?"[33] Then he gives his famous biological justification for the pleasure-pain principle. Ethics, he asserts, follows the principle of pleasure and pain quite as much as the physical well-being or ill-being of the organism does. Pain follows the injurious; pleasure, the wholesome and the good. Pain in the physical sphere produces discomfort or perhaps permanent injury, even when it is not of long duration; if it is of protracted duration, death. The same, he believes, holds good of emotional pain, which is the type felt in the moral sphere.[34]

Spencer finds that failure to recognize these truths has vitiated all moral speculation, which, as he truly points out, has assumed the

[30] *Ibid.*, pp. 61–67.   [31] *Ibid.*, pp. 271 f.   [32] *Ibid.*, p. 277.
[33] *Ibid.*, p. 76–77.   [34] *Ibid.*, pp. 79, 87 f.

independence of the mind and the body and has been interested only in the consequences of conduct to character, thereby refusing to see that physical and moral consequences cannot be separated into two distinct compartments.[35] He criticizes the popular moral philosophy that the lower should invariably be disregarded in favor of the higher. He cites convincing evidence that neglect of the body, though prompted by the highest motives of self-sacrifice and fidelity to duty, may result in loss of health and permanent disability. The consequence of too great altruism is to defeat its own purpose by depriving the person of all further chance to be of service to others, for the net result of his intended unselfishness is to make him a burden instead of a help.[36]

Out of the evolution of life springs a canon that a creature must live before it can act. The consequent corollary, which ethics, like other sciences, would do well to observe, is that the acts necessary to maintain life are more imperative than all other acts.

Besides the principles that it shares with organic evolution, such as the above, ethics has certain roots that are psychological, because emotional. Still another source of its principles is the social structure. Those that originate here are the principles of mutual aid and co-operation. Morally speaking, man's nature changes by adaptation to social living, and its line of development tends always to move from the simple to the complex. Individuals and groups that lack this power of adaptation do not survive any more than do those who lack the capacity for physical adaptation. There is a survival of the fittest on the moral as well as the physical level of being.[37]

In social evolution co-operation is really necessary for survival and follows everywhere the principle that the interests of the individual must be subordinated to those of the group, which are far more important. However, the individual, though in group life he must perforce display some capacity for altruism, remains fundamentally egoistic, and has to remain so, in order to survive. That egoism forms the background for altruism, which grows out of such drives as the parental impulse to protect the young, which, in turn, is rooted deeply in the ego. By means of his biological theory Spencer

[35] *Ibid.*, pp. 91–93.   [36] *Ibid.*, pp. 110–15.   [37] *Ibid.*, chap. viii.

was able to balance by a different formula the equation between the interests of the ego and the interests of the group. The earlier utilitarians had postulated a sort of moral laissez faire, but in the interaction between the ego interests and the group interests and their interdependence upon each other Spencer gave the neatest solution to the problem that any member of the school was ever to provide.

Indeed, Spencer's argument that egoism and altruism are necessary complements and counterparts of each other is an irrefutable answer to those skeptics who maintain that all supposed altruism is but disguised egoism. He shows quite clearly that if the individual becomes too unselfish he forfeits health or some other essential of survival. On the other hand, if he does not subordinate his own interest to that of the group in at least some degree, he incurs the antagonism of his fellows and is excluded from those protections that are necessary to his safety, which only the group can provide. Also, he is dependent upon the co-operation of others for the fulfillment of such drives as reproduction, so that the very essentials of his survival and self-perpetuation preclude the possibility of a too ruthless pursuit of his own interests. Altruism, Spencer believes, comes about in social evolution by the identification of the interests of others with one's own, and thus co-operation for good comes about. Also, the affections that flow from such impulses as parental care and family feeling dictate good conduct in society.[38]

His idea of the sanctions of morality is that these are intrinsic, not extrinsic, not the punishment of the gods, but the consequences that follow from the acts themselves. The truly moral man is deterred from wrongdoing by the thought of the harm he will cause to others and is impelled to good conduct, not by the hope of the reward he will receive, but by the hope of bringing about a good condition through his act. Both effects and motives enter into the question whether an act is moral or not.[39] The moral faculty, however, is nothing but an accretion of inherited judgments on effects.[40]

As a whole Spencer's system is by all means the most powerful and

[38] Spencer's discussion of the interplay of egoism and altruism runs through chaps. xi and xii of *The Data of Ethics*.

[39] *Ibid.*, p. 123.

[40] *Ibid.*, pp. 113–24.

convincing of any interpretation of utilitarianism. His analysis of the ethical problem against the background of biological, psychological, and social evolution was a fresh approach at the time, and his presentation contains many individual excellencies. His discussion of the part of health as a necessary foundation for the development of character and the fulfillment of opportunities for service is classic and normative on the subject; and so is that of the interrelation of egoism and altruism. His defense of the pleasure and pain principle is quite the strongest that the school produced, since he was able to support it by his knowledge of biology. However, it is possible to object that the analogy between pleasure as the good and pain as the evil in the physical organism and in the moral life is not perfect in the light of modern physiology. For pain is not itself the evil, and pleasure is not itself the good; each is merely the symptom of deeper-lying causes. But looking at the solution from the standpoint of Spencer's contemporaries we see that his is the most adequate and that the answers he returned to his contemporary critics they found difficult to refute.[41]

When all due acknowledgment has been made to the merits of Spencer's system at individual points, the fact still remains that his effort to make ethics a science cannot by any means be regarded as final, since it labors under some very serious drawbacks. To this day difference of opinion exists as to whether ethics is or ever can be a science—an indication that his pioneer attempt was not an unqualified success. Some seeds of this partial failure lay in his attack on the problem. After stressing in the Preface to *The Data of Ethics* the need to formulate its principles as an independent science, he thereupon appears to lose sight of this objective, when he becomes so involved in establishing similarities between biological and moral evolution that he does not notice the differences, the peculiarities of ethical development in contradistinction to organic. The intuitional-

---

[41] Another instance of Spencer's ingenuity is to be found in his reply to Sidgwick's contention that pleasures and pains are incommensurable. Spencer replies by admitting that they are not susceptible of exact measurement, they are real and widespread psychological states on which it is as safe to base an ethical system as it is to base the judicial system on that other incommensurable, justice. (*The Data of Ethics*, chap. ix.)

ist opponents of Spencer and his school perceived these differences that escaped him. In fairness to him, however, it must be added that the former perceived only the differences and ignored the similarities, so that each presented but one side of the reality.

Spencer's effort to come to grips with the problems set by the Darwinian theory has a vigor that still makes many of his solutions acceptable, but, essentially, what he gives us is not an independent science of ethics, but an interpretation of the development of morality in the light of biological and social evolution. Some of the concepts of evolution are not applicable to morals. The concept of automatic progress is now held to be a misinterpretation of biological evolution itself; but Spencer, like other early Darwinians, applied it wholesale. Certainly in the realm of ethics progress is anything but automatic and assured; it is slow and difficult to produce, rather than inevitable. Spencer gives us no new moral code that converges toward that rational generalization that he himself regarded as so necessary to the nature of a true science. Nor does he give us an independent method of ethics. He merely applies the method of these other sciences to the data of ethics. Instead of creating an independent science of morals, he comes close to reducing it to a department or adjunct of biology and sociology.

Spencer's influence on future investigators was great, and during the last half century it inspired a long line of researches on the evolution of morals. To the study of biology and sociology they have added anthropology. Working from studies of nearly all living primitive tribes, these investigators have traced the development of morality among them so accurately that now the main facts about it are known and systematized. The list of useful works on the subject is too long to repeat, but perhaps especially able among them have been those of Westermarck and Hobhouse. Indeed, so abundant and fertile has been the combination of evolution, anthropology, and sociology that perhaps this approach has now contributed to ethics all the light it has to shed upon the problem of the genesis of morals.

Stephen's Attempt to Make Ethics a Science.—The first to attack the study of ethics under the inspiration of Spencer's approach was his contemporary, the literary critic Sir Leslie Stephen, who tried his hand at philosophy as well as letters. Himself a convinced utilitarian, his philosophic creed was that of the altruistic wing of the school. Starting from the general position of that group, he first published his book *The Science of Ethics* in 1882, which, like Spencer's work, was an attempt to reduce ethics to a science, but along lines in which the sociological emphasis predominated over the biological. The book is not great, but it has some interest as an effort to cast ethics into the form of a science from a somewhat different point of view from that of Spencer.

Stephen believes it to be a corollary of evolution that the group is more important than the individual. This conviction he combines with the utilitarian thesis that the good is the pleasurable to produce the demonstration for the necessity of altruism, which is required for the health and preservation of the social unit. He, too, holds that progress is a more or less automatic result of evolution and that consequently the surge of morals is ever onward and upward with the development of the social organism.[42]

Morality he defines as "a function of the social forces." The individual becomes moralized as a result of group pressure continually exerted upon him from his earliest childhood, modifying his "instincts." The term "instinct" Stephen uses very loosely to mean any impulse, feeling, desire, sentiment, or tendency, according to the psychological parlance of his day.[43] The morality of the group changes constantly with the conditions of its social development, so that at any stated time group morality can only be defined as "a statement of the conditions of social welfare, the sum of the preservative instincts of society." [44]

As to the possibility of a science of ethics, Stephen admits that it, like sociology and psychology or any other social science, is not likely to be able to conform to the strict tests of a physical science, of which the most important is prediction. No social science can afford more than a minimal amount of prediction, because of the large number of variables involved. Since he makes prediction the

---

[42] Stephen, *The Science of Ethics*, pp. 208, 335, 349.   [43] *Ibid.*, p. 330.
[44] *Ibid.*, p. 208.

crucial test of true science, Stephen insists on psychological determinism as a fact of the moral life. The determinant in ethics he
discovers in the pleasure-pain principle. He contends that ethics
can be a science in the same sense as other social sciences. The moral
code, which comprises its "laws," he defines thus: [45] "I mean by
the moral code that set of rules which, as a matter of fact, is re-
spected in a given society, and so far determines the ordinary ap-
provals and disapprovals as to be an effective force in governing
ethical conduct." [46]

Now, according to Stephen's definition moral law is by no means
absolute. But this admission he is ready to make, for he says that
it is supreme only in the sense that it is superior to circumstances. It
eludes all attempts at codification, partly because no general agreement can be reached as to its content, partly because it cannot be
deduced from such universals as the laws of nature or the a priori
axioms of mathematics. If one tries to state the moral principles, it
is his opinion that they turn out to be so vague and general that
they are meaningless. In illustration of the last point he cites the
example of the Golden Rule and the command to love our neighbor.[47] Since these "rules of morality," as he prefers to call them, are
generalizations, they are no more than probabilities, not absolutes
at all. They come into being with the development of group life.
As the social unit develops, intelligence increases and sympathies
are broadened. He is sure that intelligence and sympathy keep
pace with each other. The moral generalizations do not become
genuine rules for more than a very few advanced people, until they
receive full social approval. The example he gives to show how this
process comes about is that of the rule, "Do not persecute." This
new value of tolerance arose so recently that it cannot be considered
a genuine moral law until it receives the general consent of the
community.[48] All in all, the moral code is just the prevailing practices sanctioned by the major portion of the community.

The essence of morality, in Stephen's view, is that it should be

[45] *Ibid.*, p. 19.
[46] *Ibid.*, p. 37.
[47] *Ibid.*, pp. 146, 166.
[48] *Ibid.*, p. 263.

internal, not external—that it should legislate, not about conduct, but about motive, for example, "Do not hate" instead of "Do not kill." There is a contradiction involved here. On the one hand, he insists that morality is the product of the group pressure on the "instincts" of the individual and that the individual is not free, but is completely determined.[49] On the other hand, he insists with equal firmness that true morality can only be from within, so that the two positions cannot be reconciled. In one section of his book he goes over the main traditional virtues—courage, temperance, prudence, justice, and truth and explains their origin as utility to the social group.[50] Yet in the section immediately preceding this he emphasizes the necessity for the inwardness of morality. If a man is temperate, for example, just because he is afraid of penalties following his excesses, then his conduct is not truly moral, that is, not following his inner disposition.[51]

Since the only true morality is that which has this internal character, he defines moral conduct tautologically as "what a moral man would do." [52] This truly moral man does not always have to follow the accepted rules that are the practices of the majority, because in delicate matters of morals he is so advanced that he is able to follow the dictates of his own tastes.[53]

The chief interest of Stephen's construction is not so much in the individual points of his discussions of moral problems as in the measure of success he achieved in making ethics a science. He sees and grapples with many of the same difficulties that Spencer saw, but on the whole his system is inferior to Spencer's, except that Stephen does make ethics somewhat more of an independent science, less of a department of sociology and biology than did his greater contemporary. Like all utilitarians, Stephen stresses the need for an empirical method in ethics, but he is somewhat more emphatic than the others about limiting the field by the exclusion of all metaphysical elements. On this he insists not only because, as he sets forth in the first and last chapters of *The Science of Ethics,*

[49] *Ibid.,* pp. 20–29. [50] *Ibid.,* pp. 168 ff. [51] *Ibid.,* pp. 148 ff., 182 ff.
[52] *Ibid.,* pp. 377–78. [53] *Ibid.,* p. 380.

he considers them irrelevant and unnecessary to the solution of ethical problems but also because he himself admits to a strong prejudice against metaphysics in all its branches.[54]

Although he exaggerates to some extent the influence of the social aspect of ethics in the interests of his own theory, still he has seen correctly that the social is one permanent dimension of ethics which no student of the field can afford to ignore. However, when one goes a step farther and inquires how scientific Stephen himself was in his analysis of the origin of the moral consciousness from the pressure of the social group, one finds that he is scientific only in so far as his position is supported by the facts of sociology and anthropology. Beyond that he uses, not scientific data, but philosophic analysis, as he does in his treatment of the social origin or the traditional cardinal virtues.

The most important drawback from which his construction as a whole suffers is that the conception of science into which he is trying to fit ethics is now passé. This observation holds not only of such single details as his psychology of instincts, which is utterly outmoded now, but also of his whole conception of the nature of science. This was not the fault of Sir Leslie Stephen as an individual, it was due to the state of scientific thought in his time. Nevertheless, it did prevent him from recognizing the scientific potentialities latent in his own brain child. Realizing the lack of precision of a social science, about which he expressed himself in very strong terms in the case of sociology, he tries to model ethics as much as possible according to the pattern of the physical sciences. To this effort may certainly be attributed his insistence on psychological determinism, in the hope that some day it would make possible exact prediction of conduct.[55] His determinism is traceable to the prevailing conception of causality of the late nineteenth century science, and so, too, is his notion that if there are to be any scientific laws at all, they must be *absolutes*. Hence Stephen's unwillingness to use the term "moral laws" instead of "rules" or generalizations! For Stephen, no less than Kant, must have absolute moral laws, which are universal, necessary and their opposites unthinkable, or he will have

[54] *Ibid.*, chaps. i, xi.   [55] *The Science of Ethics*, chap. ii.

none. Statistical probabilities, which he recognized his own rules to be, did not satisfy him. Now that the model of the physical sciences has changed and several social sciences have attained good standing, we can with a good conscience accept high statistical probabilities as laws. The reduction of ethics to the status of a science no longer presents that group of obstacles which so hampered Stephen's effort to fit into the cast-iron mold of the prevailing conception of science fifty or sixty years ago.

Two Nineteenth-Century Challenges to Ethics

KARL MARX

The philosophic predilections of Karl Marx were Hegelian, but his great work, *Das Kapital*, while purporting to present a philosophy of history along Hegelian lines, was of far more importance to economics than to pure philosophy. In spite of its heaviness, as a whole the book attests the humanitarianism of the author throughout. The famous challenge of the Marxian slogan, "Religion, the opiate of people," moreover, was issued more directly to religion, of course, than to ethics, or at most to the religious sanctions of ethics and to a wrong combination of religion and ethics. Indirectly, however, his work constituted an important challenge to ethics itself; for hitherto the economic element in the moral life had been ignored by the traditional schools, even by ethicians, such as Adam Smith and Bentham, who were themselves economists. More than anyone either before or after him, Marx brought home to all and sundry the importance of the economic factor in life. Of course, he overemphasized it, but overemphasis is usually necessary to gain adequate recognition for some neglected aspect of life.

The general value of Marxian doctrine is still a controversial subject, as it had been ever since the publication of *Das Kapital*, in 1867. But the point for ethics is, not whether the economic determinism of Marx is right or wrong or even whether or not the proposals he advocated are on the whole good or bad, but that ethics had neglected the economic factor in life, which Marx once and for all showed to be one of the most important determinants of this, as well as of so many other, sides of man's life. Ethics has not yet adequately come to grips with economic problems and their bearing upon moral conduct, but since the day of Marx it has no longer been possible for ethicians to go on ignoring the importance of economic relations to the good life as they did in the old days. While ethical thinking on economic issues still lags far behind what is to be desired, there has been some consciousness of them ever since Marx wrote, and recent textbooks on ethics, from whatever point of view they may be written, contain a chapter or two of more or less adequate discussion of the subject.

FREUD

As controversial as the doctrines of Marx are the psychoanalytic theories of Sigmund Freud. The present volume is not the place to go into the pros and cons of Freudian psychology, even if the writer were competent to decide these primarily psychological concerns. Whether Freud's theories are right in detail or not, the fact remains that they have set ethics some challenges and some problems which it can ignore only at its peril.

Just as Marx, by overemphasizing the importance of the economic factor in life, had unforgettably called attention to it, so Freud confronted the world with the potent influence of the sex factor in a manner that will never again permit anyone to avoid or underestimate its importance. Now, it happens that traditional ethics had not ignored sex as it had economic relationships, but the morality of the past, whether of common sense or of formal ethics, had greatly underestimated the strength of the sexual drive and ignored many of its less obvious ramifications. The Viennese doctor left only two choices open to moralists. They had to accept his challenge either by demonstrating that he was wrong or by adjusting their own thinking to some degree of conformity with his position. Most writers on ethics have implicitly or explicitly chosen the latter alternative.

One does not need to subscribe to Freud's theories *in toto* to perceive that his school, more than all the other schools of psychology, threw out another problem to ethics which it had to face: the problem of motive. The details of Freud's explanations of the ways in which covert motives manifest themselves may be incorrect in some particulars, and certain aspects of his analysis of personality may be unsound; but he, more than any other one man, produced enough convincing evidence for the complexity of motive to call for a revision of previous moral judgments on the matter.[56] It should now be as impossible for ethics to assume simplicity of motive as Einstein has made it for physics to operate on the Newtonian theory of gravitation.

A third discovery for which Freud and his school are largely responsible is the demonstration that people suffering from compulsion neuroses, fixations, and traumata (emotional shocks) cannot by volition control their behavior in the areas affected by these disorders. Such behavior therefore lies outside the sphere of moral responsibility. During recent decades considerable work has been done on the problem of psychology and moral responsibility, and ethicians have made more effort to adjust their thinking to the facts that Freud and others have brought forward here than in the area of motive, where the adjustment has been inconsiderable.

The Twentieth Century

The twentieth century has not been secure enough to conduce to thought. So far it has not seen the erection of great philosophic structures. Yet despite the wars and social upheavals science has progressed by leaps and bounds, bringing forth new discoveries and inventions and setting in motion new currents of thought, some of which have posed problems for and some given aid to ethics. Due to the revolution in the conceptions of science and scientific law that followed the overthrow of the older mechanism in physics and astronomy, the great single trend is toward relativity. The work of Einstein, Bohr, and others led to a great change in the scientific picture of the universe, which now appears to run on statistical probabilities rather than absolute laws and unbroken chains of causa-

---

[56] Though scattered through all his other works, his theories of the complexity of motive, of fixations, compulsions, and so forth, are available in convenient form in his *Psychopathology of Everyday Life*, which inspired the above discussion.

tion as scientific opinion had unanimously maintained from Newton to Einstein. The newer conception opened the way for a margin
of freedom, for chance, for new possibilities. With the overthrow
of mechanism in its great stronghold, the physical sciences, the conception soon spread to the natural sciences and from biology to
psychology. This admission of the possibility of freedom was a great
gain for ethics, which is but a contradiction in terms without the
reality of freedom.[57]

With the death of mechanism, one of the principal strongholds of
the absolutes fell. Two other intellectual developments of the late
nineteenth and early twentieth centuries combined to shake further
the faith of the new century in absolutes and axioms, the two types
of proposition that were believed previously to be apodictic, categorical, and indisputable. Two new systems of geometry had been
devised, one by Lobatschevsky and one by Riemann, each with a
different set of axioms, so that the axioms of Euclid could no longer
stand in solitary self-evidence and absoluteness. A further blow to
the older conception came with the proof of some of the supposedly
self-evident laws of logic by Whitehead and Russell in their *Principia
Mathematica*. Thus the currents of scientific thought tended to
break down the absolute and the axiomatic. A similar trend away
from absolutes was manifested in the philosophic sphere by the rise
of pragmatism, the one new system of philosophy to come into
being within the twentieth century. This was the creation of William
James (1842–1910), the only American philosopher to originate
an independent school of thought. If a date is to be assigned to its
formulation, perhaps the best one is the year 1907, in which William James published the book entitled *Pragmatism*. Although
James had been writing for many years, the appearance of this volume first presented his system as an articulated whole. It has since
been expanded and modified by others, particularly by John Dewey,
the other leading exponent of pragmatism. With its emphasis on
experience, the reaction of pragmatism on ethics is important, because it reinforced the empirical tendencies that had been the re-

[57] These changes are set forth in a form understandable to the layman by Eddington in his *The Nature of the Physical World*.

sultant of a number of nineteenth-century schools, the utilitarians, the evolutionists, and the sociologists. James did not write any book on ethics, but Dewey, in collaboration with Tufts, wrote a text on the subject that first appeared in 1909 and has touched upon it in later works, such as the chapter in *The Quest for Certainty* (1929).

A second element in pragmatism that holds potential importance for ethics, but on which it has not yet capitalized, is James's conception of truth. He deals only with that aspect of it which is created by man when tried out in experience or when, as he himself expressed it, "Truth happens to an idea." [58]

Such truth receives verification by the test of experience, by discovering whether on the whole and in the long run it *works*. Critics of James have frequently objected to his conception of truth, because it applies only to the truths of value, not to the truths of fact. However, the truths of value constitute one of the most important classes with which ethics is concerned. Since with the normative and to some extent the regulative principles man's choices, aims, and ideals decide what shall become truth, James's description of how the process comes about supplies a gap in ethical epistemology.

The intellectual currents set in motion by the transformation in scientific thought and the philosophical influence of pragmatism thus dovetailed to produce emphasis on empiricism and relativism in place of the former rationalism and absolutism. Though this purely intellectual influence was felt in ethics, the real challenges of the twentieth century to morals have been practical instead of theoretical. They have been destructive rather than constructive. While the thought of the nineteenth century had undermined many of the foundations of the popular moral code, its practical breakdown did not come until the new century. The Victorian era, radical in thought, remained as conservative in practice as the queen whose name it bears. However, the practical upheaval of World War I administered a more severe blow to the popular code of respectability than all the theories of the nineteenth and twentieth centuries combined. The post-war period of the 1920's revealed both in literature and in conduct the effects and extent of the relaxation of

[58] James, *Pragmatism*, p. 201.

the old rules that for generations had been regarded as unshakable absolutes in their own right. There followed the world-wide depression of the 1930's and upon its heels the outbreak of World War II, with its threat to civilization. The ideology of the totalitarian states, with its transvaluation of all values, constitutes the greatest practical challenge to ethics that it has known throughout its long history.

How shall ethics meet this colossal, practical challenge of the twentieth century? Shall it retreat to the past to search out some formula from the Middle Ages or the Reformation to serve as the panacea for these unprecedented ills of a new and terrible day? Shall it ignore the challenge of the present by reiterating the outworn platitudes of the traditional code? Shall it take the defeatist attitude that the "acids of modernity" have corroded all the heritage of the older systems, so that naught remains to us but the moral chaos of a hopeless relativism? These questions ethics must answer and answer at once before it is too late to influence the history of the next thousand years, which, as one leader is truly telling his followers, is now in the making. Ethics must take stock of its own position. It must turn to "things old and new" in order to meet the challenge of the twentieth century. But it must learn to distinguish among the possibility of answering the problems of the present with the solutions of the past, the obligation to devise entirely new solutions by new methods, and the possibility of combining "things old and new." Some suggestions as to the lines along which ethics should approach its task, how it can utilize its heritage from the past to aid the present, and how to build farther until it becomes a real science form the second part of this volume.

PART TWO

MAKING ETHICS A SCIENCE

CHAPTER XI

THE CONTENT OF MORAL LAW

THE STUDY of the world's great ethical systems is likely to leave those who search for unity, for universals, and for a consensus of opinion as to the nature and the content of the moral law with a disappointing sense of the relativity and subjectivity of ethics. It cannot be denied that the great ethicians of the world have differed widely not only upon minor points but also about the very fundamentals of the good life itself. Nevertheless, there has also been a substantial body of agreement about the essentials of the good life; and the passage of time, which separates the wheat from the chaff, reveals certain moral truths which have the right to be called laws. The task of the present chapter will therefore be to state and to classify the content of this code, which has already been established on a more or less scientific basis up to the present time. Such an effort is not new. Other selections have been made from time to time, some of which have been noticed in the first part of this volume. Certain laws are the same as in other lists, but the threefold classification of this treatment affords leeway for new ones to be admitted to a place in the code. In the first chapter of this volume three different classes of moral law were defined and distinguished from each other. These were: the operative laws, which are virtually automatic in their action, like the law of gravitation; regulative principles, "recipes," which govern whole classes of actions; and normative principles, a special group which differ from the regulatives only in being formulas for certain single or unusual situations rather than general ones.

The working of the laws in each of these three sets differs somewhat, since there are varying degrees of certainty regarding the results, not only in each class but also as to individual laws subsumed under each of the three. These differences in the status of the three types have not been entirely clear even to the formulators of the laws; for if they thought about the subject at all, they were prone to believe as Kant did, that only operative laws could be classed as true moral laws, or were of the opinion, as was Aristotle, that all kinds were merely value judgments and opinions. The fact is that the classes are very different. The purely operative moral laws belong to the realm of fact, where there is either a fixed sequence between cause and effect or a high statistical probability in favor of the occurrence of a certain set of effects from a given cause. Many of the operative laws are prohibitions, such as "Thou shalt not kill" or "Thou shalt not commit adultery"; but there are also a few positive injunctions among them.

The comparison of the commandment "Thou shalt not kill" with "Thou shalt not commit adultery" illustrates well the difference between the operative law with a fixed result and the operative law with a high statistical presumption in favor of certain consequences ensuing from its violation. When a life is taken, the certain consequence is that something irreplaceable has gone out of the world; therefore the law against killing is the purest example we have of a fixed operative law. The law against committing adultery, on the other hand, is statistical in its operation, since its consequences vary somewhat according to the reaction of the principal parties involved and the most radical consequences of its violation do not come to full fruition unless the act is discovered. The prohibition against stealing is another instance of a statistically operative law, with a strong probability in favor of the occurrence of harmful effects.

Those commandments of the Decalogue of Exodus 20 which are moral (and it should be borne in mind that only six of them *are* moral, the other four being purely religious) are operative in character with the exception of "Honor thy father and thy mother," which is a normative principle, and "Thou shalt not covet," a regulative. These operative laws cannot be said to belong to the realm of value, since they do not deal with qualities, but with facts, and they entail sure effects intrinsic to the process of their violation. However, the other two classes, the regulative and the normative principles, are in the sphere of value judgments, for with regard to them the question of quality enters. The analogy to recipes holds, especially for the regulatives. When baking a cake, one produces some kind of cake, more or less edible, even with an inferior recipe; but one obtains a delicious cake with a good recipe. So, too, with the regulative and normative principles, it is a matter of getting the best possible results rather than the less good or poor ones which come from following some other "recipe." With these two classes there may be some difference of opinion as to what constitutes the best effect, especially with relation to those principles within the two classes that are less well established by the test of time and experience. Matters such as tradition, group opinion, and personal preference enter into the formation of judgments of the results and may keep some from appreciating them as good, better or best, especially on first trial. For all these reasons the laws of these two classes are less indisputably in the category of laws and less widely removed from the class of opinions than are the operatives. However, the more certainly the effects of the two kinds of regulatives—for the normatives are but specialized regulatives—are established by experience, the more likely they are to belong to the class of real moral laws. Examples of regulatives that definitely have the status of genuine moral laws are, of course, the Golden Rule of Jesus and the Silver Rule of Confucius, which are regulatives governing large classes of actions, having behind them not only the authority of these ethical teachers but also the test of wide experience over a long period of time and in a great many places. The one defect of regulative principles that keeps them from being more universally recognized as laws is that ethicians have never been exact and scientific enough in their study of their application as compared with the application of some contrary or contradictory formulas for dealing with the same situations.

We are now ready to state the code of moral law that we already possess as an approved inheritance from the ethical teachers and codes of the past or that are to be formulated from approved experience of the past and the present. The laws are subjoined, and the three types are separated into appropriate groups.

The Operative Laws

From the Decalogue of Exodus 20: (1) "Thou shalt not kill"; (2) "Thou shalt not commit adultery"; (3) "Thou shalt not steal." For the Hebrew commandment "Thou shalt not bear false witness against thy neighbor," is substituted the more general precept against lying, of which the ninth Commandment is but one special case: "Thou shalt not lie."

The Ten Commandments of Buddhism agree with the Hebrew Decalogue in three of the five moral commandments.[1] However, the Buddhist commandment against lying is the more general form, as above, and the commandment against the destruction of life includes all forms, not, as in the Hebrew Code, just human life. The Buddha further forbade unchastity and the partaking of alcoholic beverages, and the use of the latter was also forbidden by Mohammed. These two codes are the most important ones that elevate the prohibition of alcoholic beverages to the rank of major moral precepts; for upon this issue there has been considerable difference of opinion among both moral and religious teachers. It seems that this prohibition should scarcely have a place in the list of operative laws; rather it is one of those borderline questions that are largely physiological, but have some moral implications.

Since there has been so much controversy among ethicians themselves as to whether "Thou shalt not lie" is a true moral law, some explanation of its inclusion among the laws of this class is in order. Plainly it belongs to the class of operatives, because like "Thou shalt not steal" it carries a statistical probability that bad and harmful consequences will result from its infraction. Like the worst consequences of adultery, those of lying are in large measure contingent upon the discovery of the real facts. In the future it is likely that we shall be able to reduce to a mathematical formula the chances of discovery of the lie, if the outcome of a sufficiently large number of lies should be studied.

The fact that the law against lying operates as a probability has not been borne in mind by most of the ethicians who have discussed the subject. Sir Leslie Stephen alone fully appreciated this fact, but even he did not draw the correct inferences from it. As a probability, however, its consequences operate impartially for lies of all kinds, regardless of whether the intention behind them is good or bad. For this reason the general law against lying seems preferable

[1] Mahâvagga i. l. 56 (Sacred Boks of the East, Vol. XXII).

to the mere prohibition of certain classes of lies, such as the commandment against bearing false witness and the special case provided against in Stephen's rule "Do not tell malicious lies." [2]

With all types of falsehoods there is always the chance that the truth will leak out and that even if told for the purpose of safeguarding some more important value than the knowledge of the facts in the case, the ruse may not serve this purpose. To consider Sidgwick's classic exceptions to the absolute rule against lying: the invalid may accidentally overhear or may guess the facts withheld from him in the hope of sparing him a dangerous shock; the child may stumble upon the truth that has been carefully concealed from him; and the falsehood may not be an adequate screen to keep the curious from penetrating the secrets they are not entitled to know. In these cases, as in all other cases, one runs the chance that the last state will be worse than the first. Because this law is operative, the probability of unfavorable consequences attendant upon its infraction works *without reference to the intention behind it.*

On the other hand, some distinctions need to be drawn with regard to the unreflecting observance of this rule as an absolute admitting of no exceptions whatsoever. Some persons fail to comprehend that there are situations in which the absolute truth is not and cannot be known, either to themselves or to anyone else, and that in such cases, what they call "telling the absolute truth" is merely giving their own opinion, value judgment, or guess. Familiar illustrations are the claim that one is telling the absolute truth in making recommendations and in volunteering to advise or to correct another; in the latter case zeal for "the absolute truth" may merely serve as a pretext for being disagreeable and censorious. Frequently, too, the absolute truth is not a matter of fact, but of future eventuality, when probabilities or even possibilities not yet realized are confused with certainties that belong only to the future.

All in all, while Kant erred somewhat on the side of rigidity in allowing no exceptions to the prohibition against lying (on the ground that we could not will these exceptions to become universal laws), yet his feeling was more nearly sound than that of those whose

[2] Stephen, *The Science of Ethics*, pp. 194–200.

usual tendency is to permit too many rather than too few exceptions. Sidgwick's rule is a wise one, that if exceptions are permitted in the hope of preserving some more important value, it is to be understood that these *are and remain* exceptions and that they shall not set a general example in favor of violating the law.[3]

THE LAW AGAINST PERSECUTING

"Thou shalt not persecute." Restatement of this law was suggested, but not used by Stephen.[4]

The only other operative law which seems to the writer to have such indisputable status that it must be included in any list of operative laws is Saint Paul's law of requital, or responsibility: "Whatsoever a man soweth, that shall he also reap" (Galatians 6:7).

It is possible that the law of compensation whose working Emerson so convincingly describes in his essay "Compensation" is a special case of the law of requital; however, it lacks some of the cogency and inevitability of the Pauline formulation. It resembles closely the statement of a similar principle from the Gospel of Luke:

And judge not, and ye shall not be judged: and condemn not, and ye shall not be condemned: release and ye shall be released: give, and it shall be given unto you: good measure, pressed down, shaken together, running over, shall they give into your bosom. For with what measure ye mete, it shall be measured to you again (Luke 6:37–38).

The list of operatives is not long; doubtless many others are waiting for some Einstein of the moral life to formulate them; for the operatives, like scientific laws, are first observed and then formulated by their discoverers. These are the laws of the moral life that exist whether or not we are conscious of their existence; we violate them with greater or less peril to ourselves, according to the inevitability of their consequences.

THE REGULATIVE PRINCIPLES

The two broadest laws of this group seem to the writer to be the two great maxims of Kant; accordingly, they are placed first: "So

---

[3] Sidgwick, *The Methods of Ethics*, p. 483.
[4] Stephen, *The Science of Ethics*, p. 263.

act that the maxim of thy will may at all times serve as a universal law"; [5] "So act as to treat humanity, whether in thine own person or that of any other, in every case as an end withal, and never as a means only." [6]

RECIPROCITY

The Silver Rule of Confucius.—"Tsekung asked, 'Is there a single word that can serve as a principle of conduct for life?' Confucius replied, 'Perhaps the word "reciprocity" will do. Do not do unto others what you do not want others to do unto you.' " [7]

The Golden Rule of Jesus.—"And as ye would that men should do to you, do ye also to them likewise" (Luke 6:31).

Perhaps to these one more principle might be added as a formulation from the knowledge accruing to us from modern psychology and experience: "Respect the personality and the human rights of every man. So far as possible, treat each man with whom you come in contact as he would like to be treated."

Criticisms of the Golden Rule as a moral law were made by both Sidgwick and Stephen, as noted in Chapter X. The latter held that it was a generalization so broad that it was meaningless and discarded it altogether. Sidgwick considered that as worded in the New Testament the statement lacked precision. He therefore stated it in negative form and added the qualification that the formula held only for identical circumstances. Although the writer is of the opinion that Sidgwick's restatement is unwieldy and somewhat pedantic, she agrees with him that the Golden Rule alone does need some kind of supplement in order to be a complete regulative principle. However, the best way to complete it seems to be to couple it with the Silver Rule of Confucius. The latter is a somewhat broader principle, since people probably have more dislikes in common than likes. So far as the psychological reactions of human beings are similar or identical, the Golden Rule and the Silver Rule can serve as regulatives for all situations, but in so far as differences in taste

---

[5] Kant, *Kritik der praktischen Vernunft*, p. 39, tr. by the author.
[6] Abbott, *Kant's Theory of Ethics*, p. 47.
[7] *The Wisdom of Confucius*, tr. by Lin Yutang, p. 166.

and sentiments exist, the third regulative, just stated, ought to be employed.

THE LAW OF BENEVOLENCE

"Thou shalt not hate thy brother in thy heart. . . . Thou shalt not take vengeance nor bear any grudge against the children of thy people; but thou shalt love thy neighbor as thyself" (Leviticus 19:17, 18).

"Love your enemies, do good to them that hate you" (Luke 6:27).

"To those who are good to me I am good; and to those who are not good to me, I am also good; and thus all get to be good. To those who are sincere with me, I am sincere; and to those who are not sincere with me, I am also sincere; and thus all get to be sincere." [8]

"Recompense injury with kindness." [9]

Sometimes this group, which together comprise the law of love or benevolence, has been reduced to a single maxim, as by Kant and Sidgwick. The statements of neither one seem an exact equivalent to the principles above. The Biblical formulation has been retained here, because the practice of using the earliest formulation has been followed throughout, provided that it is not too incompatible with the interest of precision. The only objection to the Biblical wording is that in this case the translation of the Greek word *agape* by the English "love" does not reproduce the exact connotation of the original. "Good will" or "benevolence" would be a closer equivalent, for the Greek word does not mean personal affection or attachment, but simply a more impersonal kind of benevolence that transcends the bounds of congeniality.

THE SERVICE PRINCIPLE

The Pauline Paradox.—"Bear ye one another's burdens" (Galatians 6:2a); "For each man shall bear his own burdens" (Galatians 6:5).

Jesus's Principle of Precedence.—"But he that is the greater

---

[8] The Texts of Taoism (Sacred Books of the East, Vol. XXXIX, p. 62).
[9] *Ibid.*, p. 42.

among you, let him become as the younger; and he that is chief, as he that doth serve" (Luke 22:26).

Giving All.—"Whosoever shall seek to gain his life shall lose it; but whosoever shall lose his life shall preserve it" (Luke 17:33).

THE LAW AGAINST ENVY

"Thou shalt not envy." It seems better to substitute this generalization for the special case subsumed under it in the commandment of the Hebrew Decalogue: "Thou shalt not covet" (Exodus 20: 17a).

THE MAXIM OF SIDGWICK

"I ought not to prefer my own lesser good to the greater good of another." [10]

THE NORMATIVE PRINCIPLES

THE RELATION TO PARENTS

"Honor thy father and thy mother" (Exodus 20:12).

THE KEY PRINCIPLE OF MUTUALITY

Mutuality is the constitutive principle of friendship and of all the more spiritual aspects of the love relationship between the sexes.

THE GOLDEN MEAN

In many courses of action the good lies in the middle between the extremes of excess or defect; in all such, seek the Golden Mean. This principle has not been formulated in just these words; but the writer believes that this summary preserves the spirit of both the Confucian and the Aristotelian interpretations of it. One must not claim for the principle of the Golden Mean that it is valid for good conduct of all sorts; some virtues, such as loyalty, are absolute, and to these the principle does not apply at all. Nevertheless, it deserves to be classed as a regulative principle, because it covers a wide range of moral conduct and is the principle of right action wherever moderation and temperance are in order, as in the indulgence in food,

---

[10] Sidgwick, *The Methods of Ethics*, p. 383.

drink, and some pleasures, indeed, wherever the good is a mean and the contrary extremes of excess and defect should be shunned as evils.

It has already been observed that Aristotle's classic discussion of the qualitative differences among the pleasures constitutes a normative principle. It might be summarized this way: We should follow the higher and more enduring pleasures, using those of a physical character moderately for the restorative purpose for which they are designed.

For the place and the rights of the individual against the group when the two conflict, this principle arises from Spencer's discussion of the subject in his *Data of Ethics*, though he himself does not state it in these words: Morally speaking, it is true that the whole is greater and more valuable than any of its parts; but it is also true that the welfare of the whole is in some degree endangered by injury to any of its parts.

One final normative principle arises from the experience of the many strong characters who have been afflicted with physical sufferings or handicaps or have been forced to endure great and unusual tragedy and suffering of other sorts, yet, in spite of these limitations, have served their day and generation and perhaps all days. This normative principle comes to us out of the life of a Helen Keller, a William Prescott, or a Franklin D. Roosevelt: I must transcend suffering and contribute to life in my own person and to the group about me in a measure as nearly normal as my limitations permit.

THE CODE OF MORAL LAW: GENERAL COMMENTS

Now that the moral laws of all three classes have been assembled, a few generalizations about the code as a whole suggest themselves. Most of these formulations are very old and familiar—perhaps so familiar that they seem but platitudes. However, the fact that they are well known should not disguise their authoritativeness. Most of the laws assembled here have been stated by some great ethician of the past and are presented in the traditional form. A few of them have been suggested, but not stated, by some older religious or ethical teacher. A few others are newly educed from the experience of the past or the knowledge of the present which is ripe for reduction to the form of law.

From time to time ethicians have endeavored to state moral laws or to compile them into codes. Most conspicuous of these attempts in ancient times, of course, are the religious law codes, in which some moral precepts are intermingled with purely religious, ritualistic, and ceremonial commands. From the standpoint of ethics, the greatest drawback of such codes is that they tend to confuse all these types of laws with one another and to place them all on the same level. Among more recent attempts to state moral laws, those of Kant and Sidgwick are notable, but each gives us only a very small number, not a whole code. Kant sets forth the two major categorical imperatives and mentions three or four other maxims of lesser importance, such as the prohibition against lying. Sidgwick lists only four rules, which he deemed self-evident moral axioms. Stephen refused to compile any moral code at all, because he believed no general agreement could be reached about its content.

Three different difficulties hampered the efforts of these ethicians in codifying moral law. First of all, the sources were restricted to those of the West, because until well into the nineteenth century the writings of oriental ethicians were not translated. In Kant's day the teachings of Gautama, Confucius, and other orientals were almost unknown in Europe; and even Sidgwick, writing in the second half of the nineteenth century, when oriental works were being translated into English, French, and German, displays no sign of familiarity with the ethical systems of the Far East.

The second limitation relates to the failure to sense the laws that had already been established. Here, as elsewhere, Kant took a wholly new and original line, setting aside most of what had gone before instead of building upon it as a foundation of assured knowledge for his new system. Sidgwick, however, shows the influence of Kant in his selection of the law of benevolence as one of the four rules he states as true moral axioms. Although he attempted to reduce ethics to a science, Stephen refused to call even his own formulations "laws"; he merely refers to them as "rules" that represent the belief and practice of the majority. The third difficulty which beset these attempts is that none of the older ethicians recognized any type as true moral law except the operatives, which are few in number. Even these had to be, according to them, either absolutes or nothing. This was a natural mistake, since only those of the first class were analogous to the laws of science, which were then conceived to be absolutes admitting of no variation. Now, with the most diverse sources available and with the changed conception of scientific law, it is possible to recognize the regulative and normative principles as new classes of moral law.

The three classes of law represent the established heritage of ethics so far as the content side is concerned. The laws based upon exterior and objective facts, where the external consequences are the most important ones, crystallize into operative laws. This class is most readily distinguishable, for here the factual results are present in most or all cases of the violation of the operatives according to the probability of a fixed effect that they represent. In the "recipes," the regulative and normative principles, we have the crystallization into law of the more intangible and subjective elements, values, qualities, ideals, and inner dispositions. The effects of their infraction are, consequently, more variable and intangible than are those of breaking the operatives, but are discoverable by comparing the results of these recipes with those of their contraries or contradictories. This comparison may be perceptible at first only to the minority possessed of deep moral insight, but gradually, when tested by time and experience, the regulatives and normatives come to receive general assent. Just as soon as the effect of a particular "recipe" is studied sufficiently to make clear its qualitative superiority over its opposite, it is a moral law.

The code of moral law is not large, but it is enlarged by recognizing those principles which were discerned by earlier workers in the field and new moral principles in the present. How the laws just stated were evolved has been the subject of the first part of this volume; how the new principles may be discovered or created and reduced to laws of the three classes is the subject of this part. For the addition of other moral laws to those we already know requires a more precise formulation and development of ethical method than we have hitherto possessed.

CHAPTER XII

THE PROBLEM OF ETHICAL METHOD

Now THAT a selection of laws sufficiently well established to be regarded as the moral code has been given, the problem of ethical method remains to be considered, both with regard to the identification of elements already accurately formulated and also as to means for its further development and extension into an instrument more precise and better adapted for the investigation of its object.

The precepts given in the three classifications of the foregoing chapter constitute the code of moral law as it comes down in formulations of the past or is furnished by the facts of past or present experience. Now that the code is stated, the next step is to evaluate the methods by which the statement of these laws has been reached and the means by which they have been validated, wherever validation has been attempted. If there is any general method of verification, it is the pragmatic method, confirmation by experience. In considering the process of discovery, the first observation that strikes the student of ethical history is that the laws have not all been arrived at by the same methods.

In the first part of this book the general method followed by each of the several ethical teachers was indicated in the course of the discussion of their systems, and the contributions—if any—of each to the method of ethics were also stated. Now, only a few general observations on the traditional methods used in ethics are in order. In the past these methods have been largely philosophic or religious rather than scientific in character. They may be divided into three types: the authoritarian, the intuitional or inspirational, and the rational, though combinations of two or even all three of these may be found in the teachings of the same teacher—for example, the teaching of Kant was predominantly rational, but also partly intuitional, and the method of Saint Thomas Aquinas, though predominantly authoritarian, shows a strongly rational trend as well.

With regard to the laws quoted from the Decalogue and other

parts of the Old Testament, all of them came to the writers as intuitions which were regarded as authentic Divine inspirations, and no attempt was made to check or verify them. The same is true of Saint Paul. Among the great ethicians, Jesus, Confucius, and Gautama followed a method that was also predominantly intuitional or inspirational. The ethical teachers who adopted a predominantly rational approach fall into two groups; those who, like Socrates, used induction, and those, like Aristotle and Spinoza, who used deduction. It is unfortunate that his successors in the field did not follow the pioneer example set by Socrates in the use of the inductive method.

However, regardless of what method the great classical ethicians employed, some truth was gained by all of them, and the test of time has revealed which of their teachings may be reckoned as real moral laws. That such was the case is either because these men had a wide experience of life and a profound knowledge of human nature, so that their method was more empirical than they knew, or, as with Kant and to some extent with Spinoza, because they were geniuses whose intuitions transcended their experience.

Yet a survey of ethical method up to the present highlights two facts. First, there is little continuity of method in the field, little building of later ethicians on the work of earlier ones. The great ones usually started out afresh to develop their own systems on original lines, and those who did work on the foundations of their predecessors (usually the lesser lights like the disciples of Kant) displayed no sure sense of what was truly established in the field. These facts add up to one conclusion: that little has been established in ethical method. While the contributions of some of the classical ethicians are basic to the foundation of a true ethical methodology, the thinkers of the past have but set forth prolegomena to ethical method and sketched preliminary outlines to shape it. The method of ethics has not advanced beyond the rudimentary stage in which they left it. It needs to be extended, refined, sharpened, supplemented, made more exact, and above all it needs to be tried. Most ethicians are still in the armchair stage, where they spin voluminous tomes on the true, the beautiful, and the good out of their own heads, with no foundation of facts whatever to which they may attach the tenuous threads of the complicated webs they weave.

Since the prime requisite of any science is to evolve a sound method suited to its object, perhaps the first step in formulating such a procedure for the science of ethics should be to find out how the laws of each of the three classes are in fact discovered. The operative laws have been recognized by means of all the traditional methods, and since they deal with facts, their presence can be empirically verified at any time. Kant was the first to evolve the theory that moral laws are universal, necessary and their opposites unthinkable—a conception that applies only to the fixed operative law, but is the first distinct formulation of characteristics of any absolute moral law.

The regulative and normative principles are each formulated differently. The regulative principles are derived much as economic principles are. They are, as in the latter science, the rules of the game, and as in economics the principles are generalizations resulting from observing the regulatives of competition, supply and demand, trade, and finance, so the regulative principles of ethics are derived from observing the dealings of men with each other, in co-operation, in conflict, and in the successful solution of problems, which at first may be reached by mere trial and error. Observing life until one discerns the clews to high moral living and then stating the formulas thus obtained is the true origin of such great regulative principles as the Golden Rule and the Silver Rule and the two maxims of Kant, whatever might be the origin to which their formulators ascribed them. Stating the regulative principles has usually been the work of men who have had a fine sense of human values, just as economists are aware of the worth of economic principles.

The normative principles are really created rather than discovered or derived. They may not be stated at all by the one who originated them; indeed, the statement of such principles may not take place for a long time after they come into being. Just as in music new forms of harmony are from time to time created by great composers and new styles of painting by great artists, so new moral norms are created from the experience of great souls faced with new and unique problems, and their attitudes, their formulas for solution, sooner or later are recognized as normative and become crystallized into moral laws, hypothetical imperatives for those situations in which they recur. It is among the normative principles that we see the working of William James's dictum that truth happens to an idea. This is the truly creative side of ethics, where the individual has opportunity to make his contribution, as Socrates did in his normative attitude toward his condemnation and death. On the other hand, this is the area of ethics where the most uncertainties exist and the fewest laws are securely established, because here the situations themselves are so individual that they may not recur; and also it is not always easy to perceive at first sight those which, among competing solutions to the recurrent situations, will emerge as the normative principles, though the passing of time generally clarifies the matter.

The second task for ethical method is to learn to select and to handle its sources. It has been pointed out several times that the sources of ethics are in human living (an insight that we owe to the utilitarians). But the proper data must be isolated from irrelevancies and then treated with far more care and precision than in the past, when even the ethicians who relied most on human life for their data did so in a rough and inaccurate fashion, instead of making careful records and comparisons from the mass of random facts stored in their memories. Until such records are kept from the observation of actual cases and the data are scientifically compared and correlated, the method of ethics will never be exact enough to furnish reliable results. What is needed for a sound study of the operation of moral law is the case method, with careful notations of the progress of each individual recorded and studied. These records must be kept and analyzed with an impartial and unbiased attitude of mind which will allow the facts to speak for themselves and make possible the isolation of the true causal factors. Much material that would repay such analysis is already available in the form of records of juvenile, criminal, and divorce courts, and the case records of psychiatrists and social workers. Ministers, priests, and rabbis are in an excellent position to make independent case records which would be very illuminating if they were compiled with sufficient objectivity.[1]

Kant's suggestion that biography provides an important source for study of the operation of moral law deserves to be put into effect. There are, however, some difficulties in using biography for this purpose. The greatest is that the biographer is usually too much of an interpreter who wishes either to idealize or to depreciate his subject. The older school of eulogistic biography and the recent school of debunking biography are both equally untrustworthy for the student of moral law. The biographies best suited for the ethician's purpose are those which approach their subject without a distinct bias, which make no effort to distort facts or to misinterpret them, either to justify or to damn their subject. The work of the late Gamaliel Bradford is a case in point; for in such books as his *Damaged Souls,* one sees clearly the operation of moral law in the lives of Aaron Burr, Benedict Arnold, and the others whom he studies. Mr. Bradford approached his task in the conscious effort to see how moral causes and effects actually operated in the lives of his subjects, and in his *Biography and the Human Heart,* he writes this illuminating passage about his sources:

Besides physical health, there is moral health, or ill-health, which makes the stuff and matter of biography, because it makes the stuff and matter of all life. There is moral health as regards one's self, in the aspect of temptation and yielding. Some of the amplest biographical records, like the *Confessions* of Saint Augustine, deal fully with human nature in this aspect, too fully, some of us think, with amplification of sin, for the sake of emphasizing repentance. There is the temptation of drink, as we find it minutely and curiously exposed in the narrative of John B. Gough. There are the manifold liabilities of sex, exhibited only too freely in records of every kind. There is sex, joyous, naked, and unashamed, as we find it in Casanova or in the wild *Diary* of Aaron Burr. There is sex, timid, respectable, cautious, repentant, as we find it in the *Diary of Pepys.* There are the temptations of money, mere disorder and incompetence, as they are depicted so tragically in the *Diary* of Haydon, sordid and petty as they appear in Augustine or Rousseau, on a larger and more dubious scale, as

---

[1] The closest approximation to the type of independent case record desirable for ethics is to be found in Bonnell, *Pastoral Psychiatry.*

we meet them in the lives of men like Blaine or Ben Butler. And again, there is the inner spiritual weakness, the mere infirmity of will eaten away by excessive power or subtlety of the pure intelligence, as it is analyzed in the strange histories of Amiel or Barbellion.[2]

The use of autobiographies for moral analysis has also some value, but here more caution needs to be exercised than with biography. In addition to the tendency noted by Mr. Bradford to exaggerate one's sins because of an inverted pride in being chief of sinners, there is the further fact that others are usually more truthful and more objective in dealing with one's life than one's self. Consequently, it is even more difficult for the moralist to disentangle motives and to interpret controversial facts in autobiography than in biography. A good biography is likely to be far more profitable to the student of moral law than all but exceptionally truthful autobiographies.

In homiletical and other types of edifying literature it is the custom to draw illustrations of the inexorable working of moral law from the lives of characters in fiction or drama. While the moral struggle of such characters as Hester Prynne, Eustasia Vye, Anna Karenina, Macbeth, Hamlet, and a host of others is depicted in masterly fashion, the actual lives recorded in biography and history afford far more suitable material for the serious student of moral law. However true to life the psychology of characters in literature may be, the study of them will only mislead the student; for not only are these wholly or partly imaginary, but the plot of any novel or play has a specious and artificial unity of pattern in its action which rarely occurs in life. Hence the science of ethics cannot draw accurate enough data from even the greatest masters of fiction, who on the whole tend to delineate either villains or heroes rather than real men and women in whom the good and the bad are inextricably and bewilderingly mingled together and whose lot in life does not usually show that strict correspondence with their deserts that the author can mete out to his characters in a story.

While the careful application of the case method would doubtless enable ethics to become considerably more scientific than it has been in the past, there are still other problems of ethical method that

[2] Bradford, *Biography and the Human Heart*, pp. 17–18.

remain to be solved; one of the most important is the lack of any
measuring unit for such studies. The physical sciences and to a large
extent the natural sciences have the enormous advantage of dealing
with objects that are amenable to quantitative measurement by
mathematical means. Even the social sciences, though their measures
are not so precise, have some mathematical units at their disposal to
which their data can be at least partially reduced, such as the census
(simple enumeration), statistical comparisons from which quotients
of correlation can be obtained, and, lately, polls of public opinion.
So far, ethics has developed no corresponding means of reducing
its object to some quantitative basis. While it would indeed be
difficult to imagine a measuring unit for such intangibles as motives
or those dispositions which produce either the virtues or their opposites, it would be quite possible in determining the statistical
probabilities in operatives such as lying and stealing.

Moreover, much more could be done toward ascertaining causes
and effects in ethics than has hitherto been attempted. Simple
enumeration is a method beset with many fallacies, but in studying
causal principles it would be better than nothing. More than half
a century ago Herbert Spencer complained about the uncertainty of
the causal factors in ethics, but neither he himself nor any later
ethician suggested any corrective for the difficulty. The general
method pursued by even the greatest ethicians has been simply to
assert that certain causes produce certain effects, without any effort
to check whether the supposed causes actually do produce those
particular effects or not. The result has been, of course, that all
negative instances have been ignored and no attempt has been made
to demonstrate that the cause was really moral rather than physical
or psychological. Here even the method of simple enumeration
would have been a remedy, especially if followed up by the usual
tests of inductive logic to determine whether the cause is really what
it is supposed to be or not. In ethics, as in every other field, a cause
can be separated from extraneous and accidental accompaniments
only by being subjected to one of these inductive tests, either the
joint method of agreement and difference or concomitant variation.
The functioning of the operative moral laws can be decided by the

first, that of the regulatives and normatives by the second of these inductive canons of causality.

Many riddles of the moral sphere might be greatly clarified by conducting polls of moral sentiment, for if these can predict and test with a high degree of accuracy such imponderables as the popularity of a political candidate, they should be able to deal with normatives in the moral realm, which are even less imponderable. Effects are ascertainable only by such means, and it is the duty of ethicians to use the devices that lie at hand to improve their method and to add other devices to them until it becomes really precise and as scientific as that of any of the social sciences.

We can decide whether causes are in fact such, and effects are measurable within certain limits. If we were sufficiently openminded to put aside the prejudices and preconceptions which foredoom to failure most of our attempts to learn any truth in the moral realm, we could discover how to measure the disorder caused by the exterior consequences of infractions of moral law. It is more doubtful whether we shall ever be able to measure their subjective consequences in anything but a very rough and ready fashion, by noting the observed signs of the disintegration of the personality in question—which the psychiatrist and the physician are usually in a better position to know than is the ethician. With regard to motives we shall probably not in the near future go much beyond what the courts are at present able to do in criminal cases, that is, to establish whether a deed is premeditated and what were probably the principal motives that inspired it. Indeed, far from being illuminated by the revelations of modern psychology as to the complexity of motive, the whole problem has rather been rendered more obscure. The only scientific attitude for ethics to adopt is to shift its center and emphasis away as far as possible from the obscure and tangled subject of motive toward the relatively measurable and objective sphere of effects.

Furthermore, this new science needs to have ethicians experiment with new methods and procedures in the field, since here, as in other sciences, the expert will have to supply the more technical work of his science. To him will fall primarily the task of devising the experiments and conducting the surveys and case studies that will yield the data he needs. It will be his duty to investigate the conditions favorable to the development of character by the survey of actual case records from the past in the form of biography or history, and from reliable contemporary records compiled either by himself or by other competent observers. He must then work over his observations and records and by analyzing, correlating, and systematizing the data he has gathered must reduce them to a co-ordinated body of sound and valid results. He will codify the new operative laws as he discovers them in the course of his investigations. He will formulate the new regulative principles as he discerns them and will record the new normative principles as they are created. It will then be his function to present the body of results for verification by other competent investigators, so that his findings will gain acceptance and prestige equal to those of other sciences. While the science of ethics remains in the pioneer stage, the ethician, besides having to create the methods of his science as he goes along, will be obliged to strive for the kind of impressive practical results that will command respect for his new science from the general public.

Nowadays the more thoughtful observers bemoan the fact that our ethical and spiritual progress has lagged so far behind our scientific and technological advancement. But we have worked for many centuries for the knowledge that has brought about this scientific progress. What we have *not* worked for is ethical and spiritual progress! Here and there throughout those same centuries a few ethical and religious teachers have thought and taught about moral problems; but how few have they been in comparison to the scientists, and how sporadic the labor of the ethicians compared to that of the research expert in all branches of science! Those who lament our lack of moral progress take one of two attitudes: either that we know the answers in morals and have always known them, but do not apply them, or that we cannot get the answer to moral problems because the whole field is simply a matter of opinion and preference. Neither position is true. The fact is that we do have some moral solutions and we do possess some moral laws from the past, which, though not enough to answer all the questions of the present, are still sufficient so that we can learn to find the answers to some. On the other hand, it cannot be too strongly emphasized that not all the answers to moral questions have been handed down from heaven on tables of stone or on gold plates. Rather, it is a truly religious attitude to perceive that just as God has left to man the discovery of natural law in the universe in which he must carry on his struggle for existence, so, in like manner, in the realm of ethics, God seems to have left to man a large part of the discovery of moral law. Even as man had to learn for himself how the laws of nature operate, so he must learn how the moral laws within human nature and human society operate. For the truth is that we have not yet learned a sure method of obtaining these laws, and we shall never progress morally until we get a method of dealing with the data of morals that is comparable, in sureness, to the scientific method.

When one appreciates the embryonic character of ethical methodology, one is no longer surprised that our known code of moral laws is so small in number and precision in comparison with the body of well-established scientific laws. Yet it must be remembered that science first began to progress by leaps and bounds when it formulated a precise method of dealing with its objects and accurate instruments for investigating them. Nor did the scientific method come about in a day or a century; rather it is the product of the work and thought of many minds from the time of Aristotle to that of John Stuart Mill, a period of some twenty-two or twenty-three centuries. Now the object of ethics is infinitely more complex and variable than that of any other science (except perhaps psychology, whose status as a bona fide science, be it observed, is the least assured of any); therefore, we should not be discouraged that we have not forged an ethical method within approximately the same period, from the time that Socrates first applied inductive analysis to the problems of ethics to the present day. Difficult as it is, the formulation will come in time if we are willing to learn how to work for it. Already we have some clews, and more will follow if we really work for ethical advance with anything like the industry and fervor that the scientists have shown.

Some scales must fall from our eyes if we desire ethical progress. Not only must we put aside vain lamentations that we have not attained ethical progress or cannot get it, but we must face the fact that we have not desired it enough even to learn how to get it. Furthermore, we must face the fact that we know but little about ethics, that it is still in the alchemy stage, and then, putting aside the prejudices and preconceptions that foredoom to failure all efforts to gain truth in the moral realm, we must prepare to labor hard to forge an ethical method that will enable us to make new discoveries in that realm and to find answers to the age-old problems that have come down unsolved from the past. Perhaps in the course of a few centuries the human race will be able to progress morally and spiritually at a rate comparable to that of scientific progress since Galileo.

CHAPTER XIII

UNSOLVED PROBLEMS AND UNDIS-
CERNED ENDS IN ETHICS

THE PRESENT chapter treats the third phase of the present status of ethics, its unsolved problems and undiscerned ends. Three sorts of problems will be included in this discussion: those which ethicians in the past have failed to perceive or touch upon at all, those which they have treated in a superficial or inadequate manner, so that no satisfactory solution has been reached; and, finally, those to which they have given the wrong solution.

The problem of war is one which the ethicians have treated very inadequately, though they have written about it from time to time throughout the centuries, without ever sufficiently going into the issues involved to view them realistically. This is one of the major failures of ethics. Teachers of ethics have not even been of one mind as to whether war is right or wrong, or right under certain circumstances and wrong under others. All three positions are represented in their writings. Saint Thomas Aquinas, who held the middle position, goes into the question at some length, Kant wrote a little-known treatise entitled *The Way to Perpetual Peace*, which, as the title implies, suggests certain means of securing peace.[1] Jesus, Confucius, and Gautama advocated peace, but none of them went into the issues of war and peace extensively. In fact, no traditional discussion of the subject is ethically adequate for the present century, because while wars have gone on throughout human history they have never been of global magnitude until now, and the contributory causes were not so involved and on such a large scale, nor were the implements with which they were waged so formidable as those which science has placed in modern hands. Since wars are of global magnitude, global effort must be directed, not only toward abolishing them, but toward eradicating their causes and setting up

---

[1] This treatise has recently been re-edited and published under the above title, by the Columbia University Press, 1929.

some effective international authority by which disputes shall be settled.

The average modern pacifist has failed completely to comprehend the enormity and complexity of the problems that must be solved before there can be peace in the world. The diplomat and the statesman may not be able to give a solution to these colossal problems, but they know of their existence and staggering size, while the pacifist is disposed to think that good will is all that is needed to obtain permanent peace. No doubt good will could help by eradicating some of the grievances that contribute to the brewing of wars and by obliterating some of the unbrotherly attitudes that dispose the minds of men to carnage; but it is a great oversimplification of the problem to think that good will alone could abolish wars. For that purpose it is necessary to remove the seeds of war and to set up some effective and powerful international medium for settling disputes which will have the authority to cause and, if need be, to compel all parties concerned to submit to its decisions.

The mere enumeration of a few of the problems to which at least a temporary solution must be found before we can have peace reveals their complexity. They are racial, cultural, economic, and political, and aside from removing these roots of war there are enormous obstacles to be overcome before some international organization can be set up in such a manner as to gain allegiance of the diverse nations of this globe in order to settle conflicts without resort to war. These problems must be settled by experts possessing the requisite knowledge; therefore it is wiser to confine this discussion to defining the exact function of ethics with regard to the great international problem of war and peace.

Ethics and religion can contribute to this effort chiefly by creating the disposition to settle these problems, since neither the academic philosopher who makes a theoretical study of ethics nor the ordinary religious person has the technical knowledge to do more than to make very general suggestions concerning the moral aspects of the solutions.

Ethics has a major concern in the creation of a world that is good for man, that provides a climate suited to the growth of character and the improvement of human life on the moral level. Therefore it should strive to visualize a world that would meet those conditions, so far as it is able to foresee and state them; and at the very least it should direct all its efforts toward seeing that we do not get a world that is antithetical to all ethical values. A world run on the Four Freedoms of President Roosevelt (who at his best displays ethical vision of a very high order) and the Declarations of the Atlantic Charter would provide a good climate for ethics. A world that is at peace is a far better climate for virtues to thrive in than one subject to periodic conflicts that uproot all the fine values, except the martial set, which hardly comprises a permanent pattern for character. The stake of ethics in securing a free and a stable world, no longer subject to wars, is to see that it is a world conducive to the growth of character and the betterment of personality, which is a wider concern than even economic equality and racial adjustments. Ethics should try to envision a world which is adapted to that moral progress our civilization did not make in the old world that is now in conflagration. But to sketch the blueprint of that world is the task of a science, and to meet that challenge ethics must grow into a science.

Ethics has also failed to set up moral substitutes for force in conflicts of all sorts. Aristotle and Saint Thomas Aquinas exalted the ideal of justice in society and so did the Hebrew Prophets; but there is much truth in Reinhold Niebuhr's reiteration that we shall never get a social order based on love until we first get one of justice. Justice can never prevail so long as there are unrighted wrongs and unredressed injuries; and the only way that the world knows to right these—if it is possible to right them at all—is by force. Now two conditions must be satisfied if we are ever to have a global society based on justice. First, there must be a clear insight as to what constitutes the resolution of conflicts, an exact definition of what the just conditions would be; then some moral means must be devised for realizing these conditions, or, if need be, for trying the experiments necessary to discover what they are, since it is not always possible to judge this a priori, and high-sounding schemes do not always work out in practice as they do in theory.

On the side of substitutes for force and nonviolent means of attaining ends, it is possible that Gandhi's techniques of nonviolent resistance are his most significant contribution to moral progress, whatever the verdict of history on this controversial figure may be. Granted that these techniques do not now apply in war, where one or both sides recognize nothing but the major force, they are proving a satisfactory means of redressing smaller-scale wrongs in economic and social life. The sit-down strike has annoyed out of measure certain American magnates in whose plants it has been employed; but, ethically speaking, it is a vast improvement over the old-fashioned violent strike, in which the governor called out the state militia and blood was shed before the dispute was settled.

In conflicts there is, however, the difficult matter of perceiving the right lines along which a just solution to the problem lies, and here ethics has lagged noticeably behind even its own declared principles. To take an example at our own door. In America the Negro problem has existed since 1619. As early as the Revolution there were those who, like George Washington and Thomas Jefferson, disapproved of slavery on economic grounds or moral grounds or both; but it took the Civil War to free the slaves. Now Negroes are free in the sense that they are no longer in a condition of involuntary servitude; but they are still a long way from anything resembling equality of status with their white fellow countrymen, though equality for all is one of the cardinal professions of American democracy. Moreover, up to the present time no one in either the North or the South has put forward any thoroughgoing solution to this vexing problem; meanwhile the conflict between the two racial groups grows more acute. There has not even been a clear appreciation of all the elements involved, and partial remedies and palliatives have been put forward rather than a concerted attack on the whole problem. Indeed, there has never been any widespread disposition on the part of the public to find the solution, and for that apathy ethicians must take their share of the blame along with sociologists, economists, and the clergy.

Similar comments could be made concerning other interracial conflicts. Only the anthropologists have produced any valuable data which bear on racial questions in general. They have shown the fallaciousness of any notion of racial purity; but, since they are scientists whose province is facts rather than values, they have laid down no ethical principles on racial questions in general. However, it is the particular function of ethics to discover the right regulative and normative principles, and starting from the findings of anthropology, it should indicate the broad lines of a right solution and leave the detailed application to the specialists in the field and the enforcement to the government, which has the necessary power.

Another urgent modern problem, one that directly concerns character, about which ethics has had all too little to say, is power, though this is no new problem. The only novelty about this problem in our day is that it has become so stupendous and so acute since the first World War. Gautama displayed some awareness of its dangers, chiefly because he reckoned it among the creators of karma, but he developed no extended philosophy on the subject. Jesus was keenly aware of its perils to the spirit and regarded it as a barrier to the Kingdom of God; but he believed that it would soon be displaced by service in the new era of the Reign of God (Mark 10: 42–45). Therefore we have from him only the two or three sayings about it in the passage just cited. Saint Thomas Aquinas dismissed it with a brief and superficial discussion as one of those goods which cannot be an end in itself. The others, down to our own time, have largely ignored this issue. But nowadays some philosophers and some theologians have begun to show awareness of the need to formulate principles for its ethical use. Bertrand Russell's book *Power* is such an attempt by a philosopher, and Reinhold Niebuhr, among theologians, has shown a clear conception of the problem, which he has treated at some length in several books.

We cannot avoid facing the problem of power in our generation, for it hangs like the sword of Damocles over the destinies of all living men today and already has destroyed many with its strokes. Gautama, in the India of his day, could escape from it into nirvana, and the early Christians could cherish the faith that the millennium would soon abolish it. Kant and Spinoza had slight encounters with it, but they were able to pursue their studies and forget it. However, in our time there is no better refuge from power for the philosopher than for the common man. We cannot hope to rid ourselves of power; all that we can hope for is that those who have it in their hands can learn to use it without its corroding their own souls and enslaving or destroying those under their sway.

We have some great regulatives that apply to those who wield power. There is the service principle of Jesus, and there is the second great maxim of Kant, that we should never use human beings as means, but always as ends. In addition to these general regulatives, the leaders of the democracies of today have an enviable chance to set normative principles for its ethical use, not for our generation only, but for all generations. The task of the ethician is the more humble one of recognizing and codifying these normative principles, since he is not likely to hold the power in his own hands.

A single piece of obscurantism has clung persistently to ethics throughout its entire history in both the East and the West and has been the source of four of its most signal failures and mistakes. That is the belief that the flesh and all that is connected with it is bad and that consequently the true philosopher must rise above all the drives of the flesh, that the good life consists in transcending all the physical and material side in so far as that is compatible with the maintenance of life itself. This belief is the chief cause of the failure of ethics to develop a philosophy of ends and means by which the physical and the material may foster and further the life of the mind and the spirit; it is the reason for the lack of any ethical guidance for the conduct of the economic and working relationships which are so large a part of man's total existence. It has been responsible for the warped and perverted thinking on the subject of sex of which most of even the greatest ethical teachers have been guilty. Finally it has been the chief root of their failure to understand emotions and to develop techniques for control and direction of these in the building of character.

Throughout the ages the moralist has generally been inclined to underestimate the value of the material to the spiritual, and up to the very present the ethician, holding to his dichotomy between flesh and spirit, mind and matter, has failed to realize the continuum that exists between the material and spiritual or to perceive that the former is the matrix for the latter, without which there can no more be life of the mind and spirit than there can be fire without fuel. In its simon pure form this dualism has expressed itself in Rousseau's dream of a reversion to the state of nature, where his brainchild, the good savage, flourished; it actuated Tolstoi's repudiation of modern civilization in his recession to the simple life of the Russian muzhik. In its most extreme form we find it in Lao-tze's nihilism, which was hostile to all civilization, culture, and activity; but it expresses itself even today in Gandhi's economic notions of return to the hand-loom stage of industrial development. In the present century this devaluation of the material has been particularly disastrous; for it is the chief cause of the failure of Western ethics to develop a sane and judicious appraisal of the function of material advance as a matrix for the moral and the spiritual.

In the West we have an abundance, perhaps a surfeit, of things, comforts and conveniences, appliances and technological devices made possible by the increasing mastery of science over nature. These devices are here to stay, unless our civilization destroys itself in devastating wars, so that these secrets are lost in a general reversion to barbarism. The way for ethics to deal with them is not to despise and denounce them, as has all too frequently been done; that attitude is foolish and futile. Instead, we should be trying to discover how these instruments that science has placed in our hands may serve to better the lot of humanity, how they may serve as doors to open up great new vistas of the life of the mind, and what are their potentialities for enkindling the fire of spirit. Instead of using these devices for the upbuilding of humanity, we have used them at best for the dissipation of our energies through the pursuit of inconsequential pleasures and diversions and at worst for our own destruction. No one has given us the vision of the lofty and exalting ends which these things might serve. The scientist has taken the cautious standpoint that his concern is only to give mankind the fruit of his discoveries and inventions and that the use made of them is the problem of whoever concerns himself with values, whether the philosopher or the theologian. What has been lacking is the perception of the ethical and spiritual potentialities latent in this great material advance. Instead of deploring or despising the materialism of our civilization, the moralist should be devoting himself to discovering how it can foster the life of the mind and the spirit, how it can further the progress of mankind.

Our failure to use the fruits of science for human betterment has been due partly to our lack of vision, partly to the fact that the patents for the processes and the inventions are the property of the great industrial corporations, who tend to use them principally for profit and only incidentally for the improvement of human existence. Only in medicine is the best that science knows available for the service of human beings, and even this must sometimes be bought at a price beyond the purse of the masses. Both the scientists and the government have more responsibility than they have hitherto been willing to assume to see that the fruits of science are used for the benefit of humanity and directed toward the production of finer human personalities. This enterprise should really be a co-operative one for scientists, educators, clergymen, and government officials, in order that there may be the vision, the knowledge, and the power to apply these devices for the welfare of mankind.

The benefits that might accrue from moral direction of our material advances range from the saving of mere mechanical drudgery up to the mental, moral, and spiritual levels that should be emergents from the material advances. Those possessed of moral insight should have given us this direction, but they have not. Instead they have either had nothing to say about this continuum between the material and the spiritual, or they have merely denounced the material gains as barriers and obstacles to spiritual progress. Instead of forming with this mastery of matter the matrix for a higher and more widely diffused culture than the world has ever seen, because of our lack of moral vision we have brought about the present condition: that the use and exploitation of our scientific knowledge has been hit or miss and has fallen into unscrupulous hands, so that civilization is on the high road to destruction by the formidable weapons placed by science in its hands. It may yet be that through the vision of the humane and the ethical use of things we can salvage the remnants from chaos; but we should begin at once to get insight into the latent spiritual potentialities of our material progress. For "it is later than we think."

Akin to the failure of ethics to provide the formulation of the humane and spiritual direction for these material gains is the absence of ethical ideals and principles to govern the conduct of man's economic life, particularly in the working relationship, though this is one of the oldest relationships in human society. In antiquity only Zoroaster (660–583 B.C.), the founder of the ancient and now almost extinct religion of the Persians, made the ethical discovery that there is creative value in work, which he considered to contribute to building the Righteous Order of his god, Ahura Mazda. However, his discovery is seldom noticed, and it never became the foundation of any later ethic of work. There are various reasons for the fact that the great ethical teachers have not thought about the problems related to the struggle for existence. Confucius was a scholar and a courtier who seems not to have given the matter any particular consideration. The Buddha never was a worker; as a young man in his father's house he belonged to the leisure class; later he escaped from all economic obligations, those creators of karma, into the unencumbered life of an Indian holy man, supported by the charity of the faithful. Christianity inherited from Jesus and Paul the eschatological hope that the present age, with all its manifold social, economic, and political relationships, would soon be superseded by the new age of the Kingdom of God. Although Saint Paul was obliged to correct the practice of giving up all work, to which extreme some of the Thessalonian Christians carried the eschatological hope, his intention was to do so only for the interim. Thus, all in all, the primitive church never developed any philosophy of work beyond his admonition to the Thessalonians that he who would not work should not eat. Indeed, the early church never visualized any conspicuous modification of existing society. The medieval church also failed to develop any well-rounded economic ethic, except on individual points such as usury and honesty in trade, which Saint Thomas treats. But the chief reason for the lack of interest in such matters in that era was that everyone accepted the stratifications of medieval society as divinely ordained. In the Reformation, Luther proclaimed the principle that the maid in the kitchen served God with her work as truly as the monk in the cloister, but he refused to recognize the logic of his principle when he repudiated the Peasants' Revolt. Then came Calvin, who embraced rising capitalism with fervor and exalted thrift and diligence in business into prime Christian virtues. Down to the present there has been no thoroughgoing Christian ethic of economics. A start toward one has been made in this century by the exponents of the so-called Social Gospel and by the recent Malvern Conference to formulate a Christian code; but such efforts have remained sporadic and largely theoretical. Still today no significant and normative code of economic and industrial ethics has been produced either within or without the church.

All in all, it is a fact that the ethician of the past felt unconsciously superior to anything so material as the struggle for existence. The resultant lack of ethical ideals in this important area of life is all too apparent in the present economic situation. While our great industrialists sometimes mouth the claim that the service principle is the inspiration of their enterprises, the fact has been that profit and self-interest are the real regulatives on which our industries and corporations have, with a few outstanding exceptions, been conducted. Those who hold the power in economic life have shown little disposition to mitigate voluntarily the abuses of the working relationship which give rise to conflicts with their employees; and they seldom mete out justice by righting these wrongs unless the government or some powerful labor union compels them to do so. In like manner, when the workers get sufficient power to assert themselves, they are likely to use the same tactics, especially under the influence of certain unscrupulous labor leaders. Indeed, neither the employers nor the unions have shown any noticeable aptitude for elaborating ethical codes for their various crafts and industries, and the fixing of whatever standards there are results for the most part from government regulation and legislation.

Now ethics has a stake in economic and industrial problems, because they are the principal centers of danger to the values of human personality. Here the Kantian maxim that persons should always be used as ends, but never as means, is being violated wholesale.

This second maxim of Kant is one of the three great regulatives that apply to the working relationship. The other is the key principle of reciprocity, but until now no one has elaborated its implications in the employer-employee relationship. Toward the public, service is really the right principle, but labor does not even pretend to operate on it, and capital has largely been insincere in claiming to do so. These three general principles can be indicated by the ethician, but he can do little more than define the general ends and regulative principles that apply to the working and other economic relationships. The further definition of ethical ends in industrial life and the indication of its potentialities for the development of human personality would form no mean contribution toward making this a world that is really good for man. The actual implementation of these principles and the formulation of codes for various industries must be the work of those who have both a specialized knowledge of the various phases of economic life and a fine sense of human values, such as the best labor leaders and exceptional employers do have.

The question whether riches and material comforts and possessions further or impede the individual's progress in the good life is one about which there has been the greatest diversity of opinion, and unfortunately none of the ethical teachers of the past was able to solve it in an entirely satisfactory manner. Some of them, especially those with a strong religious interest, have maintained that the good life and the life of poverty are identical, while others assert that a certain portion of this world's goods is a necessary precondition of the good life, both for its creation for oneself and for sharing it with others.

Jesus and Gautama agree that riches and many possessions are a serious barrier to the spiritual life, but the two do not draw the line at the same point as to what measure of them is desirable. Like Confucius, Aristotle taught that a comfortable backing of wealth and possessions was a necessary precondition for the good life, since

without it one could not provide the finer things of life for himself
nor have the surplus needed to share with others. Saint Thomas
Aquinas, at once a Christian and an Aristotelian, effects an ingenious compromise between his masters by means of a dual ethic for
the clergy and the laity. According to the saint, poverty is part of the
counsel of perfection prescribed for those in holy orders, but the
layman may enjoy even great wealth, provided only that it is hon-
estly acquired and that it is held as a trust from God to be shared
with those who are less fortunate. Spinoza and Kant do not take any
stand on this matter at all.

In short, the advice of the ethicians concerning wealth and poverty is conflicting and varies with almost every teacher. In the light
of this conflict, what attitude can the science of ethics reasonably
assume on this question? It cannot ignore the problem, since questions of wealth and poverty are more burning ethical issues at the
present time than they have been since the time of the Lollards.
It is, indeed, a delicate task for the ethician to determine what
measure of material comforts and possessions advances the spiritual
life and what retards or impedes it. Perhaps it is impossible to determine the exact proportion that provides the best spiritual climate
for any particular individual, since this probably varies widely; but
some statements can be made on the basis of economic necessities,
now that economic forces are better understood than they were by
past generations. Modern experience clearly demonstrates that poverty as it exists in the twentieth century by no means makes for
spirituality. Quite the contrary! Modern sociology has established
that the extreme poverty of the city slum district is a major cause
of crime. Moreover, the pursuit of spirituality through mendicant
orders has all but lost its appeal to the modern man, because it
is now plain that such a step means nothing but the evasion of economic responsibilities and involves the shifting of the obligation
to produce to the shoulders of someone else.

On the other hand, the vast fortunes that have been built up in
this machine age, often by questionable means, are likely to be as
bad a climate for the growth of the good life as the poverty of
the slum-dweller who is below the subsistence minimum. One of

the tasks of scientific ethics will be to create a mode of dealing with this problem. It is not too much to assert on the basis of sociological studies of wealth and poverty in the modern world that while the exact measure of wealth and possessions most wholesome for ethical development in individual cases may vary, for the majority it will be found to lie somewhere between that extreme poverty which has been demonstrated to breed crime and the vast fortunes which soften the moral fiber by luxurious living and carry with them the temptation to drift along without effort and to gratify one's every whim. The good life requires only enough material resources to provide a foundation and matrix for the cultivation of the higher values.

Certainly, when the problem is viewed from a social standpoint it is apparent that a more equitable economic distribution would go far toward promoting the good life. The tremendous inequalities of the distribution of wealth in modern society make for hatreds and rivalries; and the struggle to obtain wealth brings men into a ruthless and bitter competition that often renders them incapable of the altruism and co-operativeness required by life in this world, which is a geographical unit. It has been a misfortune that for the most part the great ethical teachers have displayed so little understanding of the part played by economic forces in determining man's moral life; else by now we might have had a realistic ethic of wealth, based on knowledge and fact rather than on opinion and guesswork, to guide the modern world through its severe economic upheavals and conflicts.

While the idea that the physical and material side of life is low and valueless from the moral standpoint has prevented the development of an adequate philosophy, either of the use of material advances for the development of character or of the right regulative principles for the control of economic relationships, it has furthermore been the root of much wrong thinking on the subject of sex. To be sure, the trouble is not that this subject has been neglected or passed over by traditional ethics; plenty of thinking and writing has been done about it by ethical teachers of every age. However, the problem has been badly handled on the whole, because it has been viewed from an ascetic, even monastic, standpoint. The theory of most ethicians has been that the good and wise man lived above the flesh and the evil drives inherent in it, of which sex is a major one, and in consequence their thinking has been misogynic and warped. It is probably not accidental that most of the great ethical teachers were unmarried. Their ideal tacitly or expressly contained the following propositions: that sex, being of the flesh, was largely an evil; that even the marital state was lower than that of celibacy, therefore unbecoming to a philosopher; and that woman was inferior to man and an instrument of temptation. Since the Reformation the world has been gradually outgrowing this age-old notion, wrong and perverted as it is, but it is unfortunate that not much adequate philosophy of sex has come to supplant it. Sex is one of those broad questions which has biological, psychological, and ethical aspects, all of which must be taken into account in the formulation of any well-rounded ideal on the subject, and the scientific facts known about all aspects of this powerful drive must be the foundation of any such ethical ideal.

Out of some scientific knowledge, out of much ill-advised experimentation and all-too-frequent discussions of sex matters by everybody from doctors and psychiatrists to novelists and playwrights, some canons for an ideal of sex relationships have emerged. The monogamous ideal has maintained itself as the best for both the individual and society, in spite of some advocates of other solutions, more ingenious than convincing. For the individual, the sex relationship should be such as to give him psychological and moral integration, should be expanding and enriching to all sides of his personality, and should be the source of character values and spiritual potentialities of the highest order, which are ever latent in the relationship at its best. For the couple, mutuality is the key principle; for, while unrequited love may beget selflessness, yet in general it tends to be futile and to verge on the morbid and the neurotic. For the couple, then, mutuality is essential to the finest and most integrating spiritual kinship and for that fusion of personality that includes the whole range of values higher than just the physical union alone—though this is also more important than the ethical teachers have generally perceived.

The greatest lack in our present moral philosophy of sex is the failure to set up any ideal, even in theory, for those who do not achieve the desired ideal in marriage, either because they do not marry at all or because the marriage relationship proves unsatisfactory. What shall happen to members of society who fail to realize in marriage the kind of union that is wholesome, healthful, and psychologically integrating? It is still too widely taken for granted that their state is purely their personal problem and that it is up to each individual to make whatever sublimations or compensations he can or to find whatever other outlet, licit or illicit, is open to him. The stronger persons can, of course, take celibacy in their stride, and there are probably as many well-adjusted persons among the single as among the married; but there are also a goodly number of others—though no census enumerates them—who are not only a problem to themselves and their friends because of their unfulfilled and frustrated existence but even constitute potential trouble centers to society. Has any ethician formulated adequate ideals to cover their state?

What has ethics to say to those who have not found satisfaction in the marital relationship or have had the tie severed through divorce? For a long time all that the moralists could do was to devote their efforts to keeping divorce from becoming legal; but now that it has become legal and in most circles socially acceptable, what has ethics to say of the state of the divorced person? So far, it has not even formulated a theoretical ideal concerning the conduct of such persons, and it has not shown society how to prevent divorce, to shield the children of divorcés from harm caused by the separation of the parents, or to preserve the principals from being shattered by the experience and enable them to readjust to life on a new basis.

On the whole, the ethical teachers have failed to achieve a more adequate ideal of sex because it furnishes such a powerful drive that their classic remedy has been repression; and, of course, the older ethicians knew nothing of its endocrine basis. In a lesser degree they have failed to understand how to control and direct other emotions, which they thought could be uprooted or repressed in order to secure the kind of self-control essential to the good life. The result has been that, though ethics has been able to formulate numerous ideals of the good, it has been weak on the side of implementing them, because the emotions involved were so frequently misunderstood and no adequate techniques for directing them were evolved. Indeed, to this day it is one of the major limitations of all our attempts at character education that we still understand so little about wholesome and integrating emotional education.

Various suggestions have been put forward by the ethical teachers of the past for implementing the good life by techniques of emotional control that would lead to virtue. These include the possession of knowledge of the good, strength of will, right intention, meditation and contemplation, example, and education. The merits of most of these are assessed in the course of the discussion of the ethical teachers who suggested them. None of them seems to be a perfect and complete device, though some of the suggestions are more valuable than others. The formation of good habits, for instance, was put forward by Aristotle and Saint Thomas Aquinas, and more recently by William James, as the main technique for the acquisition of virtue. Certainly habits are very important constituents of the good life, for we are told that the repetition of acts deepens the paths of the synapses in the brain and thus indelibly stamps them into its very physical structure. The persistence and force of habits are obvious on a merely common-sense basis, but there is always the chance that even though these good habits are formed, the emotions and impulses behind them may exhibit a strange and subtle lack of conformity with them. Theoretically, likewise, education should result in the discipline of character; but so far none of our educational systems has learned enough about the conditions for the formation of character and the education of the emotions so that character training can truthfully be claimed as more than an incidental by-product and concomitant of the training of the intellect and the perpetuation of the cultural heritage. No single device contains the magic formula for goodness, nor would all of them together prove the "Open Sesame" to the good life. There is still much to learn about the control of emotions and the method by which they may best be oriented to the goals of ethics.

Thus, though some individual suggestions for the discipline of the emotions have been valuable—some more so than others—all in all, traditional ethics, as Dr. Richard Cabot observed,[2] has been much stronger on the side of forming ideals than of implementing them. Usually, too, it was not perceived that the emotions, if rightly directed, could be a great asset to the good life, rather than a hindrance, as the Buddhists in the East and the Stoics in the West agreed in considering them. The strength of the emotions the ethical teachers knew, but they did not know enough about their physical and chemical bases to understand how they worked, and it seems not to have occurred to anybody but Spinoza, and perhaps Confucius, that instead of being repressed or uprooted they could be controlled and directed so as to give power and depth to the moral tone of the good life.

There are two known major methods of emotional control, one age-old, the other rather new, or at least it has been carried to new lengths. These are mob psychology and propaganda. It is scarcely necessary to state that mob psychology results only in temporary hysteria which is evanescent and that it has no ethical value. Indeed, it is significant that the sects of Protestantism which formerly employed it in evangelistic revivals have all but given up the practice.

In our own time we have seen a high development of propaganda, which in its present form is the joint creation of American high-pressure advertising and the totalitarian states. If propaganda is administered to young people, it is very effective in fixating the emotions to whatever ends have been determined by those who prepare it, and its effects can hardly be eradicated. On the more mature it is often effective also, especially among the ignorant and those whose temperament inclines them more strongly to emotion than to thought. However, there is always the chance that its evil effects upon adults may be offset by a counter-barrage of propaganda from

---

[2] Cabot, *The Meaning of Right and Wrong*, p. 354 ff.

the opposite side. The method of propaganda, though an all-too-powerful means of controlling the emotions of large groups and even whole nations, is completely antithetical to the spirit of ethics, not only because the ends for which propaganda is designed are usually highly unscrupulous but also because it nullifies the freedom of the individual to set his own ends and decide his own destiny, which are of the essence in all moral decisions and conduct. The victim of propaganda is no longer free to "change his emotions" or to attach them to a different set of ends, as a moral being must be. He is a slave to the ideas that have been administered to him quite as much as the drug fiend is to his opiate.

A third device for emotional control is found in the devotional exercises of religious communities, within and without the Christian fold. These vary in nature from simple prayers and meditations on the character and the career of the religious hero or heroes to the highly mystic disciplines whose goal is the culmination of the *unio mystica*. Familiar Christian examples of the latter type are the writings of Saint John of the Cross and of his contemporary Saint Theresa; but in whatever faith the mystic discipline originates, the psychological procedure is amazingly similar in all faiths, the main variation being the coloration of imagery and theology lent by the particular religious ideology from which each springs. Even the *Upanishads* display a distinct psychological resemblance to other mystic meditations, except that they are preceded by and accompanied by the physical discipline of Yoga. But the purely psychological aspects are similar, and when the goal of nirvana is interpreted as union with Brahma, it is qualitatively indistinguishable from other forms of *unio mystica*. Now, strange (perhaps shocking) as it may seem, the mystic disciplines are not necessarily valuable instruments of ethical progress, because their main purpose is the purely religious one of union with the deity. The importance given to ethical improvement varies from none at all to much, as in *The Interior Castle*, which makes it one of the primary tests of the reality of the whole experience of union with God. However, even in this type what ethical progress results from the pursuit of the mystic discipline is really an incidental and secondary concomitant of the reorientation and integration of the emotions which follows the culmination of the *unio mystica*. It scarcely needs to be added that the inferior types of mysticism, especially those that lay little or no stress on ethical betterment, are sheer withdrawals from life and the moral problems it poses into the less demanding world of escape and phantasy.

However, apart from the mystic disciplines, which after all have been followed only by the few who have a bent for such experiences, the Church throughout its history has relied upon prayer and religious contemplation as its chief means of transforming character. Now, the moral fruits of the Christian ethic are undeniably present in the inner circle of those who, in all generations, have taken their religion with sufficient seriousness to make ethical improvement a major end of prayer; and presumably in other faiths also a certain approximation to the ethical pattern of the faith is achieved to the limits permitted by the temperament of the individual concerned. However, it is a sad fact that the Christian Church in the two thousand years it has been at work in the Western world has not succeeded in transforming and modifying the nature of the rank and file of its members very markedly—in spite of their prayers and supplications and observance of its rites. There are two reasons for this. The first is that prayer has to be pursued with great assiduity before it results in ethical transformation and has to be expressly focused on this end in order to be effective; whereas the prayers of the masses tend largely to remain on the wish-expression level. The second reason is that prayer can operate only upon the psychological level, and emotions, which are greatly conditioned on the chemical level of the hormones from several of the glands of internal secretion, may remain unaltered by psychological treatment.

For the normal person who pursues prayer with sufficient fervor and persistence, ethical improvement as far as the limits of his temperament allow may be, and often is, the result. Prayer at its best illumines the mind for self-analysis and gives a new perspective through the sense of communion with the Divine which it establishes. The result is a sense of ethical inspiration and reorientation which is very helpful in imparting earnestness and self-awareness to ethical endeavor. The second factor is autosuggestion, which operates in both religious and nonreligious meditation. This reinforces the individual's faith in his ethical ideal and in his own ability to achieve it.

Nevertheless, the kind of meditations and prayers ordinarily in use among religious groups have some limitations from the ethical standpoint, for they are all designed to give the individual only what preparation he can get for the ethical struggle in solitude. This objection holds true of all types of religious exercises, from the extreme mystic disciplines to the mild contemplations, and applies as much to group worship as to solitary meditation, since the individual is passive in them all, not active as in ethical endeavor and struggle. Solitude can give the individual illumination and perspective on his moral problems; but moral living takes place, not in solitude, but in society, in larger or smaller groups of which the individual is a member, and which impose upon him certain obligations that he must fulfill or deny. Often he must make his moral decisions on the spur of the moment and in the thick of the struggle, without having time to go apart and meditate on how he shall react to these categorical demands of social living. For that kind of decision, the solitary religious discipline affords but scant preparation and indeed is not calculated to foster the attitudes most needed in group living, such as co-operation, friendliness, good will, faith, loyalty, truthfulness and humor. These grow only out of the practice of living with others, working with them, playing with them, participating with them in all sorts of group activities. The hermit in his cell and the mystic in his trance cannot help us to develop these social virtues that come from the give-and-take of life itself.

How, then, would a strictly ethical discipline differ from a religious one? The solitary phase might be identical, except that the ethical aim would predominate. The meditation would start with that foundation stone of the moral life, self-analysis designed to beget self-awareness, to take stock of both the assets and the liabilities of one's temperament, to see one's failures and successes and the roots in the self that caused them both. Then, having gained perspective from self-scrutiny, the meditation would proceed to discover the pattern of goodness suited to one's own temperament and to direct the ethical aspirations toward achieving it and toward rising to ever-higher altitudes of moral living, up to the very limits that the temperament permits. The sanctions for this ethical endeavor would vary according to the beliefs of the individual, but the pattern would remain the same for similar temperaments. The sanctions might be entirely religious, as they are in Christian prayers of ethical aspiration. They might be social, as in Howard Arnold Walter's little hymn:

> I would be true, for there are those that trust me,
> I would be pure, for there are those who care.

The sanctions might also be of a third type, the pure love of the good for its own sake, as in that anonymous hymn:

> Purer yet and purer I would be in mind,
> Dearer yet, and dearer, every virtue find.

The sanctions can and should differ according to the metaphysical beliefs and preferences of the individual; for ethics is not the exclusive possession of the religious or of the unreligious man, but a social mode of living identical for and equally incumbent upon both.

Along with meditation and contemplation there ought to be schools of real ethical culture, where the practice of ideals might be tried out in group living. These schools should be modeled more upon the lines of the Indian *Ashram* than the secluded cloister; for it is essential to the application of the ethical principles that they shall be tried out in heterogeneous groups living together for the purpose of training and disciplining themselves to social attitudes. Life does not allow us to choose those with whom we shall associate, but throws us with friend and foe, with congenial and uncongenial, and toward all it imposes the obligation of good will and helpfulness in a world where it is literally true that anyone who needs our help is our neighbor. Such group practices of ethical discipline should be oriented around co-operation and kindliness, and all the subsidiary attitudes that go with them to make for smooth and harmonious human relationships, instead of being oriented about competition, which, due to the dominance of "the folklore of capitalism," has been the regulative principle of most of our education. Indeed, co-operation should be deeply instilled and conscientiously practiced in this "ethical *Ashram*," since it is one of the prime needs of a world that has suddenly found itself united geographically, but so disunited psychologically that it has fallen into war and conflicts of all kinds.

The end and aim of both the meditation and the practice of the ethical discipline would be to enable the individual to achieve control and direction of his own feelings and emotions. It must enable the recipient to gain freedom in his own decisions, and the whole scheme should be carefully calculated for moral ascent comparable to the ascents of the mystic disciplines, so that he will go on to ever-higher levels of moral living right up to the maximum of his temperamental capacity. On the negative side, both the practical and the contemplative sides of the emotional discipline should be arranged to discover and to examine carefully all wrong attitudes and feelings, so that the bitter roots of these may be revealed and purged or eradicated. Particular effort should be made to see how these drives may be sublimated in such a manner that they will aid rather than interfere with the realization of good ends. So far as possible, the individual should discover this for himself, but it may be that in the "ethical *Ashram*" there will be someone able to direct each member, somewhat after the fashion that the Indian *guru* directs his pupils in the practices of Yoga.

Much could thus be learned about the moral functioning of emotions, and, in fact, much needs to be learned about them; for we still do not know some of the most fundamental processes for the good life in this realm. Both ethics and religion have long taught good will and love to our fellow men, but the process by which the transformation to them can be made is still undiscovered. It is not just a matter of will or habit, it appears to involve a genuine purging of the roots of evil and a redirection of the feelings involved, so that a new attitude is possible. Whoever discovers the process for the transmutation of hatred into love, of ill will into good will, will be

greater than Marconi or Edison. There is need for many other discoveries of the processes for the transforming of bad and wrong attitudes into good and social ones, and here the labors of many over
a long period of time will no doubt be necessary. For the ethical
processes will no more come to us by magic than the scientific processes did by alchemy.

CHAPTER XIV

THE DIMENSIONS OF ETHICS

OUR SURVEY of the present status of ethics reveals clearly the need for a fresh definition of its exact scope. Several reasons combine to make such a redefinition desirable. First of all, the variation in both method and content that has prevailed in the past should give way to a more precise delimitation of the field; since if ethics is to become a science, it must no longer mean something different to each ethician, but must have uniformity of object and method. A second reason for fixing its scope more accurately is that throughout the history of ethics there have been recurrent confusions between its territory and that of certain other branches of philosophy and science. A final reason is to be found in the fact that other lines of knowledge that formerly seemed not to have any bearing upon the subject or that did not exist at all have now yielded data which necessitate a readjustment of ethics, either by the limitation or by the extension of its territory in conformity with these new facts.

Some limitations of ethics have always been observable in the classical systems of the past, which at no time have considered its field coextensive with all human relationships. In the distant past teachers were usually aware that large areas of life are ethically neutral—a fact that did not escape the keen eyes of Saint Thomas Aquinas as far back as the thirteenth century. Much earlier, Jesus's perfect sense of moral perspective not only marked off portions of life that are ethically indifferent but also indicated clearly that the degree of moral concern was greater in some spheres of intention and conduct than in others. But there was never general agreement about all the territory that should be excluded from ethical consideration or about all the problems which should be included.

This lack of agreement about the precise boundaries of the field is to some extent justified by the fact that the fields with which ethics is concerned do vary somewhat from time to time. Since any aspect of life that vitally influences the development of character, by the creation of conditions either favorable or unfavorable to it, is necessarily the proper province of ethics, and these centers of conflict or reinforcement are not the same in every age, its territory does shift somewhat from one period to another. In our own day, for example, ethics has a more intense interest in economics and international relations than it has had for many generations, because at the moment these are the areas wherein the values of personality are being most seriously endangered. Nevertheless, while there is this variation in emphasis and in area, there are also many spheres where the degree of concern for ethics remains constant at all times. Some are ethically neutral in all ages; others, for instance, aesthetics, are always of slight concern to ethics; some, such as education, have great interest for it at all times, but the two fields are never identical.

Throughout history, however, mistakes have been made with regard to the proper scope of ethics: some unwarranted excursions have been made outside its own territory, and its field has sometimes been restricted too narrowly. Both errors date back to a mistaken analysis of the causal factors in morals; but they can be avoided by a sure appreciation for the data and concerns of human personality and character. In the past the intrusions into other fields gave rise to the confusion of morals with manners, customs, and ritual and, more recently, with the territory of sociology, psychology, and physiology. The opposite mistake, a too-narrow delimitation, comes from handling the subject as though it were concerned only with the spirit of man, the mind and the soul, and not with the body at all. In Chapter XIII a number of the failures of ethics were traced to this one-dimensional treatment of a subject that has at least four dimensions, and possibly five or six dimensions. Since the mind and the spirit are not independent of the body, but emerge from it and interact with it, this one-dimensional treatment of ethics is a grave oversimplification of the scope of that field. The effort of the present discussion of the scope of ethics will be to include in it its four proper and permanent dimensions.

The first three dimensions are those of the individual personality as such, within which the moral consciousness is comprehended. The first of the dimensions is the vegetative level of the physical organism, at which a solid foundation of health must be laid for moral as well as physical well-being. The second dimension is a new one to formal ethics: the biochemical basis of personality, intelligence, and character, due to the chemical conditioning of the hormones secreted by the endocrine glands. The third is the psychological dimension. The fourth is the social dimension, where the individual as a moral being reacts to other personalities and to his environment. Perhaps in the future eugenics may be reckoned as the fifth dimension of ethics; but at the present time the former is in a state so embryonic and negative that it cannot be included as a real dimension of ethics, since it has not as yet provided a sufficient body of positive data with which ethics can work. Metaphysics has often been regarded as a sixth dimension of ethics; but metaphysical extensions and implications are actually the concern of religion and philosophy instead of ethics, whose object is man's life on this planet between birth and death, not his possible—but unknown—destiny before or after his earthly existence. Thus, only the four dimensions of ethics first stated will be considered in this chapter.

With the first dimension of human personality, the vegetative or organic, where the foundation of moral as well as physical health is laid, ethics has only a general concern: namely, to see that this physical basis for character is the soundest and most favorable possible. The specific means by which this general end shall be accomplished must be left to the physician and the scientist, who have the expert knowledge needed for treatment of the physical organism. A persistent source of confusion in ethics has been the ethician's overstepping of the bounds of this general concern in attempting to make specific prescriptions without firsthand knowledge of the facts in this sphere. Efforts to prescribe diets, vegetarian or otherwise, regimens for simple living, sometimes drawn up by ethical teachers as aids to the higher life, whether in the past or the present, are merely ethical aberrations, since they lack the foundation of a knowledge of the physical organism, which was possessed by no one in the past and in the present is known only by the medical profession. Likewise, the use of or the abstinence from narcotics and stimulants should be determined, not by the moralist, but by the physician who knows their effects upon the body and the mind and is consequently in a much better position to determine whether or not they extend to the higher reaches of personality and so effect character adversely.

Within the first dimension, then, ethics should concern itself with fulfilling the general aim of securing a sound physical foundation for character.

The second dimension of personality is new in the study of ethics: the biochemical level of the endocrine glands. Now and then some new science or branch of human endeavor arises which proves to have prime significance for ethics, and so it is with the findings of the young science of endocrinology. The recent discovery of medicine that the hormones secreted by the endocrine glands exert a tremendous influence, not only upon the physical organism but also upon the nature of personality, intelligence, and character, is of such importance that ethics must orient itself to these findings of endocrinology and must make some readjustments of its own in accordance with them. Says R. G. Hoskins, a leading endocrinologist: "The evidence is now conclusive that what we are—physically, mentally, sexually, and emotionally—depends in no small measure upon the function of our endocrine glands." [1]

The hormones secreted by the thyroid, the adrenals, the pituitary, and the primary sex glands, the testis in the male, and the ovary in the female enter very deeply into the constitution of the personality, since they go far to control the intelligence, the emotions, the quality of personality and character. To attempt to go extensively into the physiology of the endocrine glands would be to go beyond the limits of the writer's knowledge; therefore the discussion will be confined to recording the facts about the glands of internal secretion which exert a marked effect upon the higher reaches of personality and are, in consequence, of interest to ethics. These facts, which

---

[1] Hoskins, *Endocrinology*. The discussion of endocrinology and ethics owes the underlying facts to this volume and to three other works in the field: Berman, *The Glands Regulating Personality*; to a series of three pamphlets, *Male Sex Hormone Therapy, Female Sex Hormone Therapy*, by the Medical Division of the Schering Foundation, 1941; and *Glandular Physiology and Therapy, a Symposium*, by various experts, reprinted from the *Journal of the American Medical Association*.

have not yet received consideration in formal ethics, are important, because they redistribute the areas of moral responsibility and freedom somewhat. On the negative side they eliminate from the moral sphere some traits that were thought to belong there; and on the positive side they give promise of teaching us how to secure a favorable endocrine foundation for various types of character that result from the dominance of some one or other of the glands of internal secretion.

The most familiar of these glands is the thyroid, which not only controls the metabolic rate of the body but also exerts a decided influence upon the emotions and has much to do with the proper development of the intelligence. There is one type of idiocy, cretinism, which is caused by thyroid deficiency, and if detected early enough it can be remedied by the administration of thyroid gland. Thyroid secretion is also essential to the process of maturation and reproduction.[2] The adrenals are important in the constitution of personality, both because they secrete hormones during fear and rage and because their secretions exert a pronounced influence upon the development of the secondary sexual characteristics, physical and mental, and upon sexual maturation.[3]

Still more important is the pituitary, a gland no larger than a pea, but consisting of two lobes, the anterior and the posterior joined by a medial cortex, both of which secrete hormones. Several of these pituitary hormones enter deeply into the emotional and psychological constitution of personality as well. A group known as "gonadotropins" control the primary sex glands; and in the female one of them called prolactin, the lactation hormone, influences the emotions and conduct incidental to motherhood, besides regulating the mammary secretion.[4] While the extent to which prolactin determines such traits of character as gentleness, kindness, and the other qualities associated with maternity, in men as well as in women, is not fully determined, there seems to be a strong presumption

---

[2] Hoskins, *Endocrinology*, pp. 101 ff.; Berman, *The Glands Regulating Personality*, pp. 214 f.

[3] Hoskins, *op. cit.*, chap. ii.   [4] *Ibid.*, pp. 142 ff.

in favor of the view that their appearance is associated with an abundant supply of this hormone. Concerning the influence of prolactin, Hoskins, a cautious scientist, raises these questions:

> What part prolactin may play in the determination of human instincts and emotions is as yet unknown, but the stimulus to the imagination is tempting. To what extent is mother love a matter of hormone chemistry? Could prolactin convert a cold misanthrope into a lover of his kind? Should our predatory overlords be sentenced to a course of prolactin? Such questions might be multiplied and they are not entirely fanciful. One wonders whether the folk phrase, "the milk of human kindness," betokens a vague foresensing of the functions of prolactin.[5]

One more set of endocrine glands must be mentioned as important determinants of the human personality, namely, the sex glands. Besides their primary function of reproduction, the testis in the male and the ovary in the female secrete hormones that are essential to the well-being of the body and are, respectively, important determinants of the masculine and the feminine psychological traits. These psychological traits may, of course, be modified by social and psychological influences—the experts differ as to the degree of this modification—but the fact remains that these personality traits, whether masculine or feminine, are heavily conditioned by the hormones that are largely responsible for their existence.[6] It has long been a fact of common knowledge that castration, which deprives the subject of these valuable hormones as well as of reproductive ability, alters drastically the personality and the character of the subject as well as his physical appearance, so that he differs from the normal male and from his former self before his mutilation. The cowardice displayed by Abelard after this misfortune befell him is the classic example of the loss of such masculine characteristics as courage and self-assertion.[7]

As a group, the endocrine glands are designed to operate so that they balance and correct each other, the balance being what we call the normal. The failure of any one of them, the overactivity of any one, or an imbalance among their secretions, results not only in dis-

---

[5] *Ibid.*, p. 185.   [6] *Ibid.*, chaps. vi–viii, xi.
[7] Carrel, *Man, the Unknown*, p. 143.

ease but also in personality disturbances that in some cases may be so serious that they are indistinguishable from insanity. Hyperthyroid psychosis, for example, can scarcely be distinguished from schizophrenia; emotional disturbances are frequent accompaniments of adrenal disorders; and involutionary melancholia, a symptom at times accompanying the menopause, yields to treatment with the estrogen hormones.[8] Although the hormone synthesis varies greatly in different individuals, the behavior tends to follow impulses originating from whatever gland is most active in a particular person. This is the chemical basis of temperament.

What is the ethical import of these facts about the role of the hormones in the composition of character and personality? In the first place, since this chemical conditioning takes place below the level where the volition can operate, we must revise our conception of moral responsibility and freedom of decision accordingly. Endocrinology accounts for our failure to cure certain faults and vices by the ordinary techniques of morality and religion, which cannot reach down far enough to modify this hormone conditioning and adapt it to ideals. This science also makes clear that much of our attack in ethics has been wrong, since it is impossible by psychological means to get at the level where the endocrines cause such objectionable ways of behaving. If some defect in the character of a certain individual is due to a glandular imbalance, the problem can no longer be treated as a moral one; for moral judgments, which imply responsibility, are inapplicable to it. Finally, the knowledge of the effects of the hormone conditioning upon character gives us hope that as the medical profession has learned to lay a good foundation of health at the vegetative level, so in the future it will learn to adjust the endocrine level of the personality in the interests of character.

A few instances of traits that are plainly outside the area of responsibility will suffice to show how our moral judgments must be corrected according to endocrinology. For example, one characteristic that is usually treated as a moral problem is bad temper. Of this Dr. Louis Berman says, "What is spoken of as a quick temper is an

<hr>

[8] Hoskins, *Endocrinology*, pp. 93, 183, 333.

adrenocentric trait." [9] Since the secretion of the adrenals is not under voluntary control, we are not justified in handling bad temper as a moral problem, however unpleasant and harmful to others its consequences may be. Indeed, if one analyzes his own state in anger or irritation, he will quickly conclude that there is a basic and unalterable quality about anger that eludes the control of the will, so that he is unable to deal with the situation in rational fashion, until, as we say, "he has cooled off"—which is just another way of saying, until the excess of adrenalin has subsided. Knowledge of the action of the adrenal hormones in states of fear and rage shows plainly that here we are not dealing with "original sin," but with "original endocrine glands." The recognition of one mistake in moral judgment such as this gives us to pause and wonder how many similar ones we have been making. We are not yet in a position to reckon up the full number, but we can already add some others to the list of matters that belong in the endocrine instead of the moral category.

The strength of the sexual drive is very largely conditioned by the hormone secretions regulating it and varies with their intensity or their imbalance. This impulse is controllable by the will and reason within certain limits, of course, but our conception of where these limits lie must be adjusted to fit the new factor of chemical conditioning. Like most other impulses regulated by the hormones, the synthesis in each person is very individual, so that whereas the libido of one may yield rather easily to psychological control, that of another may be but little governable by it. Where this point of responsibility lies in individual cases may have to be fixed by medical diagnosis, and the moral estimate may then be formed accordingly.

Homosexuality is another problem that has frequently been treated as moral, although recently some understanding of its psychological basis has been popularized. Recent investigation seems to reveal that there are three types of homosexuality to be distinguished before we are in any position to pass judgment upon them. There are psychological homosexuality, which is amenable to

[9] Berman, *The Glands Regulating Personality*, p. 224.

psychological therapy, but is nonetheless a moral disease—to borrow a phrase of Dr. Hadfield's—not a sin; hormonal homosexuality, which is caused by disproportion of the secretion of the masculine and feminine hormones (both of which are secreted in the bodies of all normal persons of either sex, but with the feminine predominating in women and the masculine in men); and finally, structural homosexuality, due to the presence of glands of both sexes in the body of one and the same person.[10] Saint Thomas Aquinas, in his excellent and judicious discussion of sexual perversions in his *Summa theologica*,[11] expresses the opinion that these are abhorrent because they are contrary to the design and order of God and nature for this aspect of life. Modern science, however, shows that homosexuality of the last two types is not a voluntary and reprehensible departure from the natural order; it is a definite aberration of nature itself, which we should pity and endeavor to correct (if that be possible), rather than stigmatize as moral turpitude.

The areas of conduct just considered are beyond the sway of the volition; therefore we must exclude them from the sphere of moral condemnation. In like manner, some characteristics and modes of behavior which have received high moral approbation, it has been shown by recent research in endocrinology, are not proper subjects of moral judgment at all. Traditional ethics has said little about such types as "the manly man" and "the womanly woman," but for more than a century popular sentiment has glorified them as ideal. However, since endocrinology has revealed the extent to which they (as well as their unfortunate opposites) are the creation of the sum total of their glands of internal secretions, it is evident that we should bestow no more moral commendation upon them than we should upon beauty or any other desirable physical characteristic. Even mother love, the maternal instinct, with all its psychological manifestations, while in the human mother it may be influenced by psychological and environmental factors, is at least strongly conditioned by the amount of prolactin, the lactation hor-

---

[10] Hoskins, *Endocrinology*, pp. 215–216; and Allen, *Sex and Internal Secretions*, pp. 1276–1278.

[11] The *Summa theologica*, II² Q cliii, arts. 1, 9, 11–12.

mone, present in any particular woman. Probably this fact means that we ought to view this extraordinarily valuable feeling in the same light that we appraise intelligence—as a precious gift of nature.[12]

One more revaluation should be made on the basis of endocrinological findings. In the West we have all bestowed a wholly undeserved admiration on the predatory type. To be sure, in the democracies we have not considered politics a suitable sphere for his activities, but we have applauded his expansion in the economic realm, under the name of the go-getter, the self-made man, or the tycoon. In the nondemocratic lands, politics and war have provided the predatory type with opportunities to climb into the seats of power as dictators and warlords without even the liability of social disapproval. Our valuation of the predatory type should change completely, and—it is to be hoped—our treatment of him will in the near future change accordingly. We must learn to despise him, to pity him, to look upon him as a moral deficient and, far from allowing him to grasp for himself some seat of power, be it economic, political, or some other type, we must isolate him from his fellows and give him over to the psychiatrists and doctors, who will study his curious and pathological emotional and glandular make-up in the hope of fitting him to live among his fellows once more as a co-operative and innocuous member of society.

Besides the possibility of correcting moral judgments, endocrinology holds out the hope of giving more positive aid to ethics in the near future, that is, of modifying the endocrine balance along lines most suited to the development of character and personality of the highest sort for the various glandular types. It is conceivable that we shall be in a position to decide which of these feelings and impulses that result from the conditioning of the hormones are valuable to the race and what pattern of conduct can best be followed

[12] Hoskins (*op. cit.*, p. 184) and Berman (*The Glands Regulating Personality*, p. 184) express opposing views about the functioning of the maternal instinct in the human subject. Berman believes that it is completely controlled by this hormone; Hoskins, on the other hand, is ready to admit the influence of psychological and social factors. However, that prolactin exerts a very strong effect on the maternal impulses seems clear from both views.

by each of the glandular types. It is probable that in the near future the doctors will learn to adjust and correct the endocrine balance so as to foster the traits of each type that are most valuable to society. Already they know a certain amount about the correction of the hyper- or hypo-functioning of certain endocrines, and there is a strong presumption that they will learn much more as time goes on.

If the doctors actually learn to produce such personality modifications by adjustment of the hormone secretions, the path of ethics will be immeasurably smoothed. The hope of moral progress will be vastly increased if alterations of the human material can be made to facilitate character development. Overcombativeness, too great aggressiveness, and all those manifestations of the animal inheritance that are carried by the conditioning of endocrine secretions might then be modified in accordance with an ideal and a pattern at once social and rational. Then we might look forward to a much more rapid rate of moral progress than has been possible at any previous epoch in history. That this is not the way of redemption visualized by traditional ethics is not important; for, if this potential contribution of endocrinology becomes actual, it will be one of the greatest that has come to mankind.

Prior to the discoveries of the importance of the endocrine hormones, emotional problems were treated entirely within the third— the psychological—dimension of personality. There is a complex and puzzling interaction between the two levels which is not yet fully understood, so that sometimes it is difficult to tell which of the two is causing trouble. However, the fact seems to be that some difficulties are wholly or largely on the second level, some others wholly or largely on the third level, and that there are some borderline cases in which the decision is very difficult. Since both the endocrine and the psychological levels affect the conditions of character and enter deeply into the constitution of personality, ethics has a decided concern with both. However, since psychology is an older science than endocrinology, the concerns of ethics with the former have been repeatedly discussed; hence it is not necessary to give a redefinition of them within the third dimension.

The relation between psychology and morals has been sufficiently explored so that the area of moral responsibility is defined with a fair amount of clarity. In recent years the reading public has become familiar with the idea that moral responsibility does not apply to sufferers from traumata, compulsion neuroses, and fixations in the particular reaches of conduct wherein these psychological disabilities operate. As long ago as 1925 Dr. J. A. Hadfield, in his little book *Psychology and Morals,* drew some distinctions which still seem valid. The morally diseased are those who cannot by the exercise of the volition prevent doing the evil toward which their complexes or compulsions impel them, but this moral disability applies only for some particular area. Those who can will to do otherwise, yet choose to follow wrong impulses, are not the victims of moral disease; consequently, they are fully responsible for their evil deeds.[13] The normal are those who can exercise volition in this respect, who are free to choose good or ill. They are the ones who can show moral improvement within temperamental limits by the use of methods directed toward the psychological level alone; in other words, they are free enough to be capable of moral progress. On this plane the religio-ethical devices for moral improvement, such as prayer and meditation, operate, and their success with certain groups of people in various times and places is a reliable indication that many persons are amenable to help on this plane alone. When psychological and religio-ethical means, voluntarily used, are not effective or only partially so, the leaks and lags in the moral adjustment betray that the trouble lies on a lower level, where these devices cannot reach it.

Some of the difficulties that are untouched by psychological treatment belong to the endocrine level, as Dr. Louis Berman points out. He believes that the unconscious of the Freudians should really be identified with the chemical conditioning of the endocrine hormones.[14] It would appear that there is much truth in his opinion. However, that there are some purely psychological disorders is indicated by several lines of evidence. In addition to the success in

[13] Hadfield, *Psychology and Morals,* p. 63.
[14] Berman, *The Glands Regulating Personality,* pp. 219–23.

procuring ethical improvement by the religio-ethical prayers and meditations, the successes of psychiatry itself are imposing enough so that we have every right to presuppose some independence of the psychological in normal people and in those who are sufficiently normal so that their troubles yield to psychological treatment. Then, although their emotions may be conditioned by the hormones, they are aroused on the psychological level by outward stimuli; and the activities of the portion of the nervous system subject to voluntary control also take place here, so that the psychological by no means completely depends on the endocrine level, any more than the latter does on the vegetative.

In view of the interaction between the psychological and the endocrine levels, a few observations on the perennially controversial subject of freedom are in order. Of course, there is a pragmatic argument for the reality of psychological freedom in the fact that some persons are able to improve morally by the voluntary pursuit of religio-ethical exercises and that others are able to achieve this capacity for moral progress through psychological treatment. Aside from the pragmatic grounds, the theoretical case for freedom, in which ethics has such a vital interest, looks stronger at the present time than it has looked for the last two centuries. The scientific *Weltbild* now leaves room for a margin of freedom, beginning in the domain of the physical sciences and extending up through the natural sciences to the psychological realm. Kant construed his ethics as he did, with freedom as his first postulate, because the science of his time allowed him no other place for it in a world of nature that was supposed to be a complete and unbroken mechanism throughout. The materialistic mechanism of the late nineteenth century, which the discoveries of Einstein, Bohr, and others so completely shattered, was also decidedly hostile to any hypothesis of the reality of freedom. The new science, however, discovers an element of freedom even in the realm of the physical sciences. This newer conception has spread to the domain of the natural sciences and through psychology to the human realm. In spite, then, of the discovery of further limitations to the freedom of human personality because of the chemical conditioning of the hormones there is a range of freedom for the normal and well-balanced personality on the biochemical and psychological planes, and it may be possible, though hitherto undreamed of, to extend this range by adjusting personality on the endocrine level. All in all, the case for freedom is now stronger than ever, and that fact is a great gain for ethics.

Since ethics and psychology have ever many concerns in common, it is most desirable from the standpoint of both sciences to have the benefit of a fruitful liaison and a mutual co-operation in their approach to their common problems.

The greatest concern of ethics with psychology is to see that there emerges a morally oriented psychology that will study the best conditions for the growth of character within the third dimension, together with psychological obstacles that stand in its way. Such a psychology could be of the greatest constructive value to ethics in fixing the limits of self-denial and self-expression within which they remain wholesome stimuli to the growth of character. It should locate the point where the former turns into frustration and repression, the latter into selfishness and the mere expression of whims and caprices. An ethically oriented psychology might seek to throw further light on the tangled and difficult problem of motives by ascertaining the individual's responsibility for his own motives, since if so many of them lie in the obscurity of the unconscious self as some schools of psychology teach, it would scarcely seem reasonable that responsibility should extend to them. For the determination of responsibility for motives is a psychological as well as a moral problem. These potential contributions would all be of great use in advancing ethics. On the other hand, ethics can give to psychology's efforts to heal personality a social direction and orientation that should prove far more creative and useful than the integration of personality about an egotistical self-expressionism which has been all too current among some schools of psychology. In the last analysis, however, though the common interests of psychology and ethics may have a somewhat shifting emphasis, so that now one, now another, is uppermost, yet these interrelationships are so permanent and indispensable to both fields that it will always be of advantage to both to have a firm working alliance.

Ethics must be concerned with all three dimensions of the human personality that have just been discussed, for within each of them some basic conditions for the formation of character must be either realized or neglected, and the possibility of moral progress is either furthered or hindered. Within all three the interest is purely in the individual as such; but there is a fourth dimension wherein the individual's moral life is actually lived in interaction with other individuals and groups. For the moral life is lived, not in solitude, but in society. Ethics has, consequently, an almost greater concern with this fourth dimension than with the three purely individual dimensions. Of course, it is a truism to say that the group is stronger than the individual, but this platitude the ethician must never lose from sight. For on the social level the preparation for character, be it ever so perfect on the other three levels, may all go for naught. It may be undone by conflict with the social set-up in some danger zone to personality, or it may perish in some catastrophe that, overwhelming the group, sweeps the individual on to destruction in its wake. Also, the individual's capacity for moral progress may be undermined if his views run counter to the prejudices or conventions or time-honored taboos of his group.

In relation to the conflict with approved group mores arises one of the most troublesome confusions with which the science of ethics must cope. The weight of social sanctions in determining moral or supposedly moral concerns is shown by man's tendency all through his history to confuse the group mores with moral law and to imagine that anything that bears the stamp of group approval must be the good. This confusion has assumed a twofold form. There is the confusion of manners, customs, ceremonial, and ritual with morals, which, we have already noticed, prevailed in the Jewish Law and in the ethic of Confucius. Jesus disentangled these extraneous elements from the religious and moral precepts of the Jewish Law, but unfortunately the clear-cut distinctions he drew were sometimes lost from sight later on. Kant and Spinoza lifted Western philosophic ethics above the possibility of ever again becoming entangled with questions of manners and customs. Since their time no specialist in the field has ever again fallen into this particular confusion; but popular thought still displays a persistent tendency to lapse into it.

The second form of the confusions wrought in ethics by group sanctions is the more recent one bred by misapprehensions and misinterpretations of anthropological, sociological, and historical studies of the origin and development of morality: namely, the idea that no true moral canons can be disentangled from the welter of group-sanctioned mores and that, in consequence, morality is wholly a subjective matter of group or individual preference. This error originates largely from drawing too large inferences from the evolution of morals among primitives, which are indeed largely indistinguishable from custom and group mores.

Certain considerations must be kept in mind before applying conclusions drawn from the study of primitives to the civilized situation. The first is that the individual is far more bound by the group in tribal society than in civilized society, because the self-preservation of the group demands more conformity to all its mores than is needed in more advanced communities. Since one of the chief avenues of moral progress in later communities is the criticism of old ways by the individual, this absolute conformity to the group standards retards the rate of moral progress among primitives, so that they advance but a few steps along the way.

A second misapprehension arises from the variability of moral judgments among primitive tribes, a fact which has often been interpreted as an argument to the effect that morality is entirely subjective and means something different in each social grouping. Judgments on sex relationships, murder, theft and many other fundamental problems of morality have varied greatly among primitives and still do. However, the argument from the variability of primitive codes proves nothing about the nature of true morality, for the primitive is as yet largely an amoral being. True moral laws and strictly moral judgments must be formulated on the basis of exact observation of what happens in the moral transaction, of the intrinsic and extrinsic consequences entailed, and, above all, of the accurate alignment of causal factors, which the primitive mind is quite incapable of discerning.

Naturally, just as in other realms of culture, a few foundation stones of morality are laid in primitive times with the beginning of justice, hospitality, and other virtues; but, on the whole, it is a fallacy to imagine that the origin of morality any more than of anything else explains its true nature, subsequent development, and metamorphoses.

The most valuable lesson to be gleaned from the studies of primitive morality has generally been overlooked by its investigators and by ethicians as well. This lesson runs through the history of ethics, both primitive and civilized. Progress in morals has come through such accidental, such chance factors, not as the result of any rational plan or intelligent direction and preparation for that end. Some of these changes have come about as the result of individual insights; some through conversion to a new religion, as when the barbarians adopted Christianity from the empire they overthrew; some through the development of the old religion, as with the ancient Hebrews. Some have resulted from changes in the economic or social structure of the group life; some through contacts with other peoples or in a dozen other unforeseen ways. But nearly all moral progress throughout man's history has come about as the accidental accompaniment of changes along other lines, rather than as a result of definite planning for moral advancement and of concerted and conscious endeavor to create the conditions conducive to it. Such conscious planning for moral progress would be a new departure in the history of the globe, and there is little in past experience to guide it. However, it is not alone in ethics that there has been no intelligent direction; the same has been true in other realms of life, such as economics, where planning has just begun in our own time. Nevertheless, the fact that moral progress has at no time in human history come as the fruit of wise and far-sighted planning brings us face to face with the need for a society that is deliberately guided and directed along the lines which promise most for the development of man's moral nature, for the improvement of his character.

No social system has ever been perfectly adapted to the goal of character building, nor does history know of any large-scale attempt to create such a society; but if we truly wish for ethical progress, we must learn to plan an order of society that will provide an environment not neutral toward character, but positively favorable to it. Under all systems of society there have, of course, been individuals of strong character, but their emergence has never been due to any social attempt to provide them with the right climate for moral growth. Rather, they have often flourished in spite of the social set-up. Either they were strong enough to transcend it, or their environment did not present insuperable obstacles, or these obstacles stimulated them to their best efforts instead of discouraging and suppressing them. From the standpoint of aiding character development our own social system is not much—if any—better than others that have waxed and waned before it. While in the democracies of the West undoubtedly greater educational opportunities and more political freedom are provided for the common man than under the tyrannies of the past and present, there are still many perils to character in our social and economic life and some, though fewer, in our political life. Along with our great advances in some lines have come unprecedented temptations, and against those pitfalls no adequate safeguards to character and to human values have been erected by society. If we are to build a society suited to moral progress, these danger centers must be removed and the abuses corrected along not only economic, social, and political lines but also moral and ethical lines.

Neither the threats to personality nor the aids to character in any social system remain exactly the same for all times; they vary with the peculiar individuality of each social structure and also according to the phase of development of each system—some beset a rising social order, others a decaying one. To discover the seat of these dangers to personality and to plan to guard against them is the task which the new science of ethics will face. Some of the present threats to personality were mentioned in the preceding chapter, such as the disregard of human values in the working relationship. Another instance from our economic life is the lack of media for the equitable distribution of work, which at present imperils human dignity and self-respect in a most serious fashion. The right to work is as fundamental a human right as any of those listed in the Bill of Rights, since work is not only the means of gaining a livelihood—itself a vital human necessity—but man's greatest single opportunity to contribute useful service to his world. It is an important concern of ethics to see that there is work for all who can work and that we so modify our way of life that no man shall be deprived of this fountainhead of self-respect and service. President Roosevelt's fourth freedom, freedom from want, is of enormous ethical as well as economic importance; for, if we can indeed build the order that our leader has envisioned, in which there will be work for all who are able to work, we shall have fulfilled one of the paramount conditions of a world that is good for the character of man and in which moral progress will be possible.

Equally important for the creation of the world that is good for man is the third freedom, freedom from fear, which comprehends within itself the removal of the threats to the security of our civilization: wars, depressions, and all the other social upheavals that threaten to engulf us at any moment. Character cannot grow in a wholesome and normal manner in a world as insecure as that of this twentieth century; it needs an atmosphere at least sufficiently secure so that its bearers have time to yield the ripened fruits of the spirit and are not at all times in danger of extinction in some world-shaking cataclysm that sweeps before it the normal and the abnormal alike and cuts off by untimely death some who are best prepared to live wisely and usefully. The preservation of its own values within this fourth, the social, dimension is the most urgent and immediate task of ethics, in order that even if it should be able to give individuals a perfect preparation for character within the three individual dimensions, this good work may not be swept into the abyss by upheavals of the social structure.

To modify the existing social order into a world that is good for man is a task that is not national, but global, in its sweep. The attempt is one for which there is little to guide us in the experience of the past, for it is unprecedented. However, some light we do have from the very mistakes we and our forebears have made. Some vision we do possess concerning the lines upon which this new world must be erected. And if, indeed, we have the vision and the courage to undertake the task, out of the combination of the great scientific knowledge we already possess with the new morality that shall emerge, may come a more profound civilization than has yet been seen on this planet. To begin the creation of that new civilization is both the responsibility and the privilege of ethics within its fourth dimension.

CHAPTER XV

THE AIM OF ETHICS

IN THE CLASSICAL ethical systems of the past there is no point upon which more complete disagreement has existed than upon the selection of a *summum bonum* toward which the good life should aim and in which it should culminate. That there should be such striking diversity of opinion is not strange, since the choice of a *summum bonum* is the equivalent of stating what one believes to be the ultimate end and consummation of human life in this world or the next or both. In discussing the individual systems, the various *summa bona* and the reasons for their selection have been considered and evaluated. Two general objections were found to apply to most of the traditional *summa:* that they are individual rather than social, for example, nirvana and some interpretations of Heaven, and that most of them are incapable of realization within the limits of this present world. Now, both these objections are valid from the standpoint of ethics as a science: the first, because the scope of ethics is properly social as well as individual; the second, because it must have an aim that can be realized on this planet, since the span between birth and death is the only one that any science has at the present time the capacity to know.

However, if ethics is to attain the status of a science there is a more far-reaching objection which goes deeper than criticisms of individual *summa* and extends to the whole traditional construction of ethical systems around a *summum bonum*. The whole conception of the *summum bonum* is in itself appropriate to ethics as a branch of philosophy, but inappropriate to it as a science. Philosophy may legitimately take for its object some ultimate that admittedly lies beyond the limits of the knowable, as does this overarching and all-comprehensive good, the *summum bonum* that hypothetically forms the purpose of man's life here and hereafter. But the object of a science is more limited and must be confined to the realm of the knowable. Like any other science, ethics is confined to that group of specialized facts and hypotheses which constitute its own object, the moral life. Although the range of its concerns is very wide, it is not coextensive with all of life here, and if any of these extend into the hereafter, they become *ipso facto* the province of metaphysics, not of ethical science. In short, ethics must discard the concept of the *summum bonum* as too pretentious and grandiose and must substitute an aim which is more in keeping with the nature of a science.

The aim of ethics is to find out the facts about the operation of moral life in order that it may set up the conditions conducive to the development of character and thereby bring about the moral welfare and progress of mankind upon the entire planet.

Since ethics is properly an applied, rather than a pure, science, its aim is practical and may be compared with that of the science of eugenics, which designs to learn the facts of heredity in order that it may improve the human stock physically. In a similar way the purpose of ethics is the practical one of finding out the actual capacities of man for the good life, for moral advancement, and to enhance these by more and more progressive realization and extension as long as the human race continues on this planet. This aim is not static, but dynamic and progressive, since it leads on and on to an ever-nearer approximation of that world which from the moral standpoint is the ideal climate for man. It provides a sense of continuity with the past by recognizing all those whose endeavors have helped to pave the way for united effort for the moral welfare and progress of mankind. It imparts a sense of solidarity with the future generations who will carry on and advance, in their turn, this inspiring aim. It is an aim both individual and social, inasmuch as ethics deals with the individual within all three dimensions of his personality and within the social dimension as well, where it embraces all mankind. It is not confined to a few specialists, but may be shared by all living men. Thus, over and above the theoretical merits of being more in accord with the proper scope of ethics than the traditional *summum bonum*, the aim of ethics has power to inspire the allegiance of man that is by no means inferior to that of the traditional *summum bonum*.

In order to go about the realization of its aim, the immediate

task of ethics is twofold: first, to complete the work of shaping itself into a real science, whose findings shall be so well grounded
that they will command respect; second, to gain the allegiance
not only of specialists in the field but also of the rank and file of
mankind, who can render valuable service in promoting that aim
and in increasing the sum of its knowledge.

Toward the accomplishment of the first task, that is, making ethics
a full science, this volume is intended as an earnest preliminary contribution. The writer is conscious of the many gaps and imper-
fections in this blueprint of the science of ethics, but realizes that it
will require the work of many minds over a long period of time
before the science is full grown.

The other sciences have won popular esteem because they have
been able to produce a multitude of inventions and technological
appliances whose practical benefits are too impressive to be gain-
said. Ethics is not yet in that enviable position, and may not be for a
long time to come. How can it command the allegiance of a sufficiently large section of humanity so that it will have a chance to
make the experiments necessary to demonstrate its theories and to
win the power to attempt modification of the existing order of society into one that shall indeed be good for man? The aim of
ethics is inspiring enough to appeal to the more thoughtful and the
more idealistic, but can it rely on this appeal alone to gain the adherence of more than a minority of living men and women?

There is a more cogent and irrefutable argument in favor of
an affirmative answer than appears on the surface: namely, that to
build a world that is good for man has far more significance for the
masses of people than one would imagine from the length of time
it has taken man to leave off considering the idea an empty dream
and to look upon it as the rational and proper goal for the building
of society. Why should not the masses of mankind be ready to give
their support to arranging affairs on our planet so that life will no
longer be conducted for the benefit of some small minority and
shall cease to be without rational plan, but rather be ordered so
that all humanity may realize its highest moral potentialities in a
social system wherein man himself is the supreme value? For to

himself, at least, man is that supreme value; this applies to not only one particular group of men, but to all mankind.

There is, however, an even stronger reason why the aim of ethics has in the present crisis high hopes of commanding the allegiance of the common people all around this world. From the time of the cave man to the present, human beings have solved two kinds of problems: those that are essential to their own self-preservation as individuals and groups and those that correspond to their hopes and dreams. Man has penetrated many of the secrets of nature through science, because the dream of so doing haunted his imagination, as the myths and fairytales of the race testify, until at last, after centuries, nature yielded the key to some of its mysteries into his hand. For ages men dreamed of flying, as we know from the old Greek story of Daedalus and Icarus, and at length, after centuries, the Wright brothers invented the flying machine. Indeed, most problems that have held man's fancy have yielded to his desire for their solution; for here it is a matter of seeking and finding. Throughout the ages there have always been a few who ardently longed for moral progress, but these have been rare and solitary figures. Ethical betterment has never been and is not now the dream of the masses; it has never been and is not now the consuming desire of the vast majority of mankind. A general yearning for moral progress is still to be created. The hope of ethics does not lie in an aim corresponding with the passionate desire of the multitude.

The greatest hope for ethics to gain the allegiance of humanity is that in the present crisis of the world's history we have reached a point where the need for moral transformation has become a plain matter of self-preservation for all humanity. Man has today the choice between learning to live with himself and his fellows on a basis of co-operation and good will and destroying himself and his fellows by continuing conflicts such as the present war. For our planet is now one world, whether men like that fact or not and whether they adjust to it or not. Unless we wish to lapse into a new barbarism, there is no way to keep aloof on a globe where geographical barriers have vanished. No course remains for any part of the globe but conflict or co-operation. Because of human greed, human rapacity, human hatred and jealousy the first result of our geographical unity has been that we have fallen upon each other with the powerful new weapons that science has placed in our hands and are waging a war of global magnitude. Unless we create a psychological unity to correspond to the geographical unity of our planet, we can look forward to nothing but a series of such wars. Surely the destruction of the present war shows that conflicts of such magnitude but prepare the way of death for humanity. There is no choice but co-operation if we want life instead of death for the human race. And if the diverse peoples of the earth are to get along with each other, there must be moral transformation.

The need for moral transformation has thus reached the point where it is actually a matter of self-preservation. For this reason the aim of ethics cannot but commend itself not only to all thoughtful men but also to all *sane* men, for certainly none but the insane can believe that the way of conflict has been a good even to those who willed it. In this crisis is high-lighted the moral failure of humanity. Beneath all the other contributory causes—the economic, the social, the political, and the racial—are the moral causes, the sins of omission and commission that brought about this global conflagration. Our lack of vision has kept us from directing the great material and intellectual gains of our civilization toward better ends; hence our failure to organize our life for the moral and spiritual unity that our geographical unity now demands. Amid all the gains of science and technology the human heart has remained untamed. In all of us lurk passions similar to those which when given free rein by someone in a seat of power have victimized humanity. Yet the very magnitude of the mistakes of the recent past in dealing with the dynamite of human passions ought to teach us to turn from the old ways, to lose faith in the old answers, to put away greed and hatred, revenge and force, and to try their opposites. In short, men must turn to ethics, but in a new way.

The fact that we have come no further along the old road in ethics, that we have in fact reached such a disastrous impasse, should cause us to look earnestly for the root of our failure to progress ethically and spiritually. It should bring home to us how little moral progress we have actually made, how little of moral law we know in comparison with scientific law, how embryonic is our knowledge of even a sound ethical method, how inadequate our analysis of causality in morals. We must face the fact that the primary cause of our failure is the one mentioned so frequently in this book— that we have not really desired ethical progress enough to work for it. The secondary causes follow from that central one—that what little effort and thought we have devoted to ethics has not proved more fruitful because we have not yet learned enough to be certain that the lines along which we have worked are the correct ones. We need to put away our preconceptions and prejudices and to approach the subject afresh. Some of our contemporaries should stop believing that we know all the answers in morals and have known them from the hoary past and should face the fact that while we do know some of them and have long known them, there are many key problems of our time to which there is as yet no answer at all. Others need to abandon their attitude of defeatism and to give up reiterating that in the subjective and variable realm of morals we do not and cannot know; that here no light has broken, nor ever shall break—because we do know enough so that we can with sufficient effort and persistence find out much more. Still others need to give up the notion that moral progress will come through some supernatural illumination instead of as the result of our own patient efforts and hard work to find the solutions to the most complex and difficult problems that man has to solve, the problems of his own nature. Religious faith can help and inspire us to the task of ethical discovery and moral creativity, but faith alone can no more furnish the answers in morals and ethics than in physical science. Both require for discovery hard labor and patient investigation.

Humanity has progressed slowly along even the lines most essential to the maintenance of its own life. It took men we know not how many centuries to develop the arts and crafts, to learn the techniques of basic industries, and to lay the foundations of civilization. Compared with the time consumed in the discovery of these processes, his progress in science, though extending over some twenty-three centuries, has been swift. Previously the problems of the moral life have seemed more intangible, less remote, than those surrounding man's physical existence. Now that situation has suddenly been reversed. Man must perforce solve his moral problems or else go under. The urgency of our situation should drive us to the task, should lend us the wisdom and the ingenuity to devise new methods where the old have failed. It should inspire us—not as individuals, but as a race—to undertake at once the task of building that new world of which we talk so glibly lest our efforts be too late.

How much remains to be done in the realm of ethics! The task is so large that there is opportunity for all to share in its accomplishment. So far we have discovered a few, but by no means all, of the conditions that are necessary for the development of character. Our educational systems have taught much about the training of minds, little about the training of emotions or the building of personality. Medicine has taught us much about the human body; psychologists have learned somewhat of the human mind. But we are still largely ignorant of the higher reaches of the personality most intimately concerned in the moral consciousness and development. In ethics we have formulated some, but not enough, ideals and aims; now we need to discover more and to implement some of those we already possess. Thus, to realize its aim and to accomplish its task, ethics needs help from whoever can give it, whether that be the common man or the expert, the philosopher or the man of affairs, the educator or the statesman, the scientist or the mystic, the American doctor or the Indian *guru*, the Hebrew prophet or the oriental sage, the ethical teacher or the founder of a religion.

By pooling all the knowledge at its disposal ethics can undertake to found the new morally ordered civilization, great as that task is. For this "new world" must be one in which men can entertain good will toward each other in spite of their diversity as to race, color, and creed. It must be a world where they learn to cooperate with each other in spite of conflicting interests, where they shall learn to redress their wrongs by other means than force. Finally, in it they must learn to organize the life of this entire planet into one great and all-inclusive superstate, where all shall share in the goods of life, material and spiritual, and have liberty to pursue their destinies as free men. To fit them for this world, to draw the blueprint of this new civilization, and to help to build this world that is good for man is the aim of ethics.

BIBLIOGRAPHY

Allen, Edgar, and others, Sex and Internal Secretions. Baltimore, Williams and Wilkins, 1939.

Aristotle, Nicomachean Ethics; tr. by H. Rackham. New York, Putnam, 1926. Loeb Classical Library.

Behanan, Kovoor T., Yoga; a Scientific Evaluation. New York, Macmillan, 1937.

Bentham, Jeremy, An Introduction to the Principles of Morals and Legislation. Oxford, Clarendon Press, 1907.

Berman, Louis, The Glands Regulating Personality. 2d ed., rev. Garden City, Garden City Publishing Co., 1928.

Bernard, Theos, Heaven Lies within Us. New York, Scribner, 1939.

Bonnell, John S., Pastoral Psychiatry. New York, Harper, 1938.

Bradford, Gamaliel, Biography and the Human Heart. Boston, Houghton Mifflin, 1932.

Brunton, Paul, A Search in Secret India. New York, Dutton [1935].

Buddhist Suttas; tr. by T. W. Rhys Davids. Oxford, Clarendon Press, 1900. Sacred Books of the East, Vol. XI.

Burnet, John, Greek Philosophy. London, Macmillan, 1914.

Burnham, William H., The Normal Mind. New York, Appleton, 1927.

Cabot, Richard C., The Meaning of Right and Wrong. New York, Macmillan, 1934.

Cadbury, Henry J., The Peril of Modernizing Jesus. New York, Macmillan, 1937.

Cannon, Walter B., Bodily Changes in Hunger, Fear and Rage. New York, Appleton, 1929.

—— The Wisdom of the Body. London, Kegan Paul, 1932.

Carrel, Alexis, Man, the Unknown. New York, Harper, 1932.

Comte, Auguste, Positive Philosophy; tr. by Harriet Martineau. New York, Blanchard, 1856.

Confucius, The Analects of Confucius; tr. by Arthur H. Waley. New York, Macmillan, 1939.

—— The Sayings of Confucius; tr. by Lionel Giles. London, Murray, 1937.

—— The Wisdom of Confucius; ed. and tr. by Lin Yutang. New York, Random House, 1938.

Coomaraswamy, Ananda, Buddha and the Gospel of Buddhism. New York, Putnam, 1916.

Davids, T. W. Rhys, Buddhism. New York, Putnam, 1896.

Dewey, John, and James H. Tufts, Ethics. New York, Holt, 1909.

—— The Quest for Certainty. New York, Minton, Balch, 1929.

Dhammapada; tr. by F. Max Mueller, in Sacred Books of the East. Oxford, Clarendon Press, Vol. X, 1924.

Drake, Durant, Problems of Conduct. Boston, Houghton Mifflin, 1914.

Eddington, A. S., The Nature of the Physical World. New York, Macmillan, 1929.

Emerson, Ralph Waldo, Essays and English Traits. New York, Collier, 1909. Essay "Compensation."

Freud, Sigmund, Psychopathology of Everyday Life; tr. by A. A. Brill. New York, Macmillan, 1915.

Glandular Physiology and Therapy; a Symposium. Chicago, American Medical Association, 1941. Reprints from *Journal of the American Medical Association*.

Green, Thomas Hill, Prolegomena to Ethics. Oxford, Clarendon Press, 1899.

Hadfield, J. S. Psychology and Morals. New York, McBride, 1925.

Hobhouse, L. T., Morals in Evolution. New York, Holt, 1924.

—— The Rational Good. New York, Holt, 1921.

Holt, Edwin B., The Freudian Wish. New York, Holt, 1915.

Hopkins, Edward Washburn, Ethics of India. New Haven, Yale University Press, 1924.

Hoskins, R. G., Endocrinology. New York, Norton, 1941.

Hume, David, Enquiries; ed. by L. A. Selby-Bigge. 2d ed. Oxford, Clarendon Press, 1927.

Huxley, Aldous, Do What You Will. Garden City, Doubleday, Doran, 1929.

Inge, William Ralph, Christian Ethics and Modern Problems. New York, Putnam, 1930.

James, William, Pragmatism. London, Longmans, 1925.

Johnson, Henry, The Teaching of History. New York, Macmillan, 1940.

Kant, Immanuel, Kants Opus postumum; ed. by Erich Adickes. Berlin, Reuther & Reichard, 1920.

—— Kant's Theory of Ethics; ed. and tr. by Thomas Kingsmill Abbott. 6th ed. London, Longmans, 1927.

—— Kritik der praktischen Vernunft; ed. by Karl Vorländer. Leipzig, Meiner, 1920.

—— Kritik der reinen Vernunft; ed. by Raymund Schmidt, Leipzig, Meiner, 1926.

—— The Way to Perpetual Peace. New York, Columbia University Press, 1939.

Lecky, William E. H., History of European Morals. 3d ed., 2 vols. New York, Appleton, 1898.

Lippmann, Walter, A Preface to Morals. New York, Macmillan, 1929.

Manu, The Laws of; tr. by G. Bühler. Oxford, Clarendon Press, 1886. Sacred Books of the East, Vol. XXV.

Martineau, James, Types of Ethical Theory. 2 vols., 3d. ed., rev. Oxford, Clarendon Press, 1901.

Marx, Karl, Capital; tr. by Eden and Cedar Paul. 2 vols. London, Dutton, 1932.

Mateer, Florence, Glands and Efficient Behavior. New York, Appleton-Century, 1935.

Milinda, King, Questions, see Questions of King Milinda.

Mill, John Stuart, Dissertations and Discussions. New York, Holt, 1874.

Niebuhr, Reinhold, An Interpretation of Christian Ethics. New York, Harper, 1935.

Palmer, George Herbert, The Nature of Goodness. Boston, Houghton Mifflin, 1903.

Plato, Euthyphro, The Apology, Crito, Phaedo; tr. by Harold N. Fowler. New York, Macmillan, 1913. Loeb Classical Library.

—— The Republic; tr. by B. Jowett. New York, Scribner, 1928. Modern Student's Library.

Plotinus, The Ethical Treatises; tr. by Stephen Mackenna. London, Medici Society, 1926.

Pratt, James Bissett, The Pilgrimage of Buddhism. New York, Macmillan, 1928.

Questions of King Milinda, The; tr. by T. W. Rhys Davids. Oxford, Clarendon Press, 1890. Sacred Books of the East, Vol. XXXV.

Reiser, Oliver L., The Promise of Scientific Humanism. New York, Priest, 1940.

Roberts, William Henry, The Problem of Choice. Boston, Ginn, 1941.

Rosanoff, Aaron J., Manual of Psychiatry. New York, Wiley, 1928.

Royce, Josiah, Studies of Good and Evil. New York, Appleton, 1902.

Russell, Bertrand, Power. New York, Norton, 1938.

Schering Corporation, Medical Research Division, Male Sex Hormone Therapy; Female Sex Hormone Therapy. n.p. 1941. A series of three pamphlets.

Sharp, Frank Chapman, Ethics. New York, Century, 1928.

Sheean, Vincent, Personal History. Garden City, Doubleday, Doran, 1935.

Sidgwick, Henry, The Methods of Ethics. 6th ed. London, Macmillan, 1901.

Sockman, Ralph W., The Morals of Tomorrow. New York, Harper, 1931.

Soothill, W. E., The Three Religions of China. 2d ed. London, Oxford University Press, 1923.

Spencer, Herbert, Recent Discussions in Science, Philosophy and Morals. New York, Appleton, 1880. Essay on "Morals and Moral Sentiments."

—— The Data of Ethics. New York, Appleton, 1883.

Spinoza, Benedict de, Ethic; tr. by W. Hale White and rev. by Amelia Hutchinson Sterling. 4th ed. London, Oxford University Press, 1930.

—— Ethik; tr. by J. H. von Kirchman. Vol. I, "Kurzgefasste Abhandlung von Gott, dem Menschen und dessen Glückseligkeit," 2d ed. Berlin, Heimann, 1870.

Stephen, Leslie, The Science of Ethics. London, Murray, 1907.

Studdert-Kennedy, G. A. The Warrior, the Woman and the Christ. New York, Richard Smith, 1930.

Sutta Nipata; tr. by V. Fausboli, in Sacred Books of the East, Oxford, Clarendon Press, Vol. X, 1924.

Taoism, The Texts of; tr. by James Legge. Oxford, Clarendon Press, 1891. Sacred Books of the East, Vol. XXXIX.

Teresa, Saint, The Interior Castle. London, Baker, 1906.

Thomas Aquinas, Saint, The "Summa contra Gentiles"; tr. by the Fathers of the English Dominican Province. London, Burns, Oates and Washbourne, 1928. Vol. III, Pts. 1–2.

—— The "Summa theologica," Part II; tr. by the Fathers of the English Dominican Province. 9 vols. London, Burns, Oates and Washbourne, 1927.

Upanishads, The Thirteen Principal; tr. by Robert E. Hume. New York, Oxford University Press, 1931.

Upanishads; tr. by Max Mueller. 2d ed. Oxford, University Press, 1926. Sacred Books of the East, Vols. I, XV.

Vinaya Texts, The, tr. by T. W. Rhys Davids and Hermann Oldenberg. Oxford, Clarendon Press, 1881. Sacred Books of the East, Vol. XIII.

Watson, John B., Behaviorism. New York, The People's Institute, 1925.

Westermarck, Edward A., The Origin and Development of the Moral Ideas. 2 vols. London, Macmillan, 1924–1926.

Yasna, The, Part 2, tr. by L. H. Mills. Oxford, Clarendon Press, 1887. Sacred Books of the East, Vol. XXXI.

Zend-Avesta, The, Part 3, tr. by L. H. Mills. Oxford, Clarendon Press, 1887. Sacred Books of the East, Vol. XXXI.

INDEX

Date Due

APR 1 1			
APR 1 5			
AUG 1 6	1949		
APR 1 5	1950		
	1950		
FEB 1 5	1955		
OCT	7 1959		